R. S. THOMAS TO ROWAN WILLIAMS

WRITING WALES IN ENGLISH

CREW series of Critical and Scholarly Studies
General Editors: Kirsti Bohata and Daniel G. Williams (*CREW*, Swansea University)

This *CREW* series is dedicated to the memory of Emyr Humphreys, a major figure in the literary culture of modern Wales, a founding patron of the *Centre for Research into the English Literature and Language of Wales*. Grateful thanks are due to the late Richard Dynevor for making this series possible.

Other titles in the series

R. S. Thomas to Rowan Williams

The Spiritual Imagination in Modern Welsh Poetry

WRITING WALES IN ENGLISH

M. Wynn Thomas

UNIVERSITY OF WALES PRESS
2022

www.uwp.co.uk

British Library CIP Data
A catalogue record for this book is available from the British Library.

ISBN: 978-1-78683-946-6
e-ISBN: 978-1-78683-947-3

THE *A*SSOCIATION FOR
*W*ELSH *W*RITING IN *E*NGLISH
*C*YMDEITHAS *L*LÊN *S*AESNEG *C*YMRU

MIX
Paper | Supporting
responsible forestry
FSC® C013604

Typeset by Marie Doherty
Printed by CPI Antony Rowe, Melksham

CONTENTS

SERIES EDITORS' PREFACE

The aim of this series, since its founding in 2004 by Professor M. Wynn Thomas, is to publish scholarly and critical work by established specialists and younger scholars that reflects the richness and variety of the English-language literature of modern Wales. The studies published so far have amply demonstrated that concepts, models and discourses current in the best contemporary studies can illuminate aspects of Welsh culture, and have also foregrounded the potential of the Welsh example to draw attention to themes that are often neglected or marginalised in anglophone cultural studies. The series defines and explores that which distinguishes Wales's anglophone literature, challenges critics to develop methods and approaches adequate to the task of interpreting Welsh culture, and invites its readers to locate the process of writing Wales in English within comparative and transnational contexts.

Professor Kirsti Bohata and Professor Daniel G. Williams

Founding Editor: Professor M. Wynn Thomas (2004–15)

CREW (*Centre for Research into the English Literature and Language of Wales*)
Swansea University

CREW

I'm teulu, mawr a mân

'To multiply the harbours does not reduce the sea'
  – *Emily Dickinson*

'God made me – Master – I didn't be – myself.
I don't know how it was done.'
  – *Emily Dickinson*

Sacrament sicr ym modd ei sain
'There is certain sacrament by means of its sound'
  – *Euros Bowen*

'Poetry is like the line Christ drew in the sand, it
creates a pause in the action, a freeze-frame moment of
concentration, a focus where our power to concentrate is
concentrated back upon ourselves'
  – *Seamus Heaney*

Acknowledgements

Extracts from the poetry of Waldo Williams are reproduced by permission of Eluned Richards.

Extracts from *R. S. Thomas, Collected Later Poems 1988–2000* (Bloodaxe Books, 2004), are reproduced by permission of Bloodaxe Books.

Extracts from the poetry by Rowan Williams are reprinted by kind permission of Carcanet Press, Manchester

1

INTRODUCTION:
AN UNFASHIONABLE TRADITION

'All of the major poets of twentieth-century Wales,' Rowan Williams
boldly asserted in 1993, 'whether writing in Welsh or in English, have
been deeply preoccupied with Christian themes.'[1] I would broadly
agree, but with the reservation that the claim does not hold true for
the poets of the first half of that century, several of whom – such as
T. Gwynn Jones, R. Williams Parry and T. H. Parry-Williams – were
either agnostic or atheist. Gwynn Jones, the greatest master of Welsh
strict-metre poetry since the golden period of the late Middle Ages,
drew on the unique epigrammatic power of *cynghanedd* for a pungent
summary of his bleak vision:

> Ni wŷr dyn namyn mai nos
> Ddu oer sydd i'w aros
> Ym mhen ei lwybr, am hynny
> At yr hyn a wŷr y try.

[Man knows not other than that cold black night awaits him at
journey's end, and therefore turns to what he knows.][2]

Rowan Williams's comment does, however, largely (yet by no means
wholly) apply to the poets of the second half of the last century.
Throughout that period one singular, and in some ways peculiar,
feature of the country's major poetry was not only its strong reli-
gious character but the stubbornly orthodox Christian convictions
that continued to underpin it. It is indeed an unusual characteristic,
because it runs determinedly counter to what might be termed the
prevailingly 'post-religious' character of so much of the period's most

important poetry elsewhere, particularly in Western Europe and in Anglophone cultures.

The tone for the poetic culture of twentieth-century America was set early by Wallace Stevens whose substantial output consisted of poems exploring the inexhaustible creative ingenuity of the human imagination as it operated, in a post-religious environment, to reconcile human beings to living in a universe bereft of the sustaining consolations of religious belief. His great poem 'Sunday Morning' ends with a magnificent diapason in which celebration and elegy of humankind's godless existence, lived out on an 'old chaos of the sun', fuse eloquently into one:

> Deer walk upon our mountains, and the quail
> Whistle about us their spontaneous cries;
> Sweet berries ripen in the wilderness;
> And, in the isolation of the sky,
> At evening, casual flocks of pigeons make
> Ambiguous undulations as they sink,
> Downward to darkness, on extended wings.[3]

Folded into that magical phrase 'Ambiguous undulations' is Stevens's acceptance that the enigma of dying is insoluble.

Other equally towering figures followed his lead. Robert Frost adopted a sly persona of laconic scepticism, and Pound a typically chaotic and omnivorous humanism; William Carlos Williams embraced a materialism and a purely sensuous immanentism that at times seemed almost to have charismatic overtones. T. S. Eliot was of course a conspicuous exception in his later years, but by then he had distanced himself from his homeland. After the war, the future course of American poetry was traced out early in the trajectory of Robert Lowell's move away not only from his background Puritanism but from the Catholicism to which he had briefly converted. His friend Elizabeth Bishop at times accommodated a wistfulness in her tough-minded atheistical poetry, while the early John Berryman was interested in exploring the gap between belief and unbelief. Even such poets as were willing to register a spiritual dimension in their work turned away from the Christian faith. Robert Duncan was influenced by his early Theosophist upbringing, while Gary Snyder and Allen Ginsberg turned eastward to Buddhism for their spiritual orientation. Snyder also followed the example of Native American poets in exploring aspects of the faith systems of the indigenous peoples of what, following their lead, he preferred to term 'Turtle Island' rather than the USA.

The strong post-Christian trend was also very evident in major British poetry of the period. An exception was the ageing W. H. Auden, who continued to profess a Christian belief influenced by the existential theology of Kierkegaard. There was Philip Larkin's faded English Anglicanism and Heaney's poetry, while infused with loving memories of the Marianism of his early Catholic inheritance, was that of a non-believer. Geoffrey Hill's gruellingly self-punishing poetry was never more than guiltily God-haunted, and Hughes's vision of a violent universe was that of one who never could reconcile it with traditional religious convictions; Paul Muldoon found refuge in the ludic potentialities of language from the traumatic religious disorders of his native Northern Ireland, fuelled as they were by the savage discourse of religious bigotry.

For a striking, and indeed distinguished, English-language example of the residual persistence in the recent world of major poetry written from a Christian perspective one must look further afield – as far, indeed, as Australia. That country's outstanding poet of recent decades was Les Murray, who once pithily remarked that he thought of religions as big, slow poems and of poems as short, fast religions. His most powerful voicing of that belief comes, though, in 'Poetry and Religion'. 'It is the same mirror' he writes of two modes of apprehending divine presence: 'mobile, glancing, we call it poetry,// fixed, centrally, we call it a religion,// and God is the poetry caught in any religion,/ caught, not imprisoned.'[4] God, he adds, 'being in the world as poetry/ is in the poem, a law against its closure'. And he ends by phlegmatically accepting the intermittent, though stubbornly persistent, nature of the operations of belief in the human world, likening them to 'the action of those birds – crested pigeon, rosella parrot –/ who fly with wings shut, then beating, and again shut'.

While it is likely that most, if not all, the Welsh poets examined in this volume would have concurred with Murray's comments, one of the very few American poets who would have done so was Denise Levertov, who was very conscious and proud of her Welsh spiritual heritage, through her mother. It is likewise intriguing that the famous twentieth-century Anglo-American mystic Thomas Merton should have been so proud of his Welsh descent, this time on the side of his father. Donald Allchin introduced Merton to the poetry of Ann

Griffiths, R. S. Thomas and David Jones, and three weeks before his death Merton was asking Allchin whether on a future visit to Britain he could visit Wales – a country he had already visited, he explained.

* * *

All this leads us back to the nagging question that faced us at the outset: why is it that late-twentieth-century Welsh poets (and even poets of Welsh descent like her) persisted in producing religious poetry, even though the dominant strain in the poetic culture of the West during that period was secular? The honest answer, I suspect, is that we do not know, and never will. Socio-cultural developments are so complex in origin and in character that no single explanation is ever going to suffice to account for them. That said, however, it does seem true and salient that even in the modern period religious faith has remained an important agent for maintaining the identity of a people lacking the institutions and initiatives that have played, and continue to play, such a vital role in sustaining the identity of more powerfully established societies.

Broadly speaking, the secularism that predominantly characterises such societies in the West has emerged not only from transformative intellectual movements, such as Darwinism, Marxism, Freudianism, Linguistics, Anthropological Studies, but from the many consequences of the multifaceted advance of modern science. The cumulative impact on society of all of these has been heavily mediated by the many powerful instruments of modern 'nation-states', all of which have consciously implemented a secular and secularising agenda, an important engine of which has been the education system, enthusiastically aided and abetted by market capitalist practices in a mutually reinforcing process. Wales too has obviously benefited from such developments, but has done so through the agency not of its own State institutions, but those of a British state consciously and unconsciously fashioned primarily to serve the interests of English society. Indeed, the modern consciousness of 'Englishness' – increasingly post-religious in character, whatever lip service tends still to be paid to the state church of England – has to a considerable extent been the result of an enormously influential dynamic of processes set in train by the Anglo-British state.

The disconnect between the processes of creating a distinctively English and a distinctively Welsh collective identity became dramatically apparent in the nineteenth century, at a very early stage in the development of a modern British state. It was then that, in reaction against the partially apprehended initiatives being implemented at government level, Welsh Nonconformity began to develop its own dissenting range of 'alternative' initiatives. These included the imposing country-wide network of chapels, and the many different social and cultural activities they facilitated, including Sunday Schools that provided children with basic education, and the various chapel societies and clubs that by the end of the nineteenth century covered quite a wide spectrum of different interests. So successful, on its own dissenting terms, did this counter-cultural manoeuvre prove to be that many twentieth-century Welsh historians have ruefully concluded it was the primary reason why the Welsh never instituted the kind of programme for political independence commonplace during this time amongst other small, sub-state, nationalities right across Europe.

There was a very long foreground to this Welsh practice of relying on religion as a potent social unifier. In his brilliant, seminal study of the creation and maintenance of a collective, 'national', consciousness among the Welsh people, Bobi Jones identifies ten key factors that were already firmly in place as early as the tenth century. These were: (1) a common language, (2) a common poetic inheritance, (3) memory of a collective (semi-mythic) history, (4) hatred of the English, intensified after the catastrophic defeats at the battles of Deorham, 557 and Chester, 616, with their consequent separation of the Welsh from their kindred in the 'Old North' and the erection of Offa's Dyke, (5) a shared popular culture of practices, legends, beliefs and the kind, (6) the natural, defining, boundary of the sea, (7) the experience (albeit intermittent) of being subjects of a single ruler, (8) widespread familiarity with lines of lineage it was customary to trace back to the age of Cunedda, (9) a single, unifying corpus of Welsh law, compiled at the court of Hywel Dda in Whitland during the tenth century, and (10) a distinctive religious tradition deriving from the time of St David and the Celtic saints and centring not on Canterbury but on St David's.[5]

This latter ecclesiastical tradition, later modified to accommodate successively a Welsh Catholic, a Welsh Anglican, and a Welsh Nonconformist church, proved to be a particularly strong and enduring 'national symbolic', to adopt the term used by Anthony Smith. Moreover, in his influential studies of the origins and grounds of modern nationalism, Smith specifically singles out instances of what he terms a religious myth-symbol complex as the most powerful of all the different kinds of '*mythomoteurs*' (a suggestive term of his coinage) that generate, sustain, and indeed drive, a national consciousness.[6] And in Wales the most effective vehicle for this *mythomoteur* across the centuries has been poetry. It has proved to be a reliable carrier of one of the most durable markers of Welsh identity, culminating in the great tradition of hymns that originated in the eighteenth-century Methodist revival and reached its triumphant zenith in the late nineteenth-century mass singing festivals/*cymanfaoedd canu*.

There was, however, to be no clear, smooth, transmission of this nineteenth-century religious culture to the poets included in this volume. Because in between there occurred a radical cultural dislocation. Many of the first (and it turned out brilliant) generation of Welsh intellectuals, scholars and writers to be the full beneficiaries of the new UK state system of education had ended up deeply critical of established Nonconformist culture. At the beginning of the twentieth century, several of them had, indeed, even rebelled against it, with not a few – such as T. Gwynn Jones, T. H. Parry-Williams and R. Williams Parry – ending up deeply sceptical of any committed form of religious faith – and others, such as W. J. Gruffydd, thoroughly alienated from the sclerotic form it had taken in the moribund late-nineteenth-century Victorian chapel establishment. The same tendency was if anything even more evident in the writings of the gifted generation of English-language authors who were emerging at the same time, mostly from the coalfield society of the South. To some of these the chapels seemed nothing but sinister structures 'squat as toads' defacing the Welsh landscape.[7]

That the poets in this volume emerged from such a cultural background is most evident in the various Christian traditions 'alternative' to that of late-nineteenth-century-Wales to which so many of them were attracted. Saunders Lewis controversially converted to Catholicism, Pennar Davies to a radical tradition of religious dissent (consonant with his version of Welsh Congregationalism) that he traced all the way back to the time of Pelagius and the early Celtic saints. Euros Bowen, son of a Nonconformist minister, became a priest in the Church in Wales (as, of course, did R. S. Thomas), Vernon Watkins's family had also been traditionally Nonconformist, but he became a kind of Neo-Platonic Christian and Welsh Anglican. Roland Mathias's dogged and rugged adherence to Welsh Congregationalism was largely inspired by his interest in the virtues of pre-Nonconformist religious Dissent, while Bobi Jones's

Evangelicalism was likewise an attempt to reconnect with the early, pristine, form of Welsh Nonconformity before it hardened into the practices of the Victorian chapel establishment. The tempestuous Gwenallt trialled several different churches before eventually reverting to the Calvinism of his youth, but with a fierce, consuming addiction to a radical sense of sin that, by the late nineteenth-century, had ceased to be fashionable among the chapel faithful but that is memorably evident in a great poem by Kitchener Davies. As for Waldo Williams, he was drawn to a Quakerism that was at variance with the faith of nineteenth-century Welsh Nonconformity. And the Welsh Anglican R. S. Thomas was scornfully dismissive of a chapel culture that had been so philistine in its rejection of virtually all forms of artistic expression.

In virtually every case, then, one might describe their various forms of religious faith as 'recovered', in what might be called a radically reconstituted form, rather than merely inherited. In that sense, the poets' 'discovery' of religion may be considered a very modest, characteristically Welsh variant of that staple feature of twentieth-century Modernism; the turn to cultural sources that were unconventional, and in some cases even unfashionable – such as Pound's Orientalism, Eliot's Europeanism, Olson's obsession with Mayan culture, the Zen Buddhism of Ginsberg and Snyder – in search of intellectual, poetic and spiritual renewal and orientation.

And as was the case with the Modernist examples, this recovery was counter-cultural in character. The hold of Nonconformity over Welsh life began to wane after the Great War, and a new, secular society emerged slowly but surely. This culture-shift was occasioned to a significant degree by disillusionment with the chapels, some of whose prominent leaders had been enthusiastic supporters of the conflict. But it was also the result of the radical changes that had occurred in Welsh society in the wake of the development of the South Wales coalfield into one of the world's earliest and greatest fully industrialised societies, served by a workforce that included a large number of migrants from across the border as well as from rural Wales. A predominantly anglophone society was soon created, whose connections with traditional Welsh society was complex and occasionally fraught. It increasingly turned (in some cases via Christian Socialism) to a secular Socialism as an 'alternative religion' that offered practical improvement in workers' daily lives. Additionally, the Anglo-British education system, determinedly secular in character and English both

in language and in outlook, was by then deeply entrenched in Wales
and the grammar schools in particular were alienating youngsters
from their traditional backgrounds.

The poets studied in the main body of this volume were all prod-
ucts of these developments, but they responded to them by producing
a body of writing that in its religious character ran counter to the new,
prevailing, ethos. Their output may be criticised for being reactionary
or may be appreciatively accepted as a resourceful recuperative initia-
tive; an attempt to reconnect modern Wales to one of the strongest
and most enduring markers (and indeed safeguards) of its cultural
separateness. In anglophone Welsh literature there had been distin-
guished harbingers of this poetic tradition as early as the seventeenth
century, the most pre-eminent undoubtedly being Henry Vaughan,
the Silurist and self-styled 'Swan of Usk'.[8] If one is allowed to stretch
the definition of Welshness to its uttermost limits, it includes George
Herbert, that other major religious poet of the early seventeenth cen-
tury who was a descendant of Marcher lords of mixed Welsh and
Norman stock. Further to add the name of John Donne is prob-
ably a stretch too far, although he is supposed by some to have been
descended from the Dwnn family of Kidwelly.

*   *   *

This study is obviously interested in the respective beliefs of the poets
chosen for study, but it is equally interested in their poetics, the way
in which their theological outlook is inevitably inscribed in the forms,
styles and discourses that they employ. In other words, it is interested
in the form that belief takes when it becomes a poem. Such a form can
never be merely a passive receptacle or a simple vehicle. It is inevitably
dynamic; to a greater or lesser extent it re-forms belief in the very
process of articulating it. The process of implementing a poetic is
consequently a subtle interactive process, with form modifying belief
even as belief informs the form. In his two 'Jordan' poems Herbert
famously, and defiantly, celebrated the baptismal process of turning a
secular poetics into a sacred, devotional one, a process he repeatedly
characterised as exchanging a flamboyant, self-advertising style of
writing for a plain, direct and honest one.

Much of the poetry considered here may be termed 'sacramental',
allowing for the term being used in a rather loose and general sense
that does not specifically allude to those Holy Sacraments specifically
recognised by the Catholic and Anglican churches. A usefully flexible

definition is provided by *The New SCM Dictionary of Christian Spirituality*: '"Sacramentality" has to do with how human beings are open to the promise of divine grace and the transformative Spirit of God in human affairs' (553). Euros Bowen declared of a poem that there was 'Sacrament sicr ym modd/ei sain', certain sacrament woven into its very music, clear recognition that sacramentalism can inhere in the very structure and language of a poem, and not be limited to its content or 'message'. Bowen's phrase therefore neatly identifies the 'sacramental poetics' with which this study is concerned.

As has already been noted, scarcely a single one of the poets included in this volume merely adhered to the faith of their forebears. In almost every case they embraced an alternative faith of their own choosing. In many cases, too, that elective faith emerged out of a rejection alike of the powerful spiritual heritage of nineteenth-century Nonconformist Wales and of the prevailing liberal agnosticism of their own time. And while most of these poets were aware of working within the broad cultural tradition of spiritual writing developed in Wales over very many centuries, they were certainly not operating within the chapel tradition that had dominated writing during the nineteenth century.

In studying the poems of these writers, I have made no attempt to proselytise. Rather, the study seeks only to suggest that their spirituality operated in each case as a creatively fruitful literary resource, and that such a body of writing as this is culturally singular. It is a rich inheritance, and may even constitute a 'Great Tradition' of twentieth-century Welsh writing (if I may slyly borrow and adapt a term so influentially and proudly applied to the English novel by F. R. Leavis). This is obviously not to claim that this is the only valid tradition, nor indeed that it is the major one. It is only to insist that this mode of writing, seeming so 'belated' to modern cultures beyond Offa's Dyke, is one of the glories of recent Welsh poetry. Furthermore, to the extent that many of these writers were very conscious of the existence of kindred spirits from the past of their culture, such creative awareness often reinforced their writings. In that sense, this body of work may approximate at times to a 'closed cultural system'; that is, to constitute a system that is to some extent self-referential.

* * *

Thirty years ago I had occasion to visit the old Dissenters' Cemetery in Wrexham in the company of a television crew. They were preparing a documentary about the remarkable life and glorious writings of Morgan Llwyd, the great seventeenth-century Puritan evangelist and mystic who was buried there. Imagine the consternation therefore when the tomb proved to be no longer in situ. A frantic search established that the gravestone had been lifted and casually abandoned against the cemetery wall, and there it rested in an anonymity guaranteed by the many other gravestones that kept it company. Disappointed in our purpose, we hurriedly set off cross country to visit Llwyd's old home at Cynfal, near Maentwrog. That, at least, still stood. But the door was opened by a couple from England who, it quickly transpired, had never heard of Llwyd, although they were very welcoming and readily agreed to our filming there.

Over the years, the experiences of that day have periodically returned to me. They increasingly seem to reveal modern Wales's shameful, ignorant, neglect of its rich spiritual heritage. While, as already emphasised, it is no purpose of this study to press the argument – favoured by many of the poets included here – that this heritage captures the essence of the 'true' Wales, it does attempt to bring important aspects of this valuable legacy to the attention of today's readers.

It also attempts to demonstrate that in the Wales of the post-war period at least, that legacy is manifest not only in Welsh-language poetry but also in poetry in the English language. It remains for me cause for sadness that rarely is contemporary Wales considered in its entirety, as a complex compound, so to speak, of two cultures. The country continues to be bedevilled by what the novelist Hugh McLennan, describing his own country of Canada, sadly and memorably termed the 'two solitudes'. He was referring to a perceived lack of communication, and moreover a lack of will to communicate, between Anglophone and Francophone people in Canada. The present volume is therefore yet another of my attempts to break that solitude; to broker communication between 'Welsh Wales' and what is still sometimes referred to as 'Anglo-Welsh Wales'. It is an attempt parallel to my other attempt in this book, which is to broker communication between the poets of present-day Wales and such of their recent predecessors as knew themselves to be the modern heirs of a valuable spiritual heritage.

One final note, at once explicatory and self-exculpatory: this book was written under the conditions of lockdown necessitated by the Coronavirus pandemic. Throughout this period, therefore, it was impossible for me to consult any libraries other than my own. Hence the paucity of footnotes – for which, I am sure, most of my readers will be profoundly grateful.

Notes

1 Rowan Williams, 'Foreword', in Cynthia and Saunders Davies (trans.), *Euros Bowen: priest-poet/bardd-offeiriad* (Penarth: Church in Wales Publications, 1993), p. 9.
2 Quoted in David Jenkins, *Thomas Gwynn Jones: Cofiant* (Denbigh: Gwasg Gee, 1973), p. 154.
3 Wallace Stevens, 'Sunday Morning', *Collected Poems* (London: Faber and Faber, 1965), p. 70.
4 Les Murray, *Collected Poems* (London: Minerva, 1992), p. 272.
5 Bobi Jones, *Ysbryd y Cwlwm: delwedd y genedl yn ein llenyddiaeth* (Cardiff: University of Wales Press, 1998), pp. 43–4.
6 Anthony D. Smith, *Myths and Memories of the Nation* (Oxford: Oxford University Press, 1999).
7 For the response of the English-language literary culture of modern Wales to Nonconformity, see M. Wynn Thomas, *In the Shadow of the Pulpit* (Cardiff: University of Wales Press, 2010).
8 See M. Wynn Thomas, '"In Occidentem & tenebras": putting Henry Vaughan on the map of Wales', in *Corresponding Cultures: the two literatures of Wales* (Cardiff: University of Wales Press, 1999), pp. 7–44.

2

'TRAFFIC-LESS EMMAEUS':
SAUNDERS LEWIS

In 'Art and Sacrament', a brilliant essay in *Epoch and Artist* (1959), David Jones observes that words and poems are 'signs' and thus must be sign-ificant 'of something ... some reality ... something that is sacred'.[1] Form-making is a sign-making that 'causes man's art to be bound to God', the supreme artist, sign-maker and producer of forms. Jones's statement directs our attention to an important truth: a religious conviction is not only manifest in the subject of a poem but inherent in every aspect of its form. It is operative as a choice of poetics. It is through the very sacrament of its form that a poem embodies, or incarnates, a vision of the 'spiritually signifying' natural world it has been carefully designed to convey.

Why begin with David Jones? Partly to remind ourselves that Jones was a London-born poet-artist immensely proud of his Welsh descent on his father's side. He may therefore be reasonably regarded as an 'outlier' at least of the religious tradition that is the subject of the present study. But primarily because he was a very close friend, and soul-mate, of Saunders Lewis, with whom for many decades he maintained an important correspondence – indeed *Epoch and Artist* is dedicated to Lewis, described as 'gŵr celfydd a gâr ei wlad a phob ceinder' (a cultured man who loves his country and all that is beautiful). They were both very proud of being old sweats – veterans of the First World War – and both were Catholic converts of deeply conservative tendencies, whose faith included a great respect for the role played by the arts in inculcating a spirit of worship.

Lewis (1893–1985), a pocket dynamo, was a dominant figure on the Welsh political and cultural scenes for much of the twentieth century. Unfailingly magisterial in his pronouncements, he was a founder and long-time leader of Plaid Cymru, and a fearless controversial activist who spent time in Walton jail for an arson attack in 1936, along with two mild companions who were equally inoffensive, bookish, and also intellectually distinguished. Their crime was to set fire to a government bombing school under construction, in the teeth of Wales-wide opposition, on a culturally sensitive site on the Llŷn peninsula. Lewis was also a major creative talent. He produced a controversial novella, a remarkable body of plays, and a select collection of deeply sacramental poems that were the rich residue of the Catholic faith to which he, a scion of a very distinguished Welsh nonconformist family, had dramatically converted. Such was his stature and consequential impact that before his death he was nominated (unsuccessfully) for a Nobel Prize in literature.

Lewis's short poem 'Y Pîn' / 'The Pine' is a good example of his sacramental vision and poetics. It concludes with lines invoking the miracle of the pine tree by night, when the exhilarating upward thrust of its form seems to reflect the ascension of the moon and stars. As the moon harmoniously rises, so:

> Chwipyn pelydri dithau o'i blaen a phicell dy lam
> O fôn i frig dan ei thrafael
> Yn ymsaethu i galon y gwyll fel Cannwyll y Pasg dan ei fflam:
> Ust: saif y nos o'th gylch yn y gangell glaear
> Ac afrlladen nef yn croesi â'i bendith y ddaear.[2]

[Suddenly you gleam before it and the lance of your leap/ from root to twig beneath its travail/ Pierces the heart of the gloom like the Paschal Candle in flame;/ Hush: the night stands around you in the transparent chancel/ and the consecrated wafer of heaven bestows its benediction on the earth.]

The whole structure is obviously reverently modelled on the Easter Mass, at the very heart of which rests the miracle of transubstantiation. It references, and thus discursively 're-enacts', the miracles of Resurrection and Ascension. In the fiery lancing leap of the pine there is also a hint of the wounding of Christ on the cross, from which redemptive blood is supposed to have flowed, as the tree pierces to the heart of the gloom. In the original Welsh, language itself is carefully

wrought into an elaborate lexical chalice, as 'dyrchafael' (Ascension)
is echoed in 'trafael', which suggests both 'travel' and 'travail', and
'gwyll' (gloom) is transmuted into luminosity by 'Cannwyll' (the word
for 'candle' which both incorporates and transforms the very word
'gwyll'). As night encloses both the pine and its viewer, it forms a
temenos, or sacred enclosure, like the chancel of a great church or
cathedral.

At the very centre of 'Y Pîn' there unmistakeably lies a *mysterium
tremendum*, a great epiphany, in the original sense of that word: a
sudden miraculous manifestation of a supernatural mystery. And it is
an epiphany which the reader is specifically invited to share, through
the involving rhetorical device of apostrophe, or direct exclamatory
address ('Ust'/Hush or Hark). The experience of reading thus approx-
imates to that of participating in a religious communion. As for the
register of the poem, it is appropriately elevated and dignified, its
movement stately and ritualistic.

It is worth lingering on that pivotal figure of the lit Paschal candle,
because its full, rich spiritual import may well be lost on a mod-
ern secular reader. The celebration of Easter is the most sombre, yet
joyous, festival in the whole elaborate ecclesiastical calendar of the
Catholic Church; and at its very centre lies the ritual of lighting the
Paschal candle. Its lighting marks the end of the Easter Vigil on Holy
Saturday. On Maundy Thursday the darkened church has seen the
removal of all adornments – the ceremony known as the 'stripping
of the altars' – and the Host has been withdrawn from its sacred
sanctuary. The end of the Easter Vigil marks the transition from this
period of darkness, signifying Christ's descent into the tomb and the
removal of God's presence from the world, to the light enabled by His
miraculous redemptive resurrection to life. And the lighting of the
great candle (during the Middle Ages it could be up to thirty-six feet
tall) is the symbolic enactment of this great triumph over everything
that the dark has signified.

During this ritual the priest traces the symbols of Alpha and
Omega (the beginning and the end) on the candle and five pieces
of incense are then inserted into it representing the five wounds of
Christ. Once the candle is lit, it is processed into the Church, the priest
raising it three times on high while uttering the proclamation 'The
light of Christ', to which the congregation responds 'Thanks be to
God'. After this the *Exultet* is chanted by the priest, who concludes
by blessing the candle and speaking the following words:

Accept this Easter candle,
A flame divided but undimmed,
A pillar of fire that glows to the honour of God.
(For it is fed by the holy melting wax, which the mother bee has
    brought forth to make this precious candle.)
Let it mingle with the lights of heaven
And continue bravely burning
To dispel the darkness of this night!
May the Morning Star which never sets
Find this flame still burning:
Christ, that Morning Star,
Who came back from the dead,
And shed his peaceful light on all humanity,
Your Son, who lives and reigns for ever and ever.
Amen.

There are several other poems by Lewis testifying to his sensitivity
to the sacramental aspects of the natural world. One such is 'Llygad
y Dydd yn Ebrill' (A Daisy in April) (*CSL*, 1). It is a condensed
poem, elaborately ornate and enriched with epigrams in the grand
manner of ancient *barddas*, whose bards traditionally reserved such
a majestic style for emollient praise of the powerful and the mighty.
Lewis employs that high style instead to praise that most ubiqui-
tous of plants, the commonplace daisy, so frequently overlooked and
even despised. His poem is a celebration of the miraculous advent of
augmented sight (what Coleridge called the 'armed vision'), which
has empowered him to see the daisy afresh, as if newly arrived from
the very hands of the Creator. The interlinking tropes function as
enlarging conceits. The little flower is the mirror of dawn, a crystal
shilling, a ruby and gem in a bog, a drop from the Milky way, the
heavens turned upside and placing the sky's million suns underfoot
to gild grey earth's lawns, the glittering fire of God's glow-worms
become living stars. This tour de force of troping is not a bravura
performance cunningly fashioned to demonstrate a poet's skill but a
seemingly spontaneous upsurge of astonishment at the splendours
of God's world.

As for 'Difiau Dyrchafael' (Ascension Thursday) (*SCL*, 38),
its natural sacramentalism is explicitly avowed when Lewis, sur-
veying the splendours of a May morning, sees creation staging
its own celebration of the Eucharist on the Feast Day of the
Ascension:

> The dazzle of white on the shoulders of the hawthorn,
> The attentive emerald of the grass and the still calves,
>
> See the chestnut's candelabra alight,
> The hedgerows kneeling and the birch a mute nun,
> The cuckoo's two-notes over the smooth hush of the brook,
> And the spectre of mist rising aslant from the thurible of the
>   meadows.

However, what is in general a fine poem is sadly not without its dubious note, because as Lewis moves on to the rapturous conclusion in which the earth seems to him to be 'elev[ating] an immaculate wafer', and the Father 'kiss[ing] the son in the white dew', he extends an invitation to the inhabitants of the council houses to come out to witness this revelation. In the work of other poets, such an action would naturally be construed as a generously inclusive gesture to ensure that ordinary representatives of humanity at large are graced with this epiphany. But from Lewis's other writings, we know that he abhorred public housing (as he did the Welfare State that was under construction when the poem was first published in 1951) because he thought it improper that the State should in any way interfere with what by right should be the sole, moral responsibility of the individual. Read with this context in mind, his reference to council-house dwellers cannot but seem to introduce a regrettable and wholly gratuitous note of sarcastic condescension into an otherwise moving and powerful poem.

   Lewis's particular brand of devout Catholicism did not always, then, advantage his poetry. I for one cringe, for instance, when I read his unctuous tribute to the Catholic Archbishop of Wales, Michael Joseph McGrath (*CSL*, 26–7). An awareness that it is a conscious exercise in poetic eulogy – a traditional Welsh genre of which Lewis greatly approved as 'the portrayal of an ideal which is the body of unity of a tribe or society or nation'[3] – does little to improve my opinion of it. It is a reminder of how creatively inhibiting Lewis's deep respect for the grand hierarchy of the Catholic Church could sometimes be. This was reinforced by his interest in the Great Chain of Being, a seminal concept of the late medieval mind to which attention had been newly drawn by A. O. Lovejoy (1936) and E. M. W. Tillyard (1943). Lewis became convinced that this supplied a key to understanding the social structure and poetic culture of the golden age of the Welsh strict-metre poets. He summarised it as follows:

> The Chain starts with the Trinity and descends through Our Lady and the Saints and down all the celestial hierarchies. Then we find described the corresponding orders of the Church Militant on earth, from Pope and Cardinal down to parish priest and beggar friar. There follow the hierarchies of the laity, the emperor, the kings, the Princes of Wales, dukes, lords, knights, esquires, freemen. (*SLP*, 103)

As this account of the *scala naturae* makes clear, this theologically determined model included an emphasis on a hierarchically organised human society, with each class or rank knowing its place. This chimed with Lewis's own extravagant respect for the class of the 'uchelwyr', the esquires or minor gentry of late-medieval Wales. He idealised them because they had been important patrons of the Welsh poets turned peripatetic following the death of the last Prince of Wales, Llywelyn ap Gruffydd, in 1282 and the consequent destruction of the last royal court. A substantial body of high-quality work had accordingly been produced by the prominent Welsh poets of that period in copious and sometimes fulsome praise of their munificent benefactors. Lewis believed that the process of wholesale cooption of the representatives of this Welsh squirearchy into the English social establishment, a process that accelerated markedly after the Act of Union of 1536, had been a social, cultural and political catastrophe for Wales. Society had been shorn of its natural leaders, and as the newly anglicised gentry gravitated towards the new wealth and privileges on offer in London, so they became increasingly alienated from the culture they had originally served and sustained. The country houses of Wales turned into alien settlements, pockets of English influence, and Welsh poets found they were no longer welcome in an environment where the Welsh language itself was no longer understood.

Lewis never ceased to hope that one day this tragically alienated class might be culturally repatriated and restored, albeit on modern terms, to its ancient respected and influential status. Wales, he devoutly believed, would return to the Old Faith. When, therefore, he came to know a country gentleman by the name of R. O. F. Wynne it seemed that his dream had been realised. Although a native of Hampshire, Wynne had fervently believed he was reconnecting with his ancient family roots when he acquired Garthewin, a country house in the Denbighshire countryside, following the death of a relative. There he set about learning Welsh, and was converted to Lewis's brand of nationalism at much the same time as he also became a Catholic convert. At Garthewin he proceeded to turn an eighteenth-century barn into a small theatre, home to a Welsh-language theatre company formed to stage plays that were unlikely to attract a popular audience. A prominent part of this repertoire were the late plays of Saunders Lewis, who became devoted both to Garthewin and its patrician owner.

In due course, he set out to emulate the Welsh poets of the fifteenth and sixteenth centuries by producing his own extravagantly grateful eulogy in praise of the gracious owner of Garthewin, rather as Yeats, one of his poetic heroes, had done when enjoying the enlightened patronage of the surviving Anglo-Irish aristocracy. One word to which Yeats was repeatedly drawn when celebrating the imagined gracious elegance of life in the Ancestral Houses of Ireland was 'courtesy', a term that for him comprehended due order and decorum, an absence of which had made the modern world a savagely disordered place, a 'mere anarchy'. This too was adapted as a key value for Lewis, who opened the 'awdl' he wrote for Garthewin by invoking the fabled 'seddau moes' (the seats of courtesy) of the original Welsh hierarchy.

That phrase is the first of many signals in the text that Lewis is consciously modelling his poem on the eulogies that were produced in some bulk, and in varying quality, by the wandering poets of the Golden Age in canny praise of their patrons. Accordingly, he crafts an 'awdl', which was the most elaborate and prestigious genre in the tradition, because it required the demonstration of skill in several of the demanding forms of writing approved by the strict-metre masters. Lewis therefore sets out to reproduce techniques proper to what is a highly stylised and ornamented genre. The most obvious is the rhetorical device of 'chain verse', by means of which stanzas are made to interlock by repeating the final phrase of one at the beginning of the next. Also highly conventional was extravagant praise for the host's munificent hospitality (in particular his wine cellar, that seemed always to include only the most choice of Continental vintages), his beneficence towards his social inferiors, his discriminating cultural taste, and his astute social and political leadership.

Lewis further makes it clear that he has one of the greatest of the classical eulogies in particular in mind when writing 'Garthewin'.

Written in the popular 'cywydd' strict-metre form, Iolo Goch's cele-
brated fourteenth-century poem was in praise of Owain Glyndŵr's
estate at Sycharth: 'A baron's court, place of fine manners,/ Where
many bards come, where life's good'.[4] (It was later to be razed to the
ground following Glyndŵr's spectacular, but ultimately unsuccessful,
rebellion against the English crown.)

Iolo praises the symmetry of design of the great house, with its
neatly interlocking beams ('each with a knot tied tight,/ Is interlocked
with the other', 250), and its nine halls, each with its own wardrobe.
As in Ben Jonson's later poem 'To Penshurst', deemed particularly
praiseworthy is the fabled orderliness and plenty of the Sycharth estate
in its trim entirety, with its orchard, vineyard, mill and dovecote, and
its brimming pond well stocked with pike and whiting. Peacocks and
'high-stepping heron' strut the ample grounds that also encompass
'grain-rows in well-tended fields', hay and pasture meadows, ploughs
and powerful horses, a rabbit park and a deer park.

This, then, is an idyllic Arcadian landscape, both human and nat-
ural, and it is seen as generously sustaining and nurturing the whole
society of which it is the centre and lynch-pin. Within its domain, serfs
dutifully labour, fetching and carrying beer from distant Shrewsbury;
they roast meat in the great kitchens, and bake bread in the great
ovens. It is a contented realm entire unto itself, yet it is the focal point
of an extended community, and at the gentle heart of it all are the lord
of the manor, his cultured wife and their many gracious children. Iolo
thus paints the picture of a perfectly ordered, carefully graded late-
feudal society, and it is this vision that Saunders Lewis attempts to
replicate in his eulogy to Garthewin, in his view a latter-day example
of like courtesy and munificence.

His poem provides an excellent demonstration of the interdepend-
ence of his theological beliefs and his social and cultural convictions.
Garthewin is a perfect microcosm of the glorious orderliness of God's
creation and its highly civilised and ideal structure is specifically
attributed to Robert Wynne's Catholic faith. Just as the church is, for
Iolo Goch, an integral, indeed pivotal, feature of the Sycharth estate,
so Lewis reveres Garthewin because there 'y mae'r sagrafennau/ Yn
anadlu fry dros ein cenedl frau' (CSL, 7) (the sacraments breathe on
high over our fragile nation). It is a redemptive vision, one which
brings into burning focus Lewis's fervent hopes that recovery of pride
and cultural vigour may one day be enabled by his nation's reversion
to its 'old faith.' The generating heart of Lewis's poem is therefore

its dream of a return to the pristine purity and vigour of origins. He believes that Wynne's return to the estate of his forefathers, and his restoration of it to its ancient role in serving its society, is a prefiguration of what may be to come. And, similarly, his own return in the very form of his 'awdl' to the classic genre and sophisticated strict-metre poetic of the bards of the late medieval period is a mirroring tribute to Wynne's exemplary achievements.

*   *   *

Lewis detected an underlying principle of hierarchical order both in the complex internal structure of strict-metre poetry (in many lines, for instance, the second half mirrors the first in the choice and sequence of its consonants, as also sometimes in the harmonious consort of its vowels) and in the breath-taking architectonics of medieval Europe's great cathedrals. The blueprint for both these remarkable achievements, he believed, was that Age's belief in the divinely ordained *scala naturae*, and 'Garthewin' is consciously based on the same template. In his view, the production of an appropriate form was the primary, and sacred, aim and duty of any poet. This was the subject of an important address he delivered at a symposium on the arts held at Downside Abbey, one of the greatest Catholic educational institutions in England, in 1957.

Invited to give 'some indication of how in your view art meditates truth,' he opened by remarking that what sets a poet working 'is the realisation that what is vaguely in his mind has the promise, the shapeability, of a poem'. Because 'a poet is a man who has formed the habit of making poems' (*SLP*, 182). As he further arrestingly put it, 'The Dante of the *Inferno* was not a man who had been through hell, but a man who went into hell a-making' (*SLP*, 183). Poetry was for Lewis a matter of 'making', not of 'poetic vision' – he admitted that he winced, and balked, at the pretentious adjective 'poetic', a legacy he believed of the Romantic Movement, which sought to privilege poetry by attributing to it a unique power of insight. While admitting that the 'foreconscious' certainly played a crucial part in the creative process, he much preferred to emphasise the role of an awakened intelligence that moulded what had originally been inchoate into a form, a shape that gave utterance to something previously hidden even from the poet himself. At the same time, he admitted that no consciously directed act of intelligence was involved in the initial stages of finding an appropriate shape, which rather suddenly mysteriously appeared, 'proton-like and Proteus like, having crossed no intermediate space' (*SLP*, 183). That striking reference to the proton (discovered by Rutherford in 1919) is a revelation of how wide-ranging were Lewis's interests, and how catholic as well as Catholic was his spiritual appreciation of the inherently mysterious propulsions of the natural universe and of human intelligence alike.

The achievement of an appropriate shape next required the application of further faculties before a poem emerged complete. Most important at this stage, Lewis emphasised at some length, was the critical intelligence, and its successful exercise depended entirely on the prior mastery of technique – a capacity Lewis regarded as crucial to the final achievement of what David Jones had called significant form. 'Making a poem, like making pictures,' he stressed, 'is applied criticism' (*SLP*, 186). And then he noted an interesting paradox, perhaps with his own Garthewin poem in mind: hardest of all to produce is an original poem not (as popularly supposed) in free verse but in a pre-existing genre. Finally, Lewis was absolutely insistent that a distinction had to be drawn between a poet and his poem. 'A good poem is an impersonal thing' (*SLP*, 187). T. S. Eliot had also, of course, already famously stressed as much.

Lewis was an admirer of Jacques Maritain, one of the towering Catholic intellectuals of twentieth-century Europe. The guiding light for Maritain, who consciously belonged to the Scholastic tradition of theologians and philosophers, was St Thomas Aquinas. In Chapter 3 of his volume *Art and Scholasticism* (a work of importance to writers such as Flannery O'Connor, the distinguished short-story writer from the Southern US State of Georgia), Maritain stressed that 'The Fine Arts ... stand out in the *genus* art as man stands out in the *genus* animal. And like man himself they are like a horizon where matter comes into contact with spirit.'[5] He excoriated the modern age, which in his opinion was 'founded upon the two *unnatural* principles of the fecundity of money and the *finality of the useful*, multiplying its needs and servitudes without any possibility of there ever being a limit, ruining the leisure of the soul' (*AS*, 37). The 'ultimate aim of all this frenzy', he added, 'is to prevent man from remembering God' (*AS*, 37). Maritain also observed the 'curious analogy' between the Fine Arts and Contemplation. 'They are disinterested,' he wrote, 'pursued for their own sake, truly noble because their work considered in itself is not made to be used as a means, but to be enjoyed as an end ... Their whole value is spiritual and their manner of being is

contemplation' (*AS*, 34). And he shrewdly endorses Aquinas's view
that in this respect the arts resemble games, which also have their
non-utilitarian and contemplative aspects.

> Art, which rules Making and not Doing, stands therefore outside the
> human sphere; it has an end, rules, values which are not those of man, but
> those of the work to be produced. This work is everything for Art; there
> is for Art but one law – the exigencies and the good of the work. (*AS*, 7)

It was this serene impersonality that allowed Art to soothe the anx-
ieties of the existential condition. And it seemed proper to Maritain
that the personal identities of the master-minds of the great medieval
cathedrals should remain forever unknown to history. The true artist
was an *artifex*, an artisan, a maker.

Lewis's guarded acknowledgement of the crucial role of the pre-
conscious in the formative process may also be usefully glossed by
Maritain's influential remarks on the subject in *Creative Intuition and
the Arts* (1953). There he talks of the artist's necessary 'liberation
from conceptual, logical, discursive reason', a liberation that is also
marked by a related freedom from the restrictions of language as
conventionally used.[6] An artist instead turns to 'intuitive reason –
functioning in a nonrational way'. While Maritain was in this respect
avowedly influenced by the works of his old teacher, Henri Bergson,
the concepts he deployed had, in truth, already been recognised and
creatively employed by writers of the Romantic period, although
Saunders Lewis, the fervent anti-Romantic, would no doubt have been
eager to discount this. In any case Maritain anticipated Lewis's disap-
proval of the modern heirs of Romanticism by proceeding to deplore
the distortions of the pure creative impulse by such 'Narcissists' as
Rimbaud, misguided Post-Impressionists such as Picasso, and the
whole tribe of Surrealists, although Maritain also conceded that there
had been 'genuine' poets amongst the last.

He proceeded to distinguish between the 'Freudian unconscious'
of the Surrealists and what he termed his own belief in a 'spiritual
unconscious', 'an immense and preconscious life' which is involved in
even the most mundane examples of the human will as it exercises its
freedom to choose. 'Such a life', he explained, 'develops in night, but
in a night which is translucid and fertile, and resembles that primeval,
diffused light which was created first', before God created the living
universe. And it is from this life that the poet's ability proceeds, as

Maritain nicely put it, to 'hear the passwords and the secrets that are stammering in things'.[7]

*   *   *

Lewis's concept of poetic form was, then, deeply infused with his spiritual beliefs, and for him the artistic production of form was a religious act. He advised the readers in a brief introduction to an exhibition of David Jones's work at the Tate in 1954–5 to pay heed to the Gospel inscriptions and phrases that were integral to the paintings, emphasising that 'the artist worked long at them, praying them to their shape on the paper' (*SLP*, 110). And he went on to compare them suggestively to the 'Promises' that 'pious Welsh mothers used once to embroider … into samplers on cottage walls' (*SLP*, 110).

Lewis also believed that the production of any new poem necessitated a 'preconscious' search for the form specifically appropriate to it. Accordingly, the body of work he produced, though slim, covers a range of poetic genres. For Lewis, it was vitally important in each case to ensure that form was perfectly suited to spiritual purpose. Thus, when he produced 'Pregeth Olaf Dewi Sant' (St David's last sermon), a poem in praise of the patron saint of Wales, it would have been inappropriate to have fashioned a poem as 'high church', so to speak, as is 'Y Pîn'. After all, Dewi had been a pre-Catholic Christian, a sixth-century ascetic of the Celtic Church, and he had become famous for a legendary sermon preached at the Synod of Llanddewi-brefi, in anticipation of his imminent death. For Lewis, Dewi's Celtic Christianity had been the precursor of the orthodox Catholic faith eventually brought to Britain from the Continent by the monk Augustine and accepted by the Welsh around 777. But after the Reformation, Dewi had been alternatively claimed as precursor first by the Anglican Church and later by the Welsh Nonconformist denominations. Lewis's poem is therefore a determined attempt to reclaim Dewi for his own faith.

The crowd at the sermon in Llanddewi-brefi had, according to the standard Life, recorded in the late eleventh century at Llanbadarn by Rhygyfarch, been so large that in order to make himself seen and heard by the multitude Dewi had caused the land to rise miraculously under his feet to form a hill. It was from that vantage point that he preached his celebrated sermon, in which he exhorted his followers to honour his memory by keeping the faith, and performing the ordinary 'little things' of life, as he himself had always taken such particular, humble, exemplary care to do.

The form produced by Lewis 'answered' to St David's personality and message in being plain, colloquial blank verse, a form standard since the Elizabethan age in English poetry but not at all 'native' to Welsh poetic tradition. Superficially simple, and employed initially to relate a simple narrative, as it proceeds it becomes increasingly freighted with layers of cultural and historical association. Lewis contrasts the life as recorded around 1094 by Rhygyfarch with the stories of Dewi later related by an anchorite housed in the church at Llanddewi-brefi, close to where the saint's famous 'funerary' sermon had been preached. Rhygyfarch (or Rhigyfarch), a monk, was a formidable scholar from a distinguished clerical family, who was attached to the *scriptorium* of the *clas* (the sacred enclosure with its monastic community) that enclosed the great church at Llanbadarn Fawr, on the outskirts of modern-day Aberystwyth. His account of Dewi was accordingly learned, polished, and sophisticated. By contrast, the anchorite was a humble, anonymous monk, recording such tales of Dewi as he had gleaned from popular accounts. For Lewis, the latter comes to represent the transmission of folk memories down the centuries from generation to generation, a process essential for the maintenance both of a religious tradition and a national culture. In this process, too, Lewis the Catholic believer living in the remnants of a committedly Nonconformist Wales, found consolatory evidence that the 'old, original, faith' of the nation had continued to be preserved at popular level long after Protestantism had been officially adopted as the religion of the state.

There is moreover an intriguing, partially occluded, armature to the poem, a secondary narrative operating as an important structuring principle, which traces the development of Dewi over many centuries into an icon of national resistance. Lewis's use of the definitive English poetic form of blank verse may therefore be viewed as a subtle act of counter-cultural appropriation. This subtext is first glimpsed when he describes the devastating effect Dewi's passing had on the whole country. In their lamentations, he writes, they cried out for the earth to devour them, the sea to cover the land, and the mountains to fall upon them. These are conventional Biblical utterances, of course, but they also call to mind the most famous passage of all in Gruffydd ab yr Ynad Coch's great thirteenth-century elegy for Llywelyn ein Llyw Olaf (Llywelyn the last Prince of Wales), which employs exactly the same powerful, stylised, rhetoric.

This is prelude to a number of further cultural references in Lewis's poem that cumulatively make it clear that the passing of Dewi was not only that of a saintly man, but of a 'national' leader. Acknowledging the centrality of the Life of Dewi as recorded by Rhygyfarch in his 'anxious cell' within the 'worried *clas*' of Llanbadarn Fawr around 1094, Lewis emphasises that the learned scribe had, in the immediate aftermath of the Norman Conquest, been the custodian of what remained of his people's precious, and endangered, ancient manuscripts. His Life had been an attempt to protect the traditional status of St David's cathedral (where his father Silyn had been Bishop) as the universally acknowledged centre of the Catholic See in Wales, in opposition to the Normans' (eventually successful) attempt to replace it with Canterbury. Gerald the Welshman was the most famous of several who waged the very same, futile, campaign a century or so later. In his *Life*, Rhygyfarch had pointedly claimed that when Dewi and two saintly companions had made a pilgrimage to Jerusalem, he had there been officially consecrated Archbishop of Wales.

But then, Lewis proceeds to emphasise, the work of preserving Dewi's memory had passed from the hands of the learned scribes in their great ecclesiastical enclosures into the hands of the 'gwerin', the ordinary Welsh people, thanks to the popular legends (unmentioned by Rhygyfarch) that had been recorded in 1346 in the Book of the Anchorite of Llan-ddewi-brefi. It was the 'gwerin' who had cherished the loving memories of Dewi, the people's saint, throughout the many centuries that had seen endless conflicts and brought with them the sullen tyranny of the aliens' castles. It was the 'gwerin' who had implicitly realised that Dewi in his distinctive way had been a 'Gwledig' – the Welsh term for the 'Dux Brittonum', or 'Count of the Saxon Shore', who, after the legions had departed, had rallied the peoples of Britain to the defence of their land from the ravages of the Saxon invaders. After all, had Dewi not been reputed to be the great-grandson of the legendary fifth-century Cunedda, supposedly the earliest champion of the 'West Britons' against the Saxons, and one whose ancestors were seemingly Roman citizens – hence Lewis's further association of Cunedda with 'the imperial purple'. And, although there is no mention of it in Lewis's poem, Dewi had even been hailed as a Welsh resistance hero in the ninth-century poem *Armes Prydain*, which was in a way the national epic of Welsh

resistance. Like 'Garthewin', then, 'Pregeth olaf Dewi Sant' exempli-
fies the fusion of religious belief and nationalist politics in Lewis'
poetry.

*   *   *

Although comparatively few in number, Lewis's poems are of several
different kinds, consistent with what might be termed his 'theology of
form'. In 1954 the Yale scholar Louis L. Martz published his classic
study of *The Poetry of Meditation*.[8] It demonstrated how the intense
religious poems of John Donne and George Herbert betrayed in
their composition a familiarity with St Ignatius of Loyola's *Spiritual
Exercises*. Published in 1548, this became an important document of
the Counter-Reformation, and deeply influenced the art of several
of the major painters of the sixteenth and seventeenth centuries.
This was because it explained in considerable detail how a devout
believer might deepen spiritual meditation by employing all the senses
to imagine what it must have been like actually to experience central
events of the Christian narrative, such as the Crucifixion. While not
attempting to reproduce the discipline and rigour of this exercise as
laid down by Loyola, two poems in particular by Lewis may be use-
fully understood as belonging very broadly to this meditative tradition.

'Mair Fadlen' (Mary Magdalen), technically a heptastich (seven-
line poem) regularly rhyming abbacca, opens with an arresting
observation: 'Am wragedd ni all neb wybod' (About women no one
can ever know). Mary's heart remains a sealed tomb, her existence has
been turned into a dead sea. The poem dwells in great detail on the
lethargy of profound hopelessness into which Mary sank following
the Crucifixion, and its detailed attempt to enter into her depressed
state of mind is greatly reinforced by the monotonous, unvarying
repetition of the same confining pattern of rhyme throughout. The
effect is of the form itself becoming a verse tomb, suggestive both of
Mary's state of mind, and of course of the Christ she now hopelessly
believes is no more than a corpse.

The deadening effect is intensified by the largely unvarying use of
masculine rhymes – single, monosyllabic, rhyming words on which
the final accent of every line falls with a numbing regularity. The
oppressive atmosphere of mental paralysis is intensified by the rep-
etition, or near-repetition, of words, often linked by internal rhyme,
or para-rhyme. Then there is the proliferation of conceits and other
tropes that do nothing to advance or diversify understanding as they

circle in a vortex of deepening hopelessness around the one, terrible, agonisingly inescapable fact of Christ's death.

The setting for Lewis's poem is dawn of day on Easter Sunday, but virtually the whole poem is really concerned to explore the desolation of the previous day, Holy Saturday. He therefore chooses to place particular emphasis on what some contemporary theologians have argued has become a harrowing (in several meanings of the term) lacuna, a period that Christian churches have preferred to ignore, that period of 'non-time' that the Church calls Holy Sunday. The theologian Alan E. Lewis, for instance, argues that

> The familiar rendering of the Easter story, heard as it were 'on mono', is a hopeless distortion of its true sound. For the comforting joy of Easter morning *already* from the start anaesthetizes Friday's pain; the anticipation of Sunday make casual and phoney the waiting of the second day, since there is never any doubt that there *is* a new day coming, to be waited for. It is ... only the 'stereophonic' sound of both the first time story and the familiar which gives the narrative its quality of gospel Word, and its deepest meaning.[9]

Some might object to the stereotypical association of women with passive suffering, and the strong, instinctive sympathy with women's condition, which is very apparent in all of Lewis's creative writings, may no doubt be fairly criticised as based on an essentially narrow understanding of the needs and capacities of the feminine. Be that as it may, it is by attempting to imagine himself into the state of mind (and spirit) of the desolate Magdalen as she approaches the tomb – the state of mind which has become permanent ever since the Crucifixion, throughout the darkness and silence of Holy Saturday – that Lewis enables himself to imagine the numbing chaos of a Godless world. And there are several suggestive asides in his writings that indicate he himself was far from being so absolutely certain in his faith as to be immune to the nightmare fear of the catastrophe of non-belief. He was clearly appalled by what he believed to be the fearful implications of a life bankrupt of any spiritual purpose and therefore prey to total disintegration.

The recent Pope, Benedict XVI, was born and baptised on Holy Saturday, 1927. So that day had a particular significance for him, as he made clear in his words on viewing the Shroud of Turin in 2010. He reflected on how the 'hiddenness of God' had become a common experience, and emphasised that the Church had to find effective means of countering Nietzsche's influential assertion that 'God is dead'. And he continued by speaking of how 'after the two World Wars, the *lagers* and the *gulags*, Hiroshima and Nagasaki, our era has ever increasingly become a Holy Saturday. This day's darkness challenges all those who question life, and it challenges us believers in particular.'

Underlying Saunders Lewis's poem are very similar sentiments, as he contemplates the terror of living in a 'byd heb Grist byw, Sabath dychrynllyd y cread' (a world without a living Christ, the terrible Sabbath of creation) (*SLP*, 23). 'Sabbath' here is used in its root Hebrew sense of day of rest, which the Jews believe is Saturday, and which Lewis therefore associated with the Catholics' Holy Saturday. By imagining the creation as 'resting' in deathly, inanimate form Lewis is pointedly reversing the passage of Genesis that describes God resting from His labours on the seventh day – the pause in the momentum of divine creative energy becomes transmuted into a total, seemingly permanent, absenting of life. It is a de-creation. Thus the break of day as experienced by Mary becomes a 'plygain du', a black dawn, the 'gwlith' (dew) is cold, the ground laden with ash.

At the centre of the poem is Lewis's belief that God withheld from her His pity, because pity would have been but an empty sentimental emotional reflex. In that sense, his dread God is cleansingly pitiless, as instead He hounds the flesh to its lair, and instils in her a saint's iron resolve. His burning love is a voracious, scouring, fire devouring all until it has nakedly exposed her soul, the prey that He seizes with steel claws. Mary's natural wish is only to bathe, clean and anoint Christ's beloved flesh, but God has decreed that never again will His Son be physically available to her touch – unlike Thomas, who was even allowed to plunge his disbelieving hand into His wound. In the bruise of dawn, she hastens to the tomb.

There is about Lewis's poem more than a hint of Baroque extravagance, as he multiplies his conceits with profuse ingenuity, and this is very much in keeping with its subject. After all, the story of the Resurrection is a 'scandal' to the profane multitude, an offence to reason as to nature, a manifest absurdity. As the poem nears its familiar, yet eternally unlikely, climax, so Lewis makes ever greater claims on his poetic form, exploiting its resources with prominent skill. For much of its course the multifaceted image of Mary's psychological state built up by the many conceits does nothing to alter what remains a permanently static condition. Although previously not entirely absent from the poem, feminine rhymes (where the accent falls on the penultimate syllable of a rhyming word) quietly begin to predominate, as the poem begins to open to a wider range and flexibility of experiences.

And then there is the virtuosic exploitation of the exceptionally rich repertoire of sonic effects with which Welsh, being a complex, fluid system of constant mutations, is replete. In the penultimate stanza, Lewis briefly intensifies the impression of Mary's mental paralysis by actually repeating words yet subtly altering their meanings. Thus, there is mention of Orpheus lamenting (galaru) his lost Eurydice and this is coupled with the contrasting description of Mary who cries 'heb alaru' (without lamenting). Then her cry ('llef') to disciple and angel alike for news of what has happened to her Lord is changed, without its meaning being altered, into her cry to the gardener ('ymlefaru') who is of course in truth the risen Lord. But most brilliant of all is the effect Lewis brings off at the very climax of the narrative. There, mention of God manifesting Himself in 'y grym sy'n Air' (the Power that is the Word), becomes 'a dywedodd wrthi, Mair', where 'gair/air' (word) is discovered to be incorporated within Mary's very name. It is a theologically profound use of a homonym, since it signifies the transfiguration of Mair into a new being through the in-forming and re-forming power of the divine Word.

A notable feature of the poem's conclusion is Lewis's remarkable reference to the story of Orpheus and Eurydice – a striking example of his use of a tradition as ancient as the early Church fathers of interpreting stories from Classical myth as allegorical prefigurations of events in the New Testament. Earlier in the poem, Mary is likened to Niobe, the bereaved mother weeping inconsolably for her lost children, who was eventually turned by Zeus into a stone. Then, at the end, he turns to the story of Orpheus and Eurydice, with the powerful implication that his 'song' is as powerless as that of the fabled Orpheus to recover a soul from the darkness of the spiritual underworld and to restore it to light. Yet, powerless though all Lewis's words have been, a single word from the risen Christ is enough to reanimate Mary. In that simple, heartbreakingly moving, utterance of her familiar name is an act of new creation corresponding to the original Fiat Lux in Genesis. Because it brings Mary back not to her old life but to a new one, and Christ's utterance of it is a sacred affirmation of her transfigured being – Lewis specifically mentions how He seizes her out of her flesh and crowns her.

Finally, it is worth noting the image of God that Lewis gives us at this climactic moment of the poem, because here, too, there seem to be overtones of the imperious actions of the pagan Zeus, who so often in myth swooped to possess some mortal woman. His predatory God descends on Mary 'yn sydyn fel eryr o'r Alpau'n disgyn tua'i brae' (suddenly, like an Alpine eagle descending on its prey) (*SLP*, 25), because manifest in His actions is the 'cariad sy'n symud y sêr, y grym sy'n Air' (the love that moves the stars, the power that is a Word). In his final poems, R. S. Thomas chose to refer to God repeatedly as a raptor. Lewis is similarly keen to emphasise that his God is a non-human God, a God beyond reason, a totally unpredictable God whose omnipotence can strike human beings with awe and terror, even when it manifests itself as a salvatory love. The only adequate response is that of Mary, when she addresses the risen Lord not as 'Jesus' nor as 'Christ', but simply as 'Rabboni' (spiritual master), humbly recognising that He, too, is a being totally beyond her human apprehension – although not beyond her human reach – to whose divine unfathomable wisdom she can do nothing but submit.

*   *   *

The twin of 'Mair Fadlen' is 'I'r Lleidr Da' (To the Good Thief) (*SLP*, 9). It concentrates on the moment when the thief begs Christ to remember Him when He enters His kingdom, and it opens by powerfully emphasising that he had not even been granted the privilege of seeing Jesus perform any of his miracles, nor been present when He walked on the water, nor on the Mount of Transfiguration, nor when He restored the blush of life to the corpse of Lazarus. The parables – those 'Parthenons of language' – had not been heard by him, nor had he caught Jesus's accents when speaking of His heavenly father; and he had been absent both from the miracle of the Last Supper and from the Agony in the Garden. Although Lewis never specifically mentions it, it is obvious that in all these respects the Good Thief is our representative, as we, too, believers and non-believers alike, have never had the advantage of listening to or witnessing the living words and actions of Christ. Like the Good Thief, therefore, we have to take them all on trust, to risk all, as he did, on 'blind' belief.

What the Good Thief did see, the poem emphasises, is the degradation and humiliation of Christ in His agonies of mind and spirit as well as of body on the cross. And Lewis movingly registers the vileness of it all, His flesh exposed, condemned to stew in His own filth, contemptuously abandoned like a sack of bones on a pole, reduced to a mere scarecrow. His regal retinue consists of two common thieves, each twitching comically in agony like a flayed toad. Then there are the coarse gibes and the loutish jeering that accompany the event, turning it into black comedy and vulgar parody, and all this is done to one whom Lewis fastidiously addresses as 'feistr cwrteisi a moes', 'master of courtesy and manners'. The Good Thief was the only one to realise that the crude joke rebounded against its perpetrators. Blinded by contempt to the truth in the inscription 'Rex Judorum', they failed to see that '[C]abledd [became] oracl byw', blasphemy was reversed into living oracle. Lewis's own poem is, in its way, an attempt at the same process of transformation, words being redeemed as they are changed from instruments of degradation into instruments of redemption.

Finally, in the last stanza, Lewis duplicates the Good Thief's prayer. But he addresses it not to Christ but to the thief himself, whom he recognises as the alter ego of every Christian believer, and therefore the appropriate intercessor for them all. Thus, he begs the one who has now become 'flaenor bonedd y nef', the leader of all the gracious gentry of heaven, to bring all Christians to a true view of Christ before the hour of their death. Through that spontaneous petition, Lewis concludes, the Good Thief succeeded in plucking Paradise itself off the very nails of a stake. It is, he implies, an audacious, yet totally unintended, spiritual tour de force.

There is, I think, one work in particular that can help us penetrate to the very heart of 'I'r Lleidr Da'. In 1951 an English translation (*Waiting on God*) was published of *Attente de Dieu* (1950), a collection of remarkable personal essays (that had originated as letters) by the strange French mystic and scholar Simone Weil.[10] She had died in 1943 from an illness 'aggravated', as the dust-jacket put it, 'by her refusal to eat [in England] anything more than was given to her compatriots in Occupied France'. Her work became hugely influential, in Britain as well as on the Continent, for several decades. Whether or not Lewis read it, I do not know – although it would be surprising if not – but from this slim collection, one essay in particular stands out as penetratingly illuminating that particular aspect of the crucifixion that had arrested his attention in 'I'r Lleidr Da'.

In her essay on 'The Love of God and Affliction', Weil draws what she regards as a vital distinction between suffering, which she largely equates with physical pain, including the most extreme, and affliction, where extreme suffering is accompanied by what might crudely be termed a prostration of soul and degradation of spirit. She speaks of this condition as involving 'an uprooting of life' (*WG*, 77), and likens it to being branded 'with the mark of slavery' (*WG*, 77). And she expands on its dark consequences:

> Affliction makes God appear to be absent for a time, more absent than a dead man, more absent than light in the utter darkness of a cell. A kind of horror submerges the whole soul. During this absence there is nothing to love. What is terrible is that if, in this darkness where there is nothing to love, the soul ceases to love, God's absence becomes final. (*WG*, 81)

For her, the supreme example of affliction is the crucifixion. 'Christ ... being made a curse for us,' she writes, 'it was not only the body of Christ, hanging on the wood, which was accursed, it was his whole soul also' (*WG*, 81). 'Christ was afflicted', she elsewhere writes, '[H]e did not die like a martyr. He died like a common criminal, confused with thieves, only a little more ridiculous. For affliction is ridiculous' (*WG*, 85). It was affliction, she adds, that 'constrained Christ to implore that He might be spared; to seek consolation from man; to believe He was forsaken by the Father' (*WG*, 79).

Such comments foreground for us aspects of Saunders Lewis's poem we might otherwise casually overlook, regarding them as no more than a conventional dwelling on Christ's sufferings on the cross. It brings out the bitter anguish of the phrasing, as Lewis describes Calvary as 'awr ei gignoethi' – literally speaking, the hour of his being stripped raw (Lewis turns the customary noun 'cignoeth' into an active verb, thereby deliberately producing a jarring neologism). And his disgusted emphasis on the orgiastic sadism of the baying mob is made prelude to the heartbreaking cry of their seemingly broken and defeated victim, 'Paham y'm gadewaist i?' (Why hast thou forsaken me?)

But then, as if in deliberate counterpoint to that unforgettable question, comes that other cry of the Good Thief, 'Arglwydd, pan ddelych i'th deyrnas, cofia fi' (Lord, remember me when Thou enterest Thy kingdom). It is the moment that reveals that all, after all, is not lost, and it corresponds to Weil's conclusion:

> He whose soul remains ever turned in the direction of God while the nail pierces it, finds himself nailed on to the very centre of the universe. It is

the true centre, it is not in the middle, it is beyond space and time, it is God. In a dimension which does not belong to space, which is not time, which is indeed quite a different dimension, this nail has pierced a hole through all creation, through the thickness of the screen which separates the soul from God. (*WG*, 94)

Lewis's poem is a masterly acknowledgement both of the savagery of which human beings are capable (he was, after all, a survivor of the trenches) and of the humble spiritual greatness that even the most despised humans can, with God's grace, manifest under the most unlikely of circumstances.

* * *

Stylistically, Lewis's devotional poems alternate between the hieratic and the demotic, as if aspiring to mirror the dual nature of Christ – at once human and divine – as authoritatively pronounced in the Nicene Creed. 'I'r Lleidr Da' is an example of the latter mode, because although the divine transcendence of Christ is asserted at its very centre, the focus in general is on the Good Thief, as representative of humanity in the scene. 'Et Homo Factus Est', another important poem that touches on the crucifixion, tends towards the opposite pole, without becoming wholly hieratic (*CSL*, 47).

The title is taken from the Nicene Creed: 'Et homo factus est. Crucifixus etiam pro nobis sub Pontio Pilato, passus, et sepultus est. Et resurrexit tertia die' (and became man. For our sake He was cruci-fied under Pontius Pilate, He suffered death and was buried, and rose again on the third day). In extracting only a fragment from the Creed, Lewis is emulating his friend David Jones's practice of inserting such in his Inscriptions and paintings. By these means, both encourage their readers to become active participants in the eliciting of meaning. By completing the text and thus clarifying meaning they achieve illu-mination. The snippet is not of course arbitrarily chosen. By isolating and juxtaposing that part of the Creed dealing with the humanity of Christ and His crucifixion, Lewis is recognising that, in choosing to become fully human, God inevitably rendered Himself vulnerable to the crude savagery that is inseparable from human nature.

In form the poem is a meditative hymn of thanksgiving for the salvation that comes from the cross, and it incorporates a complex interplay of sonorities that maximise its theological impact. It is woven out of several different kinds of rhyming patterns, including

internal rhyme. While some of the rhymes are long delayed, others
are immediate. The one line in the whole poem that does not rhyme
is the final one, and consequently it stands out as unassimilated into
the rich harmonic whole. This is in keeping with its message, which is
that but for Christ, God would forever have remained the unknown
God to whom, so Paul tells us in Acts 17: 22–31, the prudent citizens
of Athens reserved an altar all of his own: human existence would
accordingly have lacked all order and coherence.

What the poem stresses, therefore, is that it is the life and death
of Christ alone that can bring the whole cosmos into tune. The vary-
ing rhyming schemes testify to the fact that there is rhyme, as well
as reason, in the seemingly random occurrences of existence, even
though perception of it may be intermittent and long deferred, as
on occasion is the satisfying completion of a rhyme in the poem. In
the second stanza, for example, seven lines separate the word 'grud'
(cradle) from its homophonic partner 'byd' (world).

'To the Christian mind', Lewis wrote, 'sin is the special attribute of
man, the most human thing in existence and thus essential to poetry
and literature' (*PSL*, 43). 'The mark of Christianity, always, has been
that it laid such emphasis on sin, elevating sin to such glory and
importance that it was necessary for Christ to be nothing less than
God, and He dying as a man, to disenthrone sin.' It is to be expected,
therefore, that in 'Et Homo Factus Est' he should dwell with a kind
of venomous relish on the sinfulness that has been ingrained in the
human cosmos from the very first:

> Lladd yw greddf gyntaf dynol-ryw,
> Ysfa'r amoeba yw;
> Caneuon poen a chathlau perig'
> Fu cerddi dwysau'r myrddiynau prae
> Er pan fu naddu'r bwyeill cerrig
> Yn nrysau'r agofâu,
> Miliynau cenedlaethau gwae
> Planed ddi-nod
> Ar goll yn annherfynol gwacter bod. (*CSL*, 47)

[Killing is the primal instinct of human nature,/ the urge of the
amoeba;/ the songs of pain and the hymns of peril/ have been
the most intense poetry of the myriad victims,/ ever since there was the
chiselling of stone axes/ In the doors of memory/ Of the million gen-
erations / On an insignificant planet/ Lost in the boundless emptiness
of existence.]

Into those concluding lines – reminiscent of Pascal's shuddering comment that 'the eternal silence of these infinite spaces terrifies me' – is packed Lewis's recurrent fear: the nightmare that, in the absence of God, existence may be left bankrupt of all meaning. It is therefore in the very extremities of this hell of our fractured race, he proceeds to stress, that we need to light a candle for the newborn baby and lift it from its cradle, surprised to find how heavy it is from the burden of our sin.

The supreme example of the hieratic mode is Lewis's poem on the risen Christ's sudden mysterious appearance between the two disciples on the road to Emmaus. In addition to fashioning a strict-metre poem, he deploys an archaic and arcane vocabulary to heighten further the impression of an irreducibly strange event that refuses to be reduced to familiar contemporary terms and is impossible to reconcile with modern reason. The total inaccessibility of it to contemporary intelligence is emphasised by Lewis's removal of Emmaus entirely from present-day maps and his description of the road leading to it as totally impassable, so that

> No one will find it now,
> Its history only lasted an hour;
> Rocks and path, utterly lost
> Is trafficless Emmaus. (*SLP*, 97)

The 'apparition' that is imagined as searching for a place implied not merely to be unknown but unknowable by definition – a no-place or anti-place; a place that exists entirely outside space and time – is not that of the risen Christ. Rather, after speculating whether it could be 'Arab or Rabbi', only to dismiss the thought, he concludes by wondering

> Or, increasing woe! is it me
> Awaiting the dawn of that short hour
> Of Emmaus which exists no longer.

It is a poem that beautifully fuses the certainty of Saunders Lewis's faith with its uncertainty. He is after all a twentieth-century believer, and so ruefully and reluctantly accepts there can no longer be warranty for faith in the form of any miraculous divine revelation.

*   *   *

When he was in his eightieth year, Saunders Lewis published what is probably his greatest poem. Entitled 'Gweddi'r Terfyn' (Prayer at the End of Life), it generated some controversy when Professor Dewi Z. Phillips, a professor of philosophy at University College Swansea who enjoyed an international reputation as an interpreter of Wittgenstein's enigmatic writings on the language of religion, published three articles in the Congregationalist weekly *Y Tyst*. He interpreted the poem as the utterance of a bewildered, late-twentieth-century would-be believer confounded by the lack of a credible language for faith. In his courteous but firm reply Lewis insisted (while conceding that no poet should be regarded as the final authority on the meaning of his/her poem) that for him it was a poem in the tradition of the great mystical tradition of his Church, particularly as found in the remarkable works of such late-thirteenth- and early-fourteenth-century German and Netherlandish mystics as Meister Eckhart and his disciples Johannes Tauler and Henry Suso.

One of the seminal distinctions made by Eckhart – and one that was duly condemned as heretical by the Church of the time – was between the original Godhead (the 'Gottheit' or Godhood), which was wholly mysterious and unknowable, and Divinity as manifest in the Holy Trinity. Eckhart followed the lead set by the sixth-century Pseudo-Dionysius (who had in turn been influenced by Proclus and Plotinus) in emphasising the 'He' who 'is beyond being ... a nothingness beyond being'. Ekhart also explained how 'When I go back into the ground, into the depths, into the well-spring of the Godhead, no one will ask me from where I came or where I went. No one will miss me, for there God unbecomes.'

In 'Gweddi'r Terfyn' Lewis, confronting the prospect of the total annihilation of his mortal being, and recognising the feeble – and as he insisted the laughable – limits of human experience, intelligence and language, is left movingly to anticipate that what happens at the end is an entry into the eternal silence:

How comic are the supreme declarations of our faith,
And around us there remains muteness, and the pit of annihilation
    That the whole universe will fall into some night.
    Our words cannot reach the edges of muteness
    Nor say God with any meaning.
    There remains one prayer for everyone, to go mute to the mute.

                                          (*SLP*, 227)

The poem is all the more effective for being written in such a strikingly unadorned and plain manner that in itself it seems to instance that stripping down of language at the moment of dying until in the end nothing whatsoever of it remains. Its form is that of free verse, so free indeed (by this master of condensed, formal poetry) that it risks seeming slack and flaccid. It is easy to understand why commentators like Phillips read it as a typical twentieth-century admission of the difficulties of contriving an adequate modern language of faith, because there is an air of seeming exhaustion about a poem that opens with an unflinchingly honest admission of the loneliness and isolation that comes from recognising that in the hour of death each inevitably stands completely alone:

> It's an experience for everyone that nobody else can know of.
> Each one on his own and in his own way
> Owns his own death
> Throughout the millennia of existence. (*SLP*, 227)

Along with the conclusion, such a passage brings to mind the unnerving ending of Donne's great 'Hymne to God the Father':

> I have a sin of fear, that when I have spun
>   My last thread, I shall perish on the shore;
> But swear by thy self, that at my death thy son
>   Shall shine as he shines now, and heretofore;
> And, having done that, thou hast done,
>   I fear no more.[11]

Never have puns been used in such desperately deadly earnest. For Donne, a lifelong inveterate punster, their capacity for seriousness, along with what may be termed their good faith, has at this point become a matter of life and death.

But whereas Donne thereby reluctantly persuades himself that in death Christ may yet be as good as His word and prove to be his protector against 'perishing' and the redeemer of his soul, in 'Gweddi'r Terfyn' Saunders Lewis refuses even to allow himself such essential consolation as this. Instead, he stakes all on the uncertain hope that his utter abandonment of self, which is the condition of complete trust in the essential benignity of whatever ultimately is, may ultimately prove to be well-placed. The piece is all the more moving, of course in being a born writer's abjuring at the last of the rough magic of language, the complete mastery of which has constituted an essential part of his mortal existence from its beginning to its end, 'When the breathing ceases and the person becomes a memory'. As for the seeming exhaustion, it is rather the effect of Lewis's deliberate limiting of his linguistic resources, and his curbing of his natural poet's drive to maximise textual impact, all in conscious preparation for the 'muteness' that is to come. The prayer, to which his title alludes, and whose groping filament of words vainly seeks to probe the beyond, ends only in the eternal muteness of silence.

Notes

1. David Jones, *Epoch and Artist: Selected Writings* (London: Faber and Faber, 1959), p. 156. Hereafter *EA*.
2. R. Geraint Gruffydd (ed.), *Cerddi Saunders Lewis* (Cardiff: University of Wales Press, 1986), p. 3. Hereafter *CSL*. For an English translation of the poems, see Joseph P. Clancy (trans.), Saunders Lewis, *Selected Poems* (Cardiff: University of Wales Press, 1993). Hereafter *SP*.
3. Harri Pritchard Jones (trans.), *Saunders Lewis: A Presentation of His Work* (Springfield, IL: Templegate Publishers, 1990), p. 102. Hereafter *SLP*. For an outstanding overview of Lewis's writings and career, see Alun R. Jones and Gwyn Thomas (eds), *Presenting Saunders Lewis* (Cardiff: University of Wales Press, 1973). For an authoritative brief introduction, see Bruce Griffiths, *Saunders Lewis* (Cardiff: University of Wales Press, Writers of Wales Series, 1989).
4. Joseph P. Clancy (trans.), *Medieval Welsh Poems* (Dublin: Four Courts Press, 2003), p. 249. Hereafter *MWP*.
5. Jacques Maritain, *Art and Scholasticism* (New York: Scribners, 1929), p. 34. Hereafter *AS*.
6. Jacques Maritain, *Creative Intuition in Art and Poetry*. All quotes from Chapter Three, 'The Preconscious Life of the Intellect': *www.catholicculture.org/culture/library* (accessed 23 June 2022).
7. Ibid., Chapter Four, 'Creative Intuition and Poetic Knowledge'.
8. Louis L. Martz, *The Poetry of Meditation: A Study in English religious literature of the seventeenth century* (New Haven and London: Yale University Press, 1962).
9. Quoted in Robert McLauchlan, *Saturday's Silence: R. S. Thomas and Paschal Reading* (Cardiff: University of Wales Press, 2016), p. 6. McLauchlan's study itself is also relevant.
10. Emma Craufurd (trans.), Simone Weil, *Waiting on God: The Essence of her Thought* (London: Collins, Fontana, 1950/1959). Hereafter *WG*.
11. 'A Hymn to God the Father', in A. J. Smith (ed.), *John Donne: The Complete English Poems* (Harmondsworth: Penguin, 1971), pp. 348–9.

3

'THE FLASHED MYSTERY OF THE MOVING WORLD': VERNON WATKINS

Vernon Watkins (1906–67) is a visionary poet. By which I mean that he views, and judges, this world in the light of another, which while constantly present in this is manifest only occasionally and ephemerally. 'Come, buried light,' he wrote, 'and honour time/ With your dear gift, your constancy.'[1] If there can be such a phenomenon as sainthood in poetry – and why not, if John Donne could claim he deserved to be 'canonised for love'? – then Watkins is such, so otherworldly in its selflessness was his unwavering devotion to the blessed Muse. During all those years that he worked as a humble bank-clerk (he had a talent for numbers, and never sought promotion) he 'devoted secret time', as he put it, 'to one love, one alone' (*CP*, 21). After his death his wife complained she was never able to oust this true mistress from his affections. All this helps explain why his achievements are now airily dismissed. His poems – unfailingly lofty, bardic and vatic, and already old-fashioned before he even began, as his great hero Yeats had realised decades earlier – are treated as anachronisms and viewed as embarrassingly quaint.[2]

Yet during his lifetime he was a poet whose gifts were recognised by his close friend Dylan Thomas, admired by Philip Larkin, his polar opposite as a poet, and widely respected internationally. At the time of his death he was a leading contender for the honorary role of Poet Laureate. And for all his undeniable limitations both of vision and of expression, he remains a very considerable visionary poet of the Welsh spiritual tradition, capable of rapt and rapturous writing. Not that Watkins, unlike most of the others in this volume, would have been likely to answer readily to such a description. He

insisted in a questionnaire published during the 1940s by the maverick
Welsh Journal *Wales* that he was a Welsh man but, *faute de mieux*, an
English poet. He can, however, be viewed as an interesting example of
a Welsh European,[3] and as one whose connections with the religious
culture of Wales (his parents were of Welsh Nonconformist stock,
but study at Repton public school – under Geoffrey Fisher, a future
Archbishop of Canterbury – made an Anglican of him) may have
been much deeper than he himself cared to acknowledge.

Watkins was magician enough to readily conjure up vivid phrases:
'the sleet of the stars fall cold and thin' (*CP*, 50); 'a cold moon with
stark, magnetic will/ Sucked through the trees the blind, unerring
wave' (*CP*, 36); 'far under, flying through sleep,/ Their black fins cut-
ting the rainbow surf, the porpoises follow the shoal' (*CP*, 185); 'light
lingers/ liquid in stone' (*CP*, 260). Sadly, however, he was a poor judge
of his own poetry. As a result, he published far too many poems that
were embarrassingly bad, quite a few of which came perilously close
to self-parody: 'O God, the atom has split Werfel's brain!/ The room
is rigid with the death of his brain' (*CP*, 31). Earnestness closed his
ears to the clangorous discords in his writing, solemnity closed his
eyes to blindingly obvious absurdities, his serene poetic self-regard –
although never less than endearing – prevented him from unbending
into a lower register of expression. All-in-all he could be a deadly
enemy of his own talents, prone to produce reams of rhetorical verbi-
age. Brief (and largely fortuitous) association in his younger days with
writers of the so-called Apocalyptic school – during a period when
his poetry became particularly overwrought; an anguished response
to the devastations of the Second World War – did him no favours
for the rest of his career. In all these ways he was a poet cursed by his
own considerable gifts.

A Johnny head-in-air, fine featured, long of leg, lean of frame,
wiry of body, and with a leonine mane of hair, Watkins looked
every inch 'the poet', of whose vocation he took an exalted view.
His wife, however, insists this image was in part a mask, and adds
that, although Watkins seemed gentle-natured, and was indeed so in
general, he could be extremely exacting, and intolerant of incompe-
tence in matters that most deeply concerned him. He was also given
to occasional outbursts of violent anger.[4] An innocent in some ways,
and so very easily teased and gulled, he had his own distinctive sense
of humour and shared an adroitness at word play with both Dylan
Thomas and David Jones.

Despite his worship of Yeats, Watkins failed to follow sage advice offered him by the Irish magus: 'Cast off poetic diction first/ And find what is your own' (*CP*, 62). Reporting, in verse, a conversation he had had in Dublin with his aged hero, he recalled how, 'We talked of national movements,/ He pondered the chance/ Of Welshmen reviving/ The fire of song and dance,/ Driving a lifeless hymnal/ From that inheritance' (*CP*, 65). Of course, Watkins's lack of Welsh – his parents had neglected to pass the language on to him, a loss he came to regard as a deficiency – meant that the supposedly 'lifeless' hymn book had been closed to him in any case. But there is suggestion enough in his poetry that he did not entirely agree with Yeats's dismissal of it. In his fine early poem 'Return to Goleufryn', he returns to his maternal grandparents' home in Carmarthen, after an interval of twenty years, with a mixture of nostalgia and guilt – guilt for having 'betrayed' that family background by disappearing into the alien world of an anglicised culture into which he had been thoroughly inducted during his education at refined English public schools. The whole poem is an implicit elegy for his beloved maternal grandmother, who had given up farming just outside Carmarthen to become a lay Congregational minister.

As now he stands in the poem once more in Carmarthen (Caerfyrddin in Welsh – Merlin's town – as he well knew), with 'my eyes cast down/ To the footprint of accusations', he seems to hear 'the faint, leavening/ Music of first Welsh words; that gust of plumes/ "They shall mount up like eagles," dark-throated assumes' (*CP*, 103). There is here more than a hint of respect for the majestic, Bible-fearing culture of the Welsh chapels that had been his grandfather's native environment. The innumerable references scattered throughout his poems to places, events and people from both the Old Testament and the New, are a reminder of how steeped in the Bible was the Welsh Nonconformity to which his relatives had belonged. (His parents were members of Paraclete chapel in Mumbles, where the minister was Dylan Thomas's uncle.)

Predictive of the future trajectory of Watkins's poetic career is his memory of 'the burning mile/ Of windows. It is Goleufryn, the house on the hill' (*CP*, 103). That image of a light on the brow (here of a hill) was to become talismanic for Watkins. He had learnt that the name of the legendary Welsh wizard Taliesin, with whom he closely identified, meant 'Shining brow'. So, when his close friend Dylan Thomas died so shockingly prematurely, Watkins claimed that the

light he used to see shining in Thomas's little room upstairs in the
family home on Cwmdonkin Hill had seemed to him prophetically
Taliesinic. During the course of his career, he addressed several poems
to Taliesin, relocating him in Gower, where Watkins lived in a house
on the magnificently striated limestone cliffs overlooking the sea at
Southgate, lost in 'my coastal labouring' (*CP*, 119), as he put it.[5]

His fascination with the continuum of time explored by what he
seductively called 'the mayfly of memory' (in other words fugitive
recollections of the past, vivid with ephemeral life) seemed to call out
of Watkins enchanting poetry of lyrical simplicity. 'Loiterers' is one
of his very best, and seems to be intended to evoke not so much a past
moment in his own life as the ancient Greek mode of elegiac pastoral;
hence the reference to a 'Xanion' at the very beginning. His mind goes
back 'through bee-bustle and waspish digression' to dawn memories
of a track down a cornfield, where 'Foxgloves in midge-light hid the
turning river/ Swept by the swallows' (*CP*, 221). In modelling his
poem on an ancient bucolic Greek genre, Watkins is emphasising the
eternal, archetypal, character of his own twentieth-century experi-
ences. So the 'Book-shadows' he noticed 'in the corners' when visiting
Yeats in Dublin, 'seemed to have drawn/ Spirits from the back of the
mind/ From conception and dawn' (*CP*, 67).

From his conversation with Yeats, Watkins recalled realising that,
even though monstrously evil 'leaders' such as Hitler and Mussolini
were at that very time 'sway[ing] the crowd', a different 'Power is
underneath,/ The sword of Taliesin/ Would never fit a sheath.' As he
well knew from the *Mabinogion*, the great late-medieval collection of
wonder-narratives, the 'power' of Taliesin had resided in his astonish-
ing power to assume different shapes and forms at will: 'I have passed
through a million changes', the Welsh shaman boasts in 'Taliesin
in Gower' (*CP*, 185). But it was a power he had acquired purely by
mischance. Originally 'Gwion bach', a little assistant deputed by the
witch Ceridwen to stir a cauldron of magic brew intended for her
own misshapen son, he accidentally spilt three of its precious drops
on himself. Instantly he found himself assuming a different shape,
enraging the witch who then displayed her own prodigious powers
of shape-shifting by assuming a myriad different forms in frantic
attempts to trap him.

Eventually, she succeeded by turning herself into a hen after
Taliesin had become a grain of wheat, and gobbled him up. However,
her belly shortly began to swell, and in nine months she was delivered

of a baby, so beautiful that even she could not bring herself to kill him. Instead she cast him adrift in a coracle. Thus abandoned, he was saved only by being washed safely ashore, plucked up, and carried off to King Arthur's court. There he was instantly christened 'Taliesin' – 'shining brow' – so instinct was he with radiant beauty, and upon reaching maturity he proceeded to demonstrate his astonishing gifts as a magician. 'Taliesin and the Spring of Vision' ends with the magician from the realms of Celtic myth recognising that 'Omniscience is not for man', being the preserve of the Christian God. Accordingly, he prays to the Almighty to 'Christen me, therefore, that my acts in the dark may be just,/ And adapt my partial vision to the limitation of time' (*CP*, 225).

This legend meant so much to Watkins because he found in it rich symbolic expression of his vision both of the underlying spiritual constancy of the wondrously metamorphic world and of his own role as poet in relation to it. He was a Welsh Anglican of very strong Neo-Platonist inclination. Although very consciously a religious poet – like his friend Dylan Thomas, he always insisted – he was hazy on the details of Christian belief. 'I was keen on theological discussion', his wife Gwen Watkins recalled, 'but I never had one with Vernon without concluding by telling him that he was a heretic, not an orthodox believer' (*PF*, 13). From its emergence in the Hellenistic Egypt of the third century AD through the teachings of Plotinus, Porphyry and Iamblichus, Neo-Platonism had been intertwined with the thinking of the early Christian fathers, taking important mystical form in the work of the Pseudo-Dionysius. Its emphasis on the One, supreme, transcendent source of all being – spiritual source of all the 'emanations' or forms of life itself – corresponded closely with Christian worship of an unknowable God. As for the corresponding Christian emphasis on the incarnation of spirit in body (divinely instanced of course in the earthly person of Christ), this also corresponded to Neo-Platonic belief that the pure spiritual essence – the 'world soul' – had become immanent in every aspect of creation.

It was the Renaissance that saw this philosophy become highly influential in the realm of the arts. It was most notably productive in Florence, where the writings of Marsilio Ficino (1433–99) and Pico della Mirandola (1463–94) made an immense impression on painters such as Botticelli and Raphael. Those seventeenth-century Anglican theologians and philosophers of the mid-seventeenth century who became collectively known as the 'Cambridge Platonists' imported this mode of thinking into England. In a letter to the Welsh Behmenist mystic Morgan Llwyd, Peter Sterry, the poetic mystic of the English movement, wrote ecstatically of his experiences of 'ye Ravishing pleasures of an Undeserved, Unexpected, Irresistible Love' and of 'ye Glorious Tryumph of a Deepe, a Rich Designe comprehending ye whole Creation, carrying Eternity through Time, like a River under Ground, till Time breake up into Eternity againe'.[6] Comprised largely of limestone, the cliff landscape of south Gower, where Watkins had his home, abounded in underground watercourses, such as Bishopston stream, to which he dedicated a poem. These served him, as their kind had Sterry, as symbols of the invisible spiritual order under- lying all multiform life and breaking out in the myriad visible glories of creation. Then, in eighteenth-century England, Thomas Taylor's translation of the works of Plotinus into English for the first time had a considerable impact on William Blake, the remarkable unorthodox poet and engraver who was one of Watkins's particular favourites.

The syncretic nature of Neo-Platonist thought meant it was hos- pitable to every form of spiritual experience and system of belief, since it regarded them all as emanations from a single divine source. Hence the application to it of the term *philosophia perennis*, usu- ally translated as 'the perennial philosophy' because it was eternally renewing itself in a multitude of new forms. Like the Taliesin who was Watkins's poetic, and spiritual, muse, it therefore possessed an infinite flexible capacity to assume new shapes. In 'Art and the Ravens' he likened his poetry to the flight of the birds wheeling over the sea cliffs near his home: 'Drifting in light, they stall./ Winds' conflict keeps them true' to their constant purpose of 'defending ancient springs' (*CP*, 183).

Neo-Platonism was likewise attractive to artists and writers because it encouraged the mixing of elements from many different cultures. The interweaving of pagan myth and biblical imagery was a vital feature of Watkins's rich discourse. It was a practice essential for his spiritual poetic, and during his lifetime the syncretic beliefs upon which the practice rested seemed to have found new endorsement in the psychoanalytical findings of Carl Jung, who contended that the human dream world consisted of ancient symbols and symbolic narratives common to all times and to all cultures. These were the 'archetypal symbols' from 'ancient springs' to which Watkins was drawn. And like the early Church Fathers, he believed that such myths were 'pagan' prefigurations of the truths revealed in the Christian

faith. 'The pathos of pre-Christian love lies in its incompleteness',
he wrote in a note on 'The Death Bell', 'the prophetic nature of pre-
Christian death in its reticence' (*CP*, 215).

The sumptuously sensuous 'Music of Colours: White Blossom'
includes a particularly fine example of his Neo-Platonic fusion of
Christian and mythological imagery. Its theme is the dazzling white-
ness of pure spirituality such as can be fully encountered only in
eternity, and its faint adumbration in the innumerable instances of
the lesser, yet still enthralling, kinds and degrees of whiteness to be
found in mortal life. In the whiteness of a seashell Watkins detects
just a hint of 'the Nazarene/ Walking in the ear' (*CP*, 101), while
the sea-spray is convincingly white until 'this snowfall' reveals it to
be merely grey. Apple-blossom, flowering cherry, the 'racing cloud',
glistening raindrops, lilies of the valley, all have their momentary
seductive allure of whiteness. The whiteness of a swan seems pristine
until comparison with 'original white' reveals it to be but 'wan' – the
humbling diminution of the proud identifying noun by the simple
loss of that initial 's' enacts Watkins's experience of corrective vision.
And then, as the poem reaches the great peroration of its climax, he
realises that perfect whiteness had only ever once been apparent on
earth, when Christ's 'eyes looked down and made the leper clean'.

This then acts as springboard to recollection of 'Venus, and the
white doves', of the fabled whiteness of Leda, and of the 'web-footed
Jupiter' who possessed her in the form of a white swan. But finally,
it is the whiteness of mortal dust that seems to Watkins to promise
access at the last to that perfect whiteness for which he so yearns. It
becomes available, he realises, only in and through the final dark-
ness of death. Hence his final acknowledgement that 'I know you,
black swan.' This is the blackness that will ultimately be transfigured,
or rather miraculously reversed, into white at the very moment of
death. In 'White Blossom', then, Watkins memorably raids Classical
myth for images adequate for the expression of his mystic Christian
experience.

But Watkins was also capable of expressing reservation about
the applicability of Ancient myths to Christian experience. 'Prime
Colours' (*CP*, 6) begins by accepting that the soaring Pegasus, 'the
winged horse of myth', is now revealed to have been no more than 'a
circus horse, paid to be clever'. In comparison with the humble mule
from 'Bethpage' that carried Christ on his back in His triumphal
entry into Jerusalem, it is no more than a mere showy charlatan. All

those who devoted their lives to the commemorative recording of the Classics and their myths are dismissed as 'cramped, figured scribes, distorted by possession'. In contrast the swallows swoop free, presaging the new freedom granted the human spirit by Christian revelation, while the resurrected Saviour, so mocked at the crucifixion, offers triumphal proof in the lives of His believers that 'time stopped still, stopped when an ass went down/ Slowly from Bethpage to that still town'. Christ had died to resurrected life, he wrote, to 'make a new theology' (*CP*, 262), and he was sustained by a firm Christian faith right through his adult life.

'Cantata for the Waking of Lazarus' (*CP*, 185) is another poem – attractive and lucid once one realises that it includes several different voices – focusing on an episode from the New Testament. The play of a fountain provides a linking symbol, suggestive of the upsurge of spiritual energy at the narrative's centre. Lazarus – dead in body, but one who 'in that grave shadow sleeping/ Alone could see God's face' – is implored to emulate the fountain, as 'for you, the doves obeying/ The voice of light within the water's utmost crown/ Change all the drops to glory'. He is promised that he will awaken with eyes newly empowered

> [to] see these petals breaking near the source, and white
> Roses on thorny stems, and white acacia swaying
> Where glinting birds alight above the ringing cup. (*CP*, 186)

Lazarus responds with a plea for the assistance of God incarnate: 'The Romans drove you out, they hunted you with spears,/ Yet you have pieced my flesh, have knit me, bone to bone,/ Have kindled here this force, behind the sombre stone'. And the poem ends with Lazarus praying to Christ, the emissary of divine Love, to come down and awaken him to renewed life. 'Religious poetry', Watkins wrote (*CP*, Selected, 101), 'is sealed like the eyes of Lazarus by a refusal to be raised except by the true God'.

Lazarus is a New Testament figure who recurs in Watkins's poetry, because for him he is an emblem of vision. Another such is Zacchaeus, reviled as chief tax-collector in Jericho, who was not too proud to shin up a sycamore in order to secure a better view of Jesus. And, 'since a small man climbed/ The crooked trunk, and groped, and sat in the branch', Watkins writes in 'Poet and Goldsmith', 'The minutiae of earth are changed' (*CP*, 233). Also changed was the sycamore tree itself, as Watkins emphasises in 'Zacchaeus in the Leaves' (*CP*, 143–6), a poem that identifies that moment when the little man climbed the tree as the moment when the myths of the ancient World – Pan, Dionysus – were transcended, consummated in and supplanted by the truths of Christian revelation. In that moment, too, 'the universe race[d]' through the leaves of the sycamore, whose rustling leaves have 'thrill[ed]' ever since to the spirit's passage.

* * *

In his poetry, Watkins tries to dispel the illusion that time is linear and irreversible, since 'Timeless vision/ Discerns no past' (*CP*, 258). For him the past is omnipresent within the present, and time therefore a closed circle. 'There is a time,' he writes in 'The Turning of the Stars', 'when Apollo's tree/ Is Daphne still. The Past is not the Past/ But wound within a ring' (*CP*, 159). As witness, he calls some of the great figures of the past: Raphael – 'His mind being in its silence fixed on truth: / Unrest in calm, calm in unrest he sought' – Copernicus, and above all 'Alighieri', 'fixed yet flying', and conclusive proof that 'A man may bind the stars/ To his own bent/ By faith protected' and that a 'flash' may 'translate blind mortals into seers' (*CP*, 161).

Watkins's talent may have been a relatively minor one. But if so, it is undeniably distinctive, and authentically visionary. Many of his poems are highly confusing, and even perhaps thoroughly confused, due to the intensity and density of Watkins's thinking. On occasions, his mind works on a different, remote plane of its own, where a different calculus applies. It is possible to follow the increasingly polyphonic development of his complex thought only to be disconcerted and disorientated by a transition so unexpected, a shift so delphic and elliptic, as to be impossible to follow. Yet on other occasions he proves capable of beautifully crystalline utterance, as in the following passage, a rejection of the seductive offer made by a Neffertiti 'resurrected in Gower' (as Watkins puts it with his customary sublime innocence of irony) to initiate him into the dark mysteries of ancient Egypt:

> Dear love, could my true soul believe
> The wide heavens merciless, I still would not forsake
> The man-tilled earth to which bones cleave
> While horses race across
> The neighbouring field, and their hooves shine

> Scattering a starlike wake.
> Magnanimous morning, if we change no line,
> Shall pierce stone, leaf and moss,
> And the true creature at light's bidding wake. (*CP*, 159)

Light-intoxicated as he was, and hypnotised by the great mysterious all-engulfing silence out of which life had come and to which it would return, the visionary Watkins could not help but be as aware of the limitations of language as of its potentialities. 'Verse is a part of silence', he wrote. 'I have known/ Always that declamation is impure' (*CP*, 159). On first reading one assumes that this is a blanket confession of the inadequacy of every form of language. But reflection shows that the lines allow for a subtle, but vital, distinction between 'declamation' (understood as the glib rhetoric of ordinary speech) and 'verse' (a synecdoche for the special discourse of poems). While the latter is also inescapably 'impure', it may be so to a less limiting and damaging and distorting degree than the former, particularly in the hands of a true poet.

In a poem that opens by concentrating on the very moment when Daphne is transformed into a laurel by her father, the river god, to save her from the clutches of the libidinous Apollo, Watkins brings out the significance for him as a Christian of the miracle of transfiguration accomplished in that instant, when time and the timeless meet and briefly fuse:

> There is a touch, before the wall of bark
> Echoes the music of those timeless hands,
> The pivot of the god
> Like light revealed
> Where all the stars seem fallen in one field,
> And secret, where the underleaf is dark,
> Language is understood
> Green as a spring, translated for all lands,
> A touch to which rivers of leaves must hark. (*CP*, 160)

Those final two lines are a fine instance of Watkins's practice of discovering secret connections between seemingly unrelated phenomena. In imagining language revivified and thus 'Green as spring' – if never evergreen, as the contrite Apollo, god both of the sun and of poetry, had decreed Daphne's laurel should be – Watkins exploits the dual meaning of 'spring'. It encompasses both the seasonal 'leaves' and the waters (spring = fountain) mentioned in the final line. As for the 'Language [that] is understood', behind it lies, unspoken, Watkins's association of the musical language of an imaginary lyre, fashioned out of Daphne's laurel, with that of the legendary instrument made of gold that had been Apollo's gift to Orpheus. This complex allusion has already been prepared for earlier, when Watkins refers to the moment before 'the walls of bark' begin to echo 'the music of those timeless hands'. These hands are both those of the sun-god Apollo, the god of Music, and of the singer of the 'Orphic hymns', Orpheus himself.

Throughout his career, Watkins associated poetry closely with music, and his poems were elaborate musical settings of his visionary imagination. It was its musicality, he believed, that allowed poetry to function miraculously as a 'language' which is 'understood' at a more profound and revelatory level than ordinary speech or normal 'rational' consciousness. 'They who feel ... the worshipping dead', he wrote, 'Seek for all words responses/ Deep, and attuned to a heavenly music' (*CP*, 219). In 'The Kestrel', he contrasted the movement of verse poetry with that of the sea waves he heard 'casting rhyme on rhyme/Vainly against the craggy world' (*CP*, 244); their monotonous rhythm was as automatic and pointless as the exchanges of ordinary speech. George Herbert had defined prayer as 'something understood'. So, too, was poetic discourse for Watkins. The French Symbolists he admired had taught him much about the magical, transporting, music of poems that constituted a kind of speaking silence. They created a 'harmony' consisting of 'scales ... discernible everywhere in nature, but ... discerned only by intuition, not by the reason' (*CP*, 216). 'Natural speech may be excellent', he conceded in a manuscript note, 'but who will remember it unless it is allied to something artificial, to a particular order of music'.[7]

For him, that music was an echo of the music of the spheres that had long been dreamt of by Platonists. It was another link between him and the Elizabethans, the grace, dignified courtesy, and imagistic opulence of whose lyrics some of his later poems seem to approximate:

> nothing can weigh the inscrutable movement of beech leaves
> Silken, of brightest green, which May has transfigured like music
> Born of their trumpet-like buds; (*CP*, 241)

Such miraculous new growths of springtime could move him to rapture at the silent harmonies of nature: 'Where apple-trees move under

the wind, on fire from the wound of the grail,/ Stream of wild stars
for a fork-stemmed blossom to stanch' (*CP*, 241). Those lines come
from a lovely poem celebrating a baby's recent birth, and include a
glimpse of a woodpecker nail[ing] its cry 'to the bark of [a] fir' that
grows in the poet's garden. Beyond its protective wall lies the sea,
blue on a gorgeous summer's day. The scene is particularly evocative
for Watkins because his poet's mind was haunted by the actual and
metaphoric power of the ocean whose roar at the foot of the cliffs
directly outside his door was perpetually to be heard, supplying an
everlasting (and frequently troubling) rumbling bass accompaniment
to the song of his own imagination.

His poetry is full of references to the sea, the ultimate example of
startling metamorphosis and inexhaustible source of symbolic sug-
gestiveness. He called it 'the immane sea' (*CP*, 17), 'the saga-laden
sea', invoked it as an element where 'all things haunt back/ to a more
ancient order'. 'In the air the legend,' he wrote, 'over the sea the myth'
(*CP*, 15). He opened 'The Shell' by wondering 'Who could devise/
But the dark sea this thing,/ Of depth, of dyes,/ Claws of weed cling,/
Whose colour cries:/ "I am of water, as of air the wing"' (*CP*, 181).
One of his ambitious long wartime poems was titled 'The Griefs of
the Sea', since he readily associated it with the troubled and troubling
ghosts of the departed. He returned to it in 'Sea-Music for my Sister
travelling' (*CP*, 68ff), another long poem in which he endeavoured to
capture the anxieties of wartime: then he felt that 'the sea is awake./
The sea is a bird/ There are fluttering, beating wings' (*CP*, 77). Like
the heaving ocean, the poem supplies his restless imagination with a
plethora, and a plenitude of tropes, so that he ranges from 'listening
seas that cover ears with pearl' (*CP*, 68) to the imaginary experience
of watching 'the dolphins at your keel/ Weaving all patterns of all
unimagined deaths' (*CP*, 69). He views the distant waters 'Coiled in
destruction's great Sargasso growth' (*CP*, 69) and rising to his mind
out of the depths come the myth of the Harpies, the fabled voy-
age of Ulysses, and remote magical locations from the Bermudas to
Africa, 'where blue-net seas gush Tyrian' (*CP*, 69). In 'Ballad of the
Rough Sea' its voice seems to him to waken 'the fossil-man asleep in
the ground' on Dover cliffs (*CP*, 187). In 'Ballad of the Mari Lwyd'
(*CP*, 41ff) a mare's skull is disturbingly carried by riotous revellers
from door to door on new year's eve in Maesteg, the town where he
had been born; and he recalls it as being that of 'A white horse fro-
zen blind,/ Hurled from a seawave's hollow,/ Fostered by spray and

wind,/ Profane and priestlike thing!' (*CP*, 49). In its sinister wake come a throng of followers from the dead, all seeking admission and appeasement by the living.

As the sea is the ageless dwelling place of 'Old Triton Time' (*CP*, 9), it is a mysterious element, turbulent and uncontrollable, where the dead mingle freely with the living and the past merges with the present. The coracle-borne baby was reborn as Taliesin by emerging out of the sea, he explained in 'Taliesin at Pwlldu' ('Black Pool': a small, secluded bay just along the coast from Southgate), and so 'music' flowed through him 'as through a shell' (*CP*, 353). It had also supplied the baptismal water that had turned Taliesin Christian. The ocean was Blake's 'sea of space and time' – during those lonely early months when he was a bank-clerk in Cardiff and on the very verge of total mental breakdown he had obsessively read Blake's Prophetic Books – the destructive element in which the spirits of human beings were helplessly immersed; but it was also as magically transfiguring as it had proved to be in *The Tempest*. Out of it emerged miraculous transformations, 'rich and strange'. It was a liminal zone that enabled the perilous traffic between living and dead, a transactional process that was for Watkins essential for the working of a genuinely creative imagination.

'I stoop to gather a seabird's feather', he writes in 'The Feather', a particularly affecting poem (*CP*, 120–1). It had, he speculates, been torn from the body when the bird had fallen victim to a sea-hawk, and in the pathos of this fragile remainder, which is also a reminder, he finds an emblem of the many drowned during the War. Accordingly, this token carries with it a solemn charge to him as a poet: he must compose the melody necessary to allow the dead to find rest. 'The Feather' ends on a poignant note as it opens out in an elegy for everyone and everything that is 'lost' – at sea, metaphorically speaking:

> The perfect into night must fly,
> On this the winds agree.
> How could a blind rock satisfy
> The hungers of the sea? (*CP*, 121)

Watkins's poetry is haunted by a sense, augmented by guilt, of personal responsibility for and to the dead. It may well have derived from the trauma, already mentioned, that he experienced as a young man when a motorcyclist died in an accident to which Watkins was intimate horrified witness, and had irrationally supposed that, some-how, to have been his fault. Even the most exultantly affirmative of his poems about the sea and its creatures modulates at the end into a minor key. 'The Dead Shag' is a 'sea-flash' and 'glancing fisher-bird' (*CP*, 174), and Watkins ecstatically celebrates the extraordinary exploits of 'this under-water bird,/ Glistening, glistening low'. But it ends with a recognition that his appreciation of it comes out of the dark that is the ultimate source of all light.

Particularly intense are his two poems about the curlew, because he associated it with his dead friend Dylan Thomas, whose favourite bird it was, partly perhaps because it, too, was a 'wanderer' (*CP*, 243). He hears its unchanging cry carry 'over rocks and over sea' and contrasts its faithful annual return with Thomas's 'unreturning year'. Waiting desolate on the shore, he is convinced the cry 'carries remorse across the sea' and that it 'bears a ghostly listening to my own'. 'The Snow Curlew', its companion poem published decades later, is particularly powerful, and perhaps the best of Watkins's ele-gies for his friend. Snow has fallen during the night, blanketing the cliffs, snuffing out light, turning both sea and sky leaden, and creat-ing a landscape bereft of any sign of life, as if a 'pen has fallen from the hand of dark' so that the manuscript of earth has been erased and is now blank. Most disturbing of all for Watkins it seems as if 'Earth had forgotten where her dead go' – and as we have seen that fear of the forgetting of the dead by the living was for him a lasting concern of neurotic intensity. When he hears a curlew's 'Spring call' breaking this deathly silence, Watkins takes it for 'a good-bye/ To all things not beginning' and a challenge to him as poet to make 'the driftwood catch/ To coax, where the cry fades, fires which cannot fall' (*CP*, 367). Implicit in that is a recognition that he must let the dead lie, that he must not enter their realm. He must turn back instead to life, because only in its perpetual renewals can their memory be per-petuated. He must pick up the pen let fall by the dark and indite new inscriptions on this invitingly blank landscape, just as spring, as the curlew's plangently hopeful cry suggests, is certain to summon new life from the dead earth.

His poems about birds are amongst his finest, and they almost all feature the sea, because he had encountered them during his loping walks through gorse and heather along the Gower cliffs – he was renowned for his fearless clambering over rocks. His heron stands motionless, 'deaf to the tumult of the bay' (*CP*, 174). A 'time-killing

bird' it retains its devoted concentration though 'calamity about him
cries' – the very image of a poet of Watkins's kind, because the heron,
too, has its own calm centre of gravity, its distinctive steadiness and
serenity of vision. It is when it hovers over the sea cliffs that the kestrel
catches Watkins's eye, and he is transfixed by the way in which 'still
the inviolate wing and claw/ Hold chaos in the grip of grace' – that
last word is used advisedly, in full awareness of its Christian meaning
(*CP*, 244).

Watkins's poetry is informed by a fearful sensitivity to the threat-
ening encroachments of chaos. He confessed himself to be 'a man
walking, one alive to fear' (*CP*, 149). So when he writes about an 'eye
by darkness sanctified' (*CP*, 6), he knows what he is talking about.
Vision had been born to him out of catastrophe. Disillusioned by the
way literature was taught at Cambridge, he abruptly abandoned his
degree and opted to train as a bank clerk in Cardiff. As he walked
back to his lodgings one evening, a motorcycle with sidecar over-
turned after colliding with a car, killing the rider and leaving his
passenger bleeding profusely (*EM*, 75ff). The experience soon plunged
Watkins into mental breakdown in which he was overwhelmed by
personal guilt at the ephemerality and futility of life.

Relief came only in the form of a redeeming vision of the essential
permanence of all things, and to this he remained true for the rest of
his years. It was this experience that marked his adult self decisively
off from his youthful self, 'when I still/ knew no remedy for time's ill'
(*CP*, 266). Yet he never forgot that if 'always from joy ... my music
comes/ ... always it is sorrow keeps it true' (*CP*, 283) and he suffered
his share of losses, including the shocking death of his closest friend
and ally Dylan Thomas at an early age, and the wartime obliteration
of his beloved hometown of Swansea. Infusing his best poetry is an
awareness that 'All is so hung that harmony,/ Though pitched precari-
ously,/ Conquers uncertainty' (*CP*, 270). It was this recognition that
'Joy is woven true on a tragic vision' (*CP*, 219) that prompts him to
place the Crucifixion and Resurrection at the very centre of belief:
'For in [the] dark' of Good Friday 'the greatest light was born,' he
writes, 'which if man sees, then time is overthrown' (*CP*, 263).

So traumatised, indeed, was he by Dylan Thomas's death that
in his widow's opinion he was a changed man, and different poet
thereafter – 'the death of Dylan Thomas', she writes, 'was to change
the voice of his poetry for ever' (*PF*, 156). The elegies he compul-
sively multiplied for his dead friend were attempts to restore his 'true

image' to life – Watkins was profoundly disturbed and disgusted by the impressions of Thomas left by the many ghoulish weavers of the lurid myths and tawdry reminiscences emanating from the US in particular, and all such 'banalities of judgement' as Gwen Watkins puts it (*PF*, 174). He remained obstinately faithful to an image of his friend that was in its touching way equally partial in envisaging him as 'essentially' a poet totally devoted to his vocation. There are unmistakeable overtones in Watkins's obsessive attachment to Thomas of those serial homoerotic crushes to which he had been notoriously prone at Repton when he had been besotted with Rupert Brook, the pin-up boy of the age. Even in early adulthood, Watkins had continued to be strongly attracted to young men whose souls he regarded as uniquely kindred to his own, although he always kept his Platonic distance.

As for his Christian faith, Gwen Watkins records that, again like Dylan Thomas, he 'felt that the millions of wonderful things for poets to write about had been made by some Power, and they both recognised very strongly that the power of the Word was supernatural, and that praise was what was required by whatever Power had made the world' (*PF*, 13). 'Vernon also had a conviction,' she adds, 'acquired during his breakdown, that he had been saved from damnation by the sacrifice of Another, whom he identified as Christ. Apart from this, I think his faith in God was as nebulous and as certain as Dylan's.'

'For the dead live and I am of their kind', Watkins wrote. Beginning with that of the Cardiff motorcyclist, the deaths and losses that he had known continued to affect Watkins very profoundly, so much so that his poems are full of a highly ambivalent relationship. He was fully aware of how dangerous was this obsession. It was all very well to realise that the 'world's beauty the dead sustain' (*CP*, 117) but to dwell too long on it was to risk 'wronging' 'tenuous life' (*CP*, 116). So he was careful to counterbalance a short poem on 'Fidelity to the Dead' with 'Fidelity to the Living'. For Watkins, that word 'fidelity' had a talismanic ring, so much so that in 1968 he adopted it (in the plural) as a title of a new volume. Six years previously, he had filled another volume, this time with the title of 'Affinities', with elegies for people and places of the past – the Swansea that had disappeared in the blitz, Nijinsky the great dancer, T. S. Eliot, D. H. Lawrence, Hölderlin, Heine, Wordsworth, they were all dutifully memorialised. Watkins was a naively inveterate hero-worshipper all his life, and his muses were virtually all male. He was also familiar with German and

French literature. Both had been subjects of study during his brief period in Cambridge, and his mother, who had spent two years in Germany as a young woman, was a teacher of German.

Reverend admiration for all these giants of the arts was very much in keeping with Watkins's view of the poet as one whose very vocation was to keep company with the mighty dead. A respect for august tradition – a respect he regarded as the precondition of any authentic 'originality' – was after all a prerequisite for being a serious poet. Both Eliot and Pound had, of course, publicised the very same belief, but so aware was Pound that such trafficking with the dead was not only necessary for the fulfilment of his talent but also a real danger to it that he made that ambivalent relationship the subject of the opening poem in his magnum opus, *The Cantos*. It is a reprise of the famous episode in *The Odyssey* where Odysseus descends into the Underworld in search of guidance and there meets with Tiresias, the blind seer of Thebes, who forecasts the perils he will yet have to endure before eventually reaching the safety of Ithaca having lost all his companions. Before descending, Odysseus had been warned he should protect himself against the clamorous spirits, and so on his arrival in the Underworld he had 'unsheathed the narrow sword ... to keep off the impetuous dead'. And in like manner, Pound is careful to place a cordon sanitaire between himself and the original Greek by using as his source a Latin translation of the Odyssey published by Andreas Divus in 1538. Watkins, however, took no such precautions, and so, many of his poems are unfortunately appropriated, so to speak, by the spirits of the dead masters he so adored and were accordingly derivative. They are eerily zombie compositions.

The very best of them, however, have a vibrant life of their own and there is none better than 'Music of Colours: Dragonfoil and the Furnace of Colours' (*CP*, 322). It is a heady distillation of the sensual opulence of high summer. Its gorgeous pageantry of imagery captures the season's flagrant excess: 'Lizards on dry stone; gipsy-bright nasturtiums/ Burning through round leaves, twining out in torch-buds'. It is a signature poem of Watkins's talents, which are all here on confident, alluring display. Yes, it is Keatsian in its evocation of summer 'deep in fume of poppies', the opiate among the seasons entrancing the senses until the air seems thick with drowsiness, and leaving the mind helplessly 'drugged beneath the heat haze', so that 'All is entranced here, mazed amid the wheatfield/ Mustardseed, chicory, sky of the cornflower/ Deepening in sunlight, singing of the reapers'. Keatsian, certainly. But Watkins's poem also has an integrity of vision of its own, as at its heart lies his distinctive perception of life as the product of original whiteness fractured to produce the astonishing rainbow of colours. This fecund generative process is also likened to the emissions of a white-hot furnace, and to sound fractured to produce 'music of colours swaying in the light breeze,/ Flame wind of poppies'.

Even amidst all this plenitude, however, he is haunted by 'a spirit's absence', imagining the glorious music of the season to be that of an Orpheus mourning his lost Eurydice, and supposing that an Ophelia lies somewhere drowned 'among your shadows'. All life originates in loss, as of course must it end in loss: this is an obsessively recurrent theme in Watkins's poetry, and, as so often when reflecting on it, he recalls the 'Ocean, kindler of us, mover and mother,/ Constantly changing'. The second section of his poem is in many ways a reprise of the first, but now with the theme of loss in the ascendant. Yes, he exults still in 'Brand lit in foliage, in the heart of summer,/ Breaking from the live coals', in 'Red silk of poppies' and 'Fire-misted marigold', but these June flowers hide 'the footprints of Eurydice/ Seized by the dark kind'. 'Only by absence is the song made/ Audible', he continues, 'Orpheus, leaning above Lethe,/ Knows every note there'. Nowhere is it more clear that Watkins knows himself to be a Christian Orphic poet, whose poetry arises from the soul of absence. And in this section the Ocean accordingly looms even larger, its 'Inconstancy of pattern, eternally renewing/ Through mother-of-pearl the colours of destruction/ Dissolving'.

So, in the diapasonic final section Watkins fully integrates the twin experiences of destruction and creation, noticing even how 'unremembered shadows/ Cling, where the bloom breaks'. 'All that is made,' he realises, 'here hides another making': life and death, he is convinced, lie inextricably interwoven beneath this triumphal panoply, but we, 'waking entranced', 'cannot see the other/ Order of colours moving in the white light' because 'Time is for us transfigured into colours', even as we hear the 'breakers/ Falling on gold sand, bringing all to nothing'.

'Music of Colours: Dragonfoil and the Furnace of Colours' is a complex, consummate achievement, and in itself masterpiece sufficient for Watkins to be acknowledged as a considerable poet of the Welsh religious tradition. And he was certainly very conscious of his place in the long continuum of Welsh literary history, as was to be expected of one sensitive to the way in which 'lost years are mixed with years to come' (*CP*, 404). 'Only where holy sources are obeyed', he continued, 'The spirit knows its home'. He knew that the very cliffs of South Gower continued to store remnants of the distant past, nowhere more famously than in the Paviland Cave where human bones, covered in red ochre and dating back to the Upper Paleolithic period (*c*.33,000 BCE), were the earliest bones found in Britain when discovered in 1823, and originally supposed to be that of a young girl of the Roman period. Subsequently they were realised to be the remains of a young man. Watkins devoted two poems to this subject, and emphasised yet again in the first that such a discovery was an appeasement of an unquiet spirit. The 'rock's reticence', he writes, 'Pulls our awareness/ Downward, to ease/ The forebears' stress/ Of soul'. In 'Digging the Past' he identifies with those originally involved in the funeral rites for the dead youth, as 'their shadows danced upon the tide/ Protecting still, unknown to air,/ The slender tissue in their care' (*CP*, 385). What he did not know, apparently, was that at the time of burial, the site would have been located some seventy miles inland, and would have overlooked a great plain.

No wonder, therefore, that Watkins was proudly aware, as he made clear in 'The Swallows', of his relationship to almost two thousand years of literary activity in Wales. He there compares artists to swallows, since they, too, may wander far yet always inevitably return to their place of birth. So 'Welsh ambassadors' such as himself 'break down colours from an earlier day' (*CP*, 369). Pursuing this thought, he finds himself harking back to that early age when 'Bow and harpstring both/ Sound the one hand'. The great representatives of the age who thus combined its savagery and its creativity were, first Aneirin, who 'drew anguish from stone for youth cut down and then the aged and incapacitated warrior leader Llywarch Hen, whose poems (although now known by scholars not to have been his compositions) 'threw/ Remorse at Death, who took his every son'.

But while he clearly admires these poets and acknowledges them as distant kin, he identifies most closely, as ever, with Taliesin because he associates the former two with a pre-Christian age of savagery whereas he regards Taliesin as a representative of Christian vision, and thus as his alter ego. 'Still Taliesin stays', he writes, 'Touching, more near than all we know,/ The pulse of praise,/ Deeper, more strong, than string of harp or bow.' Viewed in this civilised context, Aneirin and Taliesin seem representatives of a bygone age whose poetry now serves only to show 'how vain Earth's morning are' 'without Christ's birth'.

For Watkins, then, Taliesin is the great representative of the Welsh tradition of praise, a tradition to which he was very proud to belong. And being a shape-changer, Taliesin would have experienced no difficulty in moving from a Welsh-language to an English-language medium, just as, Watkins obviously felt, the Welsh instinct to praise would survive the catastrophe of culture-break and language shift – 'my verse is characteristically Welsh', he insisted, 'in the same way that the verse of Yeats is characteristically Irish ... because rhythm and cadence are born in the blood' (*EM*, 6). 'Speaking of "the finest early poetry in Britain," that of Aneurin [*sic*], Taliesin and Llywarch Hen, which he could not read in Welsh, he would say "I feel the affinity with these poets which does not come from study of history, but from instinct. Their roots go very deep"' (*EM*, 6).

Hence his particular concern to locate Taliesin in Gower, a region nowhere associated with him in the several medieval Welsh treatments of his character. 'Taliesin in Gower' opens with the magician-poet's triumphant assertion 'Late I return, O violent, colossal, reverberant, eavesdropping sea./ My country is here' (*CP*, 184). The shaman has returned home, as becomes clear when he declares 'I witness here in a vision the landscape to which I was born' and proceeds to itemise its details lovingly, because he 'know[s] every inch of [the curlew's] way'. He notices 'the smouldering bushes of willow, like trees of fire', 'the iris break from its sheath' and 'the dripping branch in the ache of sunrise frost'. His native language here is thus neither Welsh nor English, but rather the vocabulary of nature itself: 'I have been taught the script of the stones, and I know the tongue of the wave.' His is a restorative vision – 'In the hunter's quarry this landscape died; my vision restores it again' – because it restores to this landscape the magical, religious significance that has been long lost to secularising history. So the ageless Taliesin naturally gravitates to that distant era when 'rhinoceros, bear and reindeer haunt the crawling glaciers of age' because the hunters of that age 'where a javelin'd arm held stiff' were in awe of the mysterious spiritual powers inherent in the creatures they hunted. And the poem ends with him preparing to fashion his harp by cutting the wood and 'exactly measur[ing]'. He is, though, fully aware that his song, old-fashioned by modern standards, is certain to be scorned, as he makes clear in 'Taliesin and the Mockers' where, in the person

of the shaman he in turn hits back at 'those hired musicians,/ They
at Court/ Who command the schools' (*CP*, 321).

The little bay of Pwlldu (Black Pool) lies some two miles east
of Watkins's home at Heatherslade, Southgate, and is easily reached
by a walk along the cliffs from there. The place where Bishopston
stream – emerging from deep within the limestone – surfaces and
reaches the sea, it was for him a numinous spot, 'an eternal place!/
The black stream under the stones/ Carries the bones of the dead,/
The starved, the talkative bones' (*CP*, 189). It was with this liminal
region, the place where the dead and the living met, that he associated
Taliesin, as is made clear in 'Taliesin at Pwlldu' (*CP*, 353). Touching
this spot the shaman knows 'my native land' because all around him
he discerns trinitarian signs – suggestive both of the Holy Trinity and
of the ancient Welsh Triads. 'There are three about me where I stand',
he notes, and by such tokens he knows this to be a 'secret place within
the source of tears/ Caught by stream's light, uniting all that's gone'.

By such signs, too, Watkins knew himself to belong to the Welsh
Taliesinic tradition of praise. In the years after the war, he formed a
close friendship with the distinguished Welsh painter Ceri Richards,
a native of nearby Dunvant who spent all his summers in a holiday
cottage near Watkins's home on Pennard Cliffs. And after Watkins's
death, Richards was to produce several magnificent elegiac prints
commemorating his friend's poetry. In her classic memoir *Portrait of
a Friend*, Gwen Watkins perceptively commented on this important
friendship. They both, she wrote, 'looked on nature and humanity
from the same viewpoint; both saw creation as praise, and both were
aware of the suffering and sacrifice that must make a part of praise'
(*CP*, 147). And, one might add, they both thus instanced one ancient
and highly valuable form of Welshness, one that for Watkins was
epitomised by the legendary figure of Taliesin.

Notes

1   Ruth Pryor (ed.), *The Collected Poems of Vernon Watkins* (Ipswich:
    Golgonooza Press, 1986), p. 260. Hereafter *CP*.
2   For a sound biographical overview, see Richard Ramsbotham, *An Exact
    Mystery: The Poetic Life of Vernon Watkins* (The Choir Press, 2020). Hereafter
    EM.
3   See 'Symbyliad y Symbol: barddoniaeth Euros Bowen a Vernon Watkins',
    in M. Wynn Thomas (ed.), *Di-Ffinio Dwy Lenyddiaeth Cymru* (Cardiff:
    University of Wales Press, 1995), pp. 179–94.

4 Gwen Watkins, *Portrait of a Friend* (Llandysul: Gomer, 1983), p. 53. Hereafter *PF*.

5 See 'Vernon Watkins: Taliesin in Gower', in *All That is Wales: The Collected Essays of M. Wynn Thomas* (Cardiff: University of Wales Press, 2017), pp. 213–33.

6 Letter of Peter Sterry to Morgan Llwyd, 23 July 1654. In J. Graham Jones and Goronwy Wyn Owen (eds), *Gweithiau Morgan Llwyd o Wynedd, 3* (Cardiff: University of Wales Press, 1994), p. 173.

7 Richard Ramsbotham (ed.), *Vernon Watkins: New and Selected Poems* (Manchester: Carcanet, Fyfield Books, 2006), p. 101.

4

'Enfysu'/Rainbowing: The Anglican Sacramentalism of Euros Bowen

R. S. Thomas was apt to smile wryly whenever he mentioned Euros Bowen (1904–88), an acquaintance during his early days in Manafon who had helped him become fluent in Welsh. Though both were priests in the service of the Church in Wales, they were contrasting personalities, R. S. Thomas the spare, attenuated and reticent 'Gog' (North Walian), Bowen the squat, bull-necked and rather belligerent 'Shoni' or 'Hwntw' (from the industrial valleys of the southern coalfield) who exhibited all the undisciplined garrulousness Thomas loathed in the natives of those parts. It sometimes seemed that Bowen's round collar could barely contain the irascibility and brusque impatience of one who looked rather like a combative Rhondda miner turned scholarly and genteel. Yet it was this coiled-up energy that the ever-forthright Bowen tapped to produce poems electrically alive with the current surging through nature. To achieve this, he invested every element of language with a corresponding dynamism. But R.S. (ever jealous of potential rivals) simply refused to take 'Euros' seriously as a poet at all, which is a pity because Bowen possessed striking antithetical qualities of his own. The fact that he idolised Dylan Thomas only served to confirm R. S. Thomas in his prejudices. At his exceptional best, Bowen was an intemperate, extravagant poet, a singular talent who produced sumptuous poetry.[1]

R.S. was an Apollonian, Bowen a self-proclaimed Dionysiac. In his poem on that wild and wayward god, he pointed out that in Greek myth Dionysus had been associated not only with the vine but with the ivy, symbol of eternal life.[2] But he was also aware, as Nietzsche had been in *The Birth of Tragedy*, that in Ancient Greece the cult of

Dionysius had enabled the development of a golden age of tragedy. While R. S. Thomas was an inveterate minimalist, Bowen, ever the erratic Dionysian ecstatic, was prone in his weakest moments to take linguistic extravagance to the point of excess. His poems can then seem like a fall-out from an explosion in a hefty lexicon, although he noticeably curbed this instinct in later years. Reading them is on occasion an intensely exasperating experience. But at his best, his texts are illuminating and can even be transporting.

Bowen loved archaisms and neologisms. He writes 'enfysu'/rainbowing, for example, a coinage appropriate to a spiritual and poetic vision glorying in the fractured spectrum of earthly light.[3] He relished all the arcane exotica of vocabulary. That is because his poems are paeans to the glorious largesse of creation, its superabundance. They are celebrations of a plenitude so overwhelming as to require the exploitation of all the rich resources of vocabulary and a searching of its hidden recesses to do such opulence justice. Like the natural world, he revels in over-production, and his output is powered by the recognition that words are not just tools for managing the world but the myriad eyes that alone can furnish us with appropriate sight and insight. An accomplished Classicist, he might well have chosen Argos as Muse. Fascinated by synaesthesia, and inspired by what Dylan Thomas termed 'the colour of saying', he strove to create poems as restless with verbal colour as shot-silk, or as flamboyant as a peacock's tail. And his penchant for linguistic adventure resulted in collections that floated a perilous argosy of poems.

He was a devotee of light, constantly associating it with creative energy. One poem finds him, in a striking modification of the myth of Zeus's manifestation in a shower of gold, marvelling at the shower of shadows cascading into nooks and crannies from the loins of light (*LIT*, 219). Elsewhere, it is light that breaks through the lowering mist that envelops a field as the sun steadies itself to force a path through the gloom. Its success, Bowen writes, is 'like ardent conviction ringing out in a peal of church bells' (*LIT*, 22). A standard device of Bowen's is to trope light as sound – or as colour. Whenever he finds himself beleaguered by the darkness that is abundant in life, it is usually in light that he reposes his trust. The first stanza of 'Lux in Tenebris' deals sombrely with the movement from thickening twilight to a full darkness that gradually envelops the senses like the deepest innards of a great cave.[4] The second stanza repeats the stylised syntax and images of envelopment of the first but transforms them into a celebration of the light that breaks on the senses, the light that breaks *in* the senses, revealing a great capacious cave of discovery. In his fascination with light as it emerged from the very heart of darkness he resembled the iconographers of Eastern Orthodox tradition, who always built their images by first establishing the dark ground out of which the golden splendours of their icons then proceeded to shine.

A fine explanation of the theological implications of the special techniques involved in fashioning an icon, a 'small jewel of the sacred', may be found on the website of St Cecilia's Abbey, Ryde, on the Isle of Wight:

> When using tempera one is really painting with light. If one floats successive thin glazes of colour across the white gesso ground, light travels through these glazes, reaches the gesso and travels back outward again, giving the colours glowing luminosity. Light plays at the edge of an intense colour, or is suffused in it as in a sapphire. As Goethe has said, 'colour is light's suffering and joy ... all colour is half-light.' ... This quality is lost if the tempera is used over gold or straight onto wood neither of which matches the reflective strength of gesso. But when fields of gold are juxtaposed with the tempera it enhances its spiritual power, for example in icons.
>
> ... Egg tempera on gesso ground ... can create a shadow without breaks which is not opaque black but has the tones of its object within its depths. As Goethe has it, '... Colour in itself is a degree of darkness ... darkness is a colour nearest the light ...' He meant that darkness is an active ingredient rather than a place where light is absent.[5]

This chimes well with Euros Bowen's understanding of the matter in the terms appropriate to him as poet rather than as visual artist.

Bowen's 'Dan Oleuad' (*D*, 191) is a complex poem of his late period. It dwells on the mysterious intertwining of qualities that constitutes the very quick of earthly existence, and it opens with an extended meditation on the creative mingling of light and dark under an ordinary street lamp. Recalling the great proclamation at the beginning of the Gospel according to Saint John that divine light penetrated the darkness and the darkness knew it not, Bowen adds the rider that darkness is nevertheless compelled to become the cradle of light. Then his vision broadens to encompass the many mingling of opposites and unlikely enlivening juxtapositions visible everywhere in the world of nature: dull light seeps through the gloom of fog, yellow moss clouds lawns; a hedgehog lurks in the cracks of a path, a dandelion spills the sperm of its seed in the grass. At night, the eyes of some sleepers take root in the dark, while those of others flower – there is, one suspects, just a hint in such an antithesis of Bowen's conviction that a few, although not all, of his fellow-mortals were instinctively drawn like himself to trust in hope rather than succumb to the lethargy of indifference. And as the poem proceeds, emphasising the mysterious creative powers of the union of opposites, it finally brings Bowen to the realisation that all such moments of encounter are liminal in character, occasions where our world unexpectedly encroaches on another wholly other to itself. They are the products of a borderland, which is literally a no man's land because it does not allow of familiarising, normalising human occupation. It is a strange, disorientating, zone intermediate between this life and the next.

Given Bowen's passion for light, no wonder that he found an analogy, both for his poems and for the life abroad that, as Shelley put it, stains the white radiance of eternity, in the blazing medieval technicolour of Chartres cathedral. But in his tour de force of a poem on that subject it is in music he finds a lexicon adequate for expressing the eloquence of the colours in the great stained-glass windows (*D*, 39). For him, musical instruments seem to make themselves audible in these rich harmonies: in the very act of seeing, he hears the blue of a violin's passion, the ruddiness of sensual trumpets, and the shifting shades of yellow fluting, while all this gorgeous diapason of colours rings out in sonorous counterpoint to the strum of white that for Bowen reposes like a smile on the seats. For him, peacocks sing their hearts out in the medieval glass, light pours its ruby in profusion, sunshine sounds its ecstatic note of sapphire, and the sweet sounds of topaz soar between the taut pillars of confession and the calming quiet of the roof. Bowen was as sensible of the emotional impact of colours as Kandinsky, as ready to associate the changing moods of the world with them as was Wallace Stevens. Then the rumble of the organ begins in the great cathedral's depths, seeming to set candles flickering in the dark, and sending lightening flashing on high, as the roar of thunder pours from the uttermost secret recesses. The cumulative effect, he adds, resorting to a kind of surrealist oxymoron, is of a lightening that blinds the eyes with the unforgettable deafness of hearing.

The Welsh language is particularly rich in homophones, a feature enhanced by mutations and fully exploited by the classical strict-metre poets who employed it to create their intricate and tightly regulated patterns of sound. Bowen was a highly accomplished strict-metre poet, twice winner of the coveted crown at the National Eisteddfod of Wales. But in his mature poetry, he preferred to avail himself freely of every manner of striking aural correspondences. In the process he discarded sacred conventions so cavalierly that he scandalised the straight-laced fraternity (almost all being male) of *barddas*, practitioners of the arcane bardic arts. But there was a purpose behind his bold breaking of hallowed conventions. For him, the web of sound created by the elaborate patternings and interconnections of a poetic text signified a divinely ordered and harmonious universe.

He always fiercely defended his provocative 'free *cynghanedd*' (a concept that conservatives of the tradition dismissed as a contradiction in terms). It was, he insisted, an attempt to perpetuate an august tradition not by mummifying it but by reinvigorating it through audacious innovation. And he attacked the stuffy practitioners of orthodoxy, who succeeded, in his typically belligerent view, only in condemning *cynghanedd* to stiffen in a refrigerator of cliches (*LIT*, 97). But a much deeper and more consequential concern underlay this spat. Bowen was haunted by a fear that the Welsh language was slowly withering away, its vocabulary steadily shrinking, its constituencies of use increasingly limited. In his poem 'Boncyff' he found an image for this linguistic and cultural crisis in an old tree-trunk, stripped of life, its branches drooping above a cold profusion of grasses. The tree's roots, he suggested, had aged like an old language. They had once been a profusion of delights, all vigorous growth and leaves in the company of a forest of relatives, and joyous as bells that honoured the ear of meadows and dales. But now it withers away in an acid rain, having lost its old vital power of self-renewal (*M*, 11).

Each of Bowen's poems was a defiant attempt at tapping the capacity for new life still stubbornly lingering in those old roots to produce a poetry that displayed anew all of his beloved language's ancient, rich resources. After all, as he wrote in 'Ieuenctid yr Iaith' (*D*, 114), if Welsh was ancient, it was also eternally youthful. So he urged his readers to open their windows wide so that they could once more smell the Welsh language ploughing the fields, and see it graft new skin on to schools and universities. Welsh was the culture of the land, as it had been the original cultivator of it. It was the language that had sculpted the mountains to make a home for the goats among the crags. For centuries it had embraced the whole country in its amplitude, from valley to broad acres, and it had taken into its care hay fields and corn meadows, pits and quarries, kitchens and parlours. The language was for Bowen a latter-day Galatea, still given breath enough by the abiding love of its people to enable it to marry the present age (*D*, 119).

*   *   *

Bowen's poetics is not only underpinned by religious conviction, it is intimately in-formed by it. A native of the industrial Rhondda, he wasn't a cradle Anglican, his father having been a Welsh Congregationalist minister and Bowen himself at one time a candidate for ministry in the same denomination, undergoing training at the Presbyterian College in Carmarthen. That, however, turned out to be a mere preliminary to his subsequent education at Bangor (where he graduated in Classics), at Oxford (where he studied theology at Mansfield and St Catherine's colleges), and finally at the Anglican College of St David's at Lampeter (where he prepared for the priesthood).

He was never reluctant to parade his considerable resultant erudition (he was ever the *poeta doctus*), and his proficiency both in Greek and Latin, as well as in several modern languages, enabled him to produce a large number of translations into Welsh. These included several plays by Sophocles, a theological classic by Athanasius on the Incarnation of the Word, Virgil's *Eclogues*, and an excellent selection of French Symbolist poetry. Although a late starter, he was a very productive poet as well as a highly distinctive one and published nineteen collections over a writing career spanning some forty years. During most of that time he was rector at Llangywair and Llanuwchllyn, villages near the rural mid-Wales town of Bala.

It is worth pausing over two of the above translations in particular: those of Athanasius and of the French Symbolists. Both have extensive implications for Bowen's own poetic theory and practice. Athanasius, a fourth-century Bishop of Alexandria and a sainted and revered Father of the early Church, was a leading proponent of a theological doctrine that was eventually accepted as orthodoxy at the Seventh Ecumenical Council of Nicea (787). For the previous three centuries, however, it had been involved in a violent life-or-death struggle with a rival doctrine propounded by Arius, another leading churchman of the period. Centred on rival versions of Christology, the fierce disagreement occasioned a fatal rift between the Catholic and Eastern Orthodox churches, healed only with the Triumph of Orthodoxy in 843.

Arius stubbornly pointed to passages in Scripture clearly stating that Christ had been begotten by God. Christ, he argued, could not therefore be regarded as an eternal integral aspect of the Godhead. Rather, he was the son of God, made flesh and become a man. This Arian doctrine came to be described as 'subordinationist', since it denied Christ parity with God. Its antithesis was Monophysitism, which denied the human nature of Christ. Athanasius pointed by contrast to the famous opening of the Gospel according to St John, and the unambiguous proclamation there that Christ had existed with God from all eternity. This being true, it followed that He must have been an essential aspect of Divinity itself. Therefore, when the Word became flesh, the divine nature of Christ had been miraculously fused with his human nature. Christ, Athanasius crisply asserted, was irrefutably 'of one being with the Father', and the Holy Trinity was an instance of 'consubstantiality' – three persons of a single divine substance. Some Eastern icons subsequently sought to capture this dual nature of Christ by depicting him as dressed in a red garment: this underlay another garment which was blue-green in colour. The former symbolised his divinity, the latter his earthly life, the period during which, as the Byzantine liturgy had it, 'The illuminated Word of the Father imposed a limit on itself in the incarnation [and] restored the corrupted image of the primitive archetype and filled it with divine beauty.'[6]

It was the constant insistence on recognising the transcendent nature of God as well as His immanence that perhaps eventually led Bowen, in his old age, to develop an interest in the Greek Orthodox faith. His appreciation of the emphasis, evident in all its elaborate rituals, on the unassailable majesty and impenetrable mystery of Godhead was no doubt refined and deepened by his exposure to contemporary Greek Orthodoxy during his travels, late in life, both to Greece and to Crete. But much earlier he had written a poem marvelling at the image of the Pantocrator displayed in a great Byzantine church at Cefalu, a peninsular town in northern Sicily:

> Gold mosaics bursting into leaf
> The praise of
> Archangels, cherubim, seraphim,
> And the magnifying
> Of the Virgin Mary,
> Apostles, patriarchs,
> Prophets and saints,
> To the eternal head.[7]

At its conclusion, the poem makes clear Bowen's acknowledgement of ingrained human sinfulness. The eyes in that 'eternal head' are those of Christ the Judge, Lord of Creation, and they are 'a fire searing the root/ of the earth's guilt'. The image is similar to that of 'The Saviour with the Fearsome Eye', an early fourteenth-century icon in the Kremlin Cathedral of the Dormition (*IS*, 242).

Athanasius had emphasised that Christ was the Word, the Logos, and this suggestive metaphor resonated profoundly with Bowen. It seemed to allow for the possibility that there might be a special, spiritual affinity between human language, fallible and inadequate though that was, and the divine Word whose power created and sustained the whole of creation. By grace, a poet could be granted the privilege of exploiting this affinity for the greater glory of God. The Nicene Creed's further declaration that Christ was 'Light from light' also spoke to one who was such a devotee of light, both as a priest and as a poet.

Bowen was adamant, though, that no spark of this divine Light was immanent in human beings. Such a belief, he insisted, belonged to the world of the Greeks not to that of the Hebrews. Here, again, his respect for God's irreducible transcendence is evident, as is his acknowledgement of human sin. His sonnet on God's image ('Delw Duw', *D*, 15) opens accordingly with the authoritative statement 'Nid oes gwreichionedd ddwyfol ynom ni' (there is no divine spark in us). We are instead the handiwork of God the supreme craftsman, specifically fashioned to be the wonder of the world. The relationship of God to any human being is similar to that of a master with a keen apprentice. God likewise carefully nurtures in us creative skills. And although Bowen is careful not to claim as much explicitly, it is obvious that one such skill is that of the poet with language.

In his poem 'Y Gair' he 'grounds' the theology of his poetics in the findings of modern science, tracing the origins of life to the impact of a comet or asteroid which was already 'yn ferw o leferydd' ('boiling with speech') (*LIT*, 86). This 'speech' eventually migrated 'o lygad i glust/ o lygaid i glyw' (from eye to ear, from eyes to hearing). Thus the Word emerged out of chaos. Testing its power against the night, it triumphed and reduced darkness to mere cargo of the boat rowed by Charon across the Styx at the end of every human life.

Bowen understandably chooses to emphasise the ancient orthodox theology of his poetics. But it also owes much to the theorising of the great English Romantics, most particularly of Coleridge. He it was

who, in a famous passage in *Biographia Literaria* that owed much to
the late-eighteenth-century German idealists, described the Primary
Imagination – the mental faculty that brings order to the chaos of
sense impressions – as 'the living power and prime agent of all human
perception, and as a repetition in the finite mind of the eternal act
of creation in the infinite I am'. In Bowen's theological terms (and
Coleridge had modelled his phrasing on the Book of Genesis), this
living power was that of the Word operative at a basic human level.
As for the Secondary Imagination, it was a higher faculty possessed
only by those of an artistic nature. Translated again into Bowen's
theological terms, this was the Word as dimly reflected in the poetry
as in other arts.

Appreciation of the depth of Bowen's devotion to the Word/word
is vital for understanding his carefully qualified interest in French
Symbolist poetry. In 1980 he published masterly Welsh translations
of Baudelaire, Mallarmé, Rimbaud, Verlaine, Corbière, Laforgue,
Valéry and Claudel. In the introduction he furnished a succinct
account of the movement and its philosophy, concluding with a
pen-portrait of its main poetical practitioners. Bowen was care-
ful to distinguish between the different inflections given to the core
ideas of Symbolism by each of these key figures. The translations
that followed were embedded in an impressive essay that traversed
the wide and varied mental landscape of the Symbolist movement.
But for all his interest in the French Symbolists, Bowen insisted that
theirs was a poetics that gave precedence to the image; his, by con-
trast, was one in which the word was absolutely paramount. It is
a distinction some of Bowen's readers have understandably found
hard to swallow, given his poems are chock-a-block with particularly
audacious imagery.

There can certainly be no doubt that Bowen learnt a very great
deal from the French Symbolist masters. Indeed, so inward was
his connection to them that he produced several poems that con-
sciously entered into dialogue with some of their most distinguished
work. Very shortly after turning his hand to poetry in middle age,
he launched a vigorous new journal, *Y Fflam*, and its early num-
bers featured spirited disagreements between two young rising stars
of Welsh poetry, Gareth Alban Davies and Bobi Jones. The former
(who became a distinguished Professor of Spanish) fervently believed
French Symbolism could help supply deficiencies in Welsh culture.
In particular, he valued its treatment of symbols as an indispensable

medium for accessing the transcendent, and the priority it placed on the musicality of poetry. But Davies remained wary of the disconnect that tended to follow in the case of such as Mallarmé between sound and sense. Bobi Jones's response came a year later when he published a vigorous attack on what he characterised as the archaic and decadent character of French Symbolism, whose taste for the exotic had actually resulted in limiting and specialising discourse, thus weakening it. He also condemned Symbolism for preparing the way for Surrealism, which he largely associated with a specific kind of automatic writing.

Bowen himself declined to enter the fray, but his interest in Symbolism was no doubt developed under the influence of such discussions. It may also have been mediated by his enthusiasm for the neo-Symbolist poetry of Dylan Thomas, the self-styled 'Rimbaud of Cwmdonkin Drive'. Shortly after Thomas's passing, Bowen dedicated an 'englyn' to his memory. It invoked him as a Dionysiac figure whose avid raids on the vineyard of poetry had turned his lips red. Drunk on the fruit of the vine, he had passed prematurely away, leaving wine widowed (*D*, 19). Thomas's chosen manner of expression therefore, or so Bowen believed, revealed him to be a poet of European rather than English stock, and Bowen considered himself likewise to be a Welsh European.

Behind the memorial englyn there lies, one suspects, the memory of Baudelaire's warning to the poet that permanent intoxication is the only reliable protection against becoming a prisoner of time. This apothegm is quoted in a note to a poem composed by Bowen in response. In 'Sobri' ('Sobering up') flight from time is seen as already implicit in the history of stars and birds, and palpable in such moments of silence and stillness as when stars steady the hours of night, a bird meditates on the tip of an ash tree at midday, while the imagination remains sober (*D*, 155).

Bowen resembled Baudelaire in his love of the prose poem. As we have seen, sight of the renowned stained glass windows of Chartres moved him to an extravaganza of synaesthesia, again in the manner of his great French predecessor: 'I listened to them striking up their chords on wall and pillar, in the bays and on the floor.// I saw the musical instruments in the windows, an intense violin blue, red impassioned trumpets, a yellow fluting alternating with harps in their setting bright and gay.' His whole approach to the poetic imagination was informed by the credo announced in Baudelaire's 'Correspondences', a classic poem acknowledged by Bowen in one of his commentaries and duly translated by him. There the intermingling of the senses enables unique symbolic apprehension of the secret underlying unity of all creation. Time after time Bowen transfigured the world in this fashion in his torrential poetry. Viewing sunflowers through the eyes of Van Gogh, he discovered them to be 'like a yellow emotion on the blue wave of trees; like a sea-shell intent on oystered pearls:// Like drops of lemon rain on the high windows of the wood: like a deep whirlpool circling to the acclaim of bannered rocks' (*EB*, 39). 'When the wind is green,' he elsewhere writes, 'seaweed in the sea,/ the ivy's flesh/ and the glass of the lake's windows.// When the wind is yellow,/ sand and shells,/ and the moon on the floor of the lake' (*D*, 214). Rimbaud's famous remark about *dérèglement de tous les sens* comes to mind.

As was the case with Baudelaire, Bowen's aim, he explained in 'Y Gelfyddyd' (the Art), was to use art to reveal the secret sources of all creation. It allowed a glimpse of the ultimate mystery – what Mallarmé had termed *sens mysterieux de l'existence*. But, unlike the Frenchman, Bowen had a Christian understanding of that mystery. He saw his poetry as a natural extension of his work in the priesthood. At the very centre of the act of worship, as of the act of writing and of reading a poem, lay ritual and sacrament, both indispensable means, for him as an Anglican priest, of communicating with ultimate spiritual reality and of transmitting it to others. 'Sacrament sicr ym modd/ ei sain', wrote Bowen in his poem on the mystery of a poem; the sound of poetry was a certain means to sacramental experience (*LIT*, 88). As a poet he was, he insisted, not a Symbolist (which he equated with an occult atheism) but a devout Christian sacramentalist. In accordance with the twenty-four Articles of the Anglican Church, he believed a sacrament to be the visible sign of invisible Grace. Such were for him particularly apparent and eloquently significant in the life of the natural world. His was primarily a 'natural sacramentalism' and in some ways a Christian extension of what has been described as the 'Natural Supernaturalism' of the great English Romantic tradition.

In a fine essay of 1993 on Bowen's poetry, A. M. Allchin, at that time Canon of Canterbury Cathedral, glossed the Welsh poet's devotion to the sacraments very illuminatingly. When speaking in public about his poetry, Allchin recalled, Bowen would sometimes refer to 'the sacramental order' of the goodness to be found throughout creation (*EB*, 14). Allchin recognised that 'Euros would have wanted to see a close analogy between the imaginative work of the poet and the role of faith in grasping hold of the inner realities given in the Church's sacraments' (*EB*, 25). But he also emphasised how important it was both to Bowen the priest and to Bowen the poet to root 'universal, divine significance and power ... in the particular created reality of which they partake'. Hence, Allchin explained, Bowen's rejection of the Catholic belief that the mystery of transubstantiation lay at the very heart of the Eucharist. It seemed to him that to believe that was to undervalue the inherent spiritual dimension of the most ordinary, even the most banal, elements of life. It was to assume the insufficiency, the sacramental deficit, of the everyday.

Allchin perceptively took his argument one stage further. For an Anglican such as Bowen, he added, 'the Catholic Christian faith needs to incarnate itself in particular peoples and particular cultures, in the one case English, in the other Welsh'. Such an insight allows us to understand why Bowen was so ready to include a poem about Owain Glyndŵr, for example, or about the site of the court of the Prince of Powys at Mathrafal, alongside his poems of explicit spiritual experience. His poem on 'Bugail Kares' (the Shepherd of Kares) even draws a parallel between Glyndŵr's foiled attempt to become the saviour of Wales and the equally unsuccessful efforts of Petros Philarges, who began life as a shepherd on Crete, to close the gap between the Papacy and the Anti-Papacy when in 1409 he became Pope Alexander V (*D*, 245). Elsewhere Allchin also acutely detected in Bowen's sacramentalism a preference for a suggestively symbolic rather than a reductively literal articulation of religious mysteries. As Bowen himself succinctly put it at the end of his poem on 'The Word' (Y Gair), the sacraments were uniquely capable of communicating that glow in the world that 'breaks forth from the mystery,/ so that the words of grace shall not be an ideology of Christ' (*EB*, 49). This was also very much the core conviction of R. S. Thomas.

Bowen tried to explain this trust in symbols, essential for his poetry, to a sceptical and philistine Welsh Nonconformist readership brought up on a strict diet of didacticism. He spoke of 'rhesymeg y dychymyg' (the rationale of the imagination), explaining that a poem was best thought of as a 'river of symbols', its flood carrying the mind to a different world from that of mundane apprehension and communication. It is an impeccable Symbolist poetic. Yet, as already emphasised, his was far from an uncritical acceptance of the revelations of the French Symbolists. He felt a Christian unease at some of the more extreme tendencies apparent in their work, with the belated exception of the Catholic Claudel. For Baudelaire he felt a mixture of admiration and repugnance. He was wary of a poet whose own peculiar vision of original sin lingered lasciviously over the close affinity between divinity and Satanism. His two-part poem on Baudelaire compares and contrasts him with Dafydd ap Gwilym. Like the great Welsh medieval poet, the Frenchman, too, had rebelled against the restrictive moral outlook of the church of his day (a rebellion exemplified in Dafydd's work by his debate with 'Y Brawd Llwyd', a Greyfriar). But unlike the Welshman, Baudelaire had, by way of reaction, allowed himself to be seduced by the fatal allure of sinful, ultimately syphilitic, flesh (D, 225–6).

As a confirmed Christian incarnationist, Bowen was also disapproving of the tendency of the greatest Symbolists to treat the given, visible, world, glorious in all its ambivalent character and manifest imperfections, as a mere springboard towards some more pure transcendent reality. There are some occasions when, as in his two poems to the swan, he appears to be locking horns with key Symbolist texts on this very issue (D, 5; 189). He had translated the famous poems by Baudelaire and Mallarmé on the same subject, pointing out that, while very different, both treated the swan as a symbol of the poet's alienation from the ordinary world and proof of his complete devotion to the transcendent realm of beauty. This reading is specifically repudiated by Bowen, who sees the bird (with, in the second poem, more than a nod to Yeats's 'Wild Swans at Coole') as dazzlingly bright, inevitably transient, and evidence of the presence of divine creativity abroad in all common things and creatures.

While Bowen's swan, too, is ultimately a visitor from a superior spiritual realm, it does not offer transport to the transcendent. Instead, this elegant and dazzling bird on Bala lake brings with it for mortals the gift of discerning the signature of the divine perfection legible under the dull surface of surrounding mundane reality. Hence the poem's opening lines. These rapturously acknowledge the swan's power to bestow the gift of new (in)sight on a human observer who thereby acquires the visionary ability to glimpse spiritual significance and mystery everywhere. Except that at this crucial point Bowen uses the active continuous present tense of the verb 'argoeli' (to signify, or to promise), where normally the noun-form 'argoel' would have been employed. He thus underlines the permanent dynamics of this

new, transfiguring, act of looking enabled by the visitation of grace
in the form of the swan.

* * *

At times, Bowen's poetry can pall because it seems so tiresomely
intent on 'hurrahing the universe', as one critic once contemptu-
ously wrote of Walt Whitman. Its obvious weakness is a tendency
to limit itself to the one register of praise and celebration. It seems to
imply an inability (or is it perhaps a reluctance?) to face fully up
to the pain, suffering, evil and anguish in the world. But at its best
his poetry can be incomparably exhilarating. Bowen could glory
in 'anterth perthi/ a goleuni'r glannau' (the climactic glory of the
hedges and the light of shores) (*LlT*, 40), wonder at 'morfilod yn
morio i folawd/ tôn y tonnau' (whales surging seaward to the tune of
waves) (*LlT*, 40), and revel in 'rhithm angerdd/ cerdd' (the rhythm of
a poem's passion) (*LlT*, 40). He would have agreed with Shelley that
'the universe,/ In nature's silent eloquence, declares/ That all fulfil the
works of love and joy'.[8]
He was far from unaware, however, that his upbeat vision might
be suspect to many of his readers for whom life had been darkened by
the legion of twentieth-century atrocities. His most succinct defence
came in the form of the short poem 'Pabi Coch', 'A Red Poppy' (*EB*,
117). The first stanza recognises that such Christian belief as his might
seem to others no more than a 'crefydd cysur', an escapist consolatory
faith. But how can that be, he asks, since the sower of the poppy seed
has to bleed for his pains as he picks off the rocks, stones and weeds
that threaten the flower's growth? The allusion is obviously first to
Christ (with a sidelong glance no doubt at the famous parable of the
sower) but secondly to a priest such as Bowen himself. Then in the
second stanza the poem opens onto its concluding affirmative vision:

> Ond ar yr awel
> Fe ollyngodd ei friwiau
> Gerdd
> O fryncyn y dalar,
> Fel y pabi coch yn y gwenith
> A'i galw'n ddiddanydd arall.

[But on the breeze/ his wounds released/ a poem/ from the hillock
of the headland,/ like a red poppy in the corn,/ and called it another
comforter.]

Bowen is obviously thinking of the crucifixion. But he is also sug-
gesting that his own affirmative vision is paradoxically made possible
by the pains and the sufferings of the rough world of human experi-
ence from which it emerges.

And on occasion he does indeed allow his readers to glimpse the
dark hinterland of this poetry of hope – a hope that he insists is not
unrelenting but rather irrepressible, because it springs from the fountain
of life itself. One such poem is entitled 'The Age of Anxiety', in homage
to Kierkegaard. The Dane, he there writes, captured the bare, blank
expanse of clouds that loom heavy over our modern path as it skirts
the abyss. But then Bowen typically finds a counterpart to Kierkegaard
in Van Gogh. The Dutchman's paintings were infected with the fever
of his existence, and he found sustenance in a madman's cell by turn-
ing mental derangement into a rush of colours he released to capture
the essential serenity and sanity of his genius. Both these figures, he
concludes, had heard the howl of anguish rising from humans lost in
a wasteland. Theirs had been the knowledge granted only to privileged
souls. But it survived them to be eventually acknowledged by human-
kind at large in the wake of the disaster of Chernobyl (*LIT*, 62–3).

The two world wars, the gas chambers, the looming Millennium,
to all these was added in Bowen's mind the disaster of Chernobyl. It
struck home because it visited a catastrophic blight of acid rain on the
fields of Bala, where Bowen served out his life as a priest. For decades
afterwards lamb and beef, crucial elements in the rural Welsh econ-
omy, became totally inedible – and unmarketable. He blamed these
catastrophes on the hubris that had allowed free rein to mankind's
arrogant drive to dominate nature, leading to the unprecedented
modern evils enabled by scientific 'advances'. In spite of humanity's
towering achievements, Bowen wrote in 'Icaros' (*D*, 205), godhead
remained permanently beyond human reach.

> Ond er cael y gorau ar yr afael gan gorwynt
> A malais pob cymylau,
> Niwl nos
> Ac annelwig anialwch
> Y gofod digysgodion,
> Didduwdod yw dyndod ei waed.

[Despite getting the better of the grip of whirlwind/ And the malice of
all clouds,/ the fog of night/ and the intangible desert of shadowless
space,/ non-divinity is in the mortality of his blood.]

In one collection he turns to the myth of the Medusa for an image grotesque enough for a modern age whose powerhouse is the laboratory ('Labordy'n bwerdy yw ein byd') (*M*, 109). He is thinking not only of the winged female creature's fabled power to turn all who gazed upon her to stone but of the nest of serpents that was her hair and the boar's tusks that served her as teeth. All these attributes are fused to produce the monstrous composite image appropriate to the image of the 'Age of the Medusa' with which his poem ends. As a corrective to such malign examples of hubris as this, Bowen the Classicist, accomplished translator of several of Sophocles' tragedies, produced his own, redemptive, version of the myth of the over-reacher. He found it in Prometheus, the Titan who stole fire from the gods out of pity for humans, only for Zeus to punish him for his daring by chaining him to a rock and setting eagles to feast on his liver to all eternity.

Perhaps recalling that in ancient Athens Prometheus had been worshipped by potters, Bowen turned the legendary 'thief of fire' into an image of the artist, thereby implicitly producing a mythic self-portrait. His Prometheus carries a torch whose flame is light. He is deft as a magician as he steals the sparks of the sun, the heavenly body which leaves tracks that are light green and beautiful as beryl as its wheels race over the bare troubled expanse of clouds. And in return for his daring, Prometheus asks only, 'throughout the many generations of his vigour', for eternal passage in the sun's carriage as it dashes intoxicatingly on high across our heavens (*LIT*, 52).

Bowen's Promethean poet is, then, the daring bringer of light and flame to troubled humanity. But he is also, as explained in another poem on this figure, a prefiguration of Christ and one who passes on to poets 'A fire that awakens the gift of men's imaginations/ and thus breaks into leaf in the peace of images that suggest the tree of life' ([T]ân sydd yma'n dihuno/ dawn dychymyg dynion,/ yn deilio hedd delweddau/ biau pren bywyd').[9] And in keeping with his excursion into the world of ancient myth, Bowen fashions a brief stanza out of a largely archaic lexicon. The spirit of the god,

> Merchyg merched eigr eigion
> Y môr hen morwynol,
> Naiadau a'u nodiant
> Yn egru dagrau.

[is a rider of women from the ancient virginal depths of the sea, naiads whose notes are sour tears.]

But the final stanza recalls how Tertullian had detected a resemblance to Christ in Prometheus. Both had been noble figures who had voluntarily undergone excruciating suffering for the sake of humanity. Additionally for Bowen, he is a reminder of the travails a poet may have to endure in his service to humanity, particularly if he is a poet of religious conviction.

Bowen's repeated mining of the Prometheus myth is just one instance of many where he discovers suggestive analogies in the ancient stories of Greece and Rome both for the modern condition and for the miraculous metamorphoses of the world of nature. He found these myths particularly useful when evoking the ecstatically sensual dimensions of experience. He was quite as aware, and every bit as appreciative, as Whitman of 'the promiscuous urge of the world'. He was ever ready to recognise the sexual energies that lay at the root of nature's prodigal fertility. Nowhere is the celebration of them more overt than in 'Y Tarddle', a poem in honour of Courbet's notoriously frank painting of female genitalia. Likewise entitled 'The Source', the painting recognises and honours the secret site where all human beings first emerge into the realm of life.

It opens with a shot of a young woman naked, her flesh an electrifying flash of colour, standing alluringly under a cascade of water as it emerges from the womb of a rock, and catching it in the 'spoon' of her palm. It then moves on to a reflection on the wide spectrum of colours used by nineteenth-century painters to marvel at the adventure of a woman's being. Such an image of joy made flesh is a fertile stimulant to the imagination, he writes, as the blaze of female thighs transfixes the viewer. Then as he registers the life boiling in her body, he senses in her an awareness that every homage paid to her 'neuadd lathr' (the smooth hall of her genitalia), including that in Courbet's painting, is a recognition of it as the source of all human life. It is because Bowen knows himself humanly subject to the attractions of the flesh that he instinctively understands, when visiting the Acrocorinthos (the Acropolis of Corinth), why the ancient Greeks were as willing to obey Aphrodite's command to 'follow me', as were the Christians to follow Christ's identical summons centuries later (*D*, 206).

Paintings, particularly those invoking the myths of the Ancient world, provided Bowen with many an occasion for glorying in the sensual allure of the female body. His poem on 'Paradwys' (*LlT*, 79–80) opens with an evocation of the earthly paradise. Summer is seen in its full vigour by rivers, striding along valleys, bringing peace to the mountains, and energising lakes, while the power of colours is made evident on the floor of the plains. Set nimbly leaping by such a variety of sights, the imagination realises that this is no otherworldly Eden but rather the common earth which is home to young men and women. In such a place as this, Bowen imagines, did the tumescent Zeus once gently visit the daughters of men. He appeared as a fathering power to sow, and thus bestow, his sublime beauty on earth. From his seed was the luminous, fatally alluring, Helen born, whose magic brought a shiver of astonishment to cities.

Then, in the final section of the poem, Bowen identifies Renoir as the previously unmentioned subject of his thinking. He had summoned up all the energy remaining in his old age, despite being mocked by rheumatism:

> i fynnu peintio
> Y gyfaredd a gyforiai'n
> Gnawd merch dan gnydiad mawl
> Yr haul, a'i oed â gwawr ei haelodau
> Yn peri i adwyth brofi paradwys. (*LIT*, 80)

[to insist on risking all by venturing on a painting to capture the magic that overflowed in a girl's flesh beneath the fertile opulence of the sun's praise, as it kept its tryst with the dawn of her limbs, turning what was flawed into a paradise.]

Bowen was ever ready to acknowledge, as here, that the glory of God could become manifest in epiphanic moments of the flesh, and he readily accepted it was his duty as a religious poet to capture these transfigurative instances. His related appreciation of the ceaseless flow of life – Heraclitus was a philosopher he admired – meant his poetic imagination had a naturally Ovidean cast. The 'Invocation' with which *The Metamorphoses* opens, captures the essence of Bowen's poetic vision in this respect:

> Now shall I tell of things that change, new being
> Out of old: since you, O Gods, created
> Mutable arts and gifts, give me the voice
> To tell the shifting story of the world
> From its beginning to the present hour.[10]

Likewise alive to the captivating metamorphic character of the world, Bowen relied on the swift 'river of imagery' upon which his poems swam to convey the quicksilver nature of existence. And a major asset in this undertaking was the Welsh language itself, whose endless slippages through constant mutations are themselves examples of the astonishing restless metamorphoses of sound.

The mixing of images, such as happens above in 'Lleidr Tân' when Promethean fire suddenly changes into leaves suggestive of the Tree of Life, understandably disconcerted Bowen's readers and often confused them. But it is understandable from his point of view, as they reflect his visionary sense that it is the one source of spiritual energy that inhabits all the multiple forms of life. From first to last, his poetry is dedicated to the praise of the prodigiously shape-shifting character of creation. His fluidity of tropes may also distantly reflect the favourite custom of the medieval strict-metre poets who, employing a rhetorical technique known as 'dyfalu' (roughly meaning 'to riddle'), often cascaded startlingly different images to conjure up a particularly arresting phenomenon, whether it be a woman's golden hair or a gliding swan.

In his poem to a seagull, Bowen notices how, as the big bird rises with flailing wings from the surface of a lake, its commotion sends water rippling outwards in ever-widening circles, 'un siâp yn codi siâp arall/ a'r naill yn marw i fywyd y llall//goleuni'n suddo yn y cysgod/ a chysgod yn llunio goleuni' (D, 141). One shape gives rise to another, with the first dying into the life of the next, as light sinks into shade and shade swells into light. These are comparisons suggestive of Bowen's handling of images. For him a poem mirrors the process of creation in the processual progress of its images. Dylan Thomas (acknowledged by Bowen as a poetic kinsman) had famously said much the same thing, when explaining that his method was to let one image breed another. 'Gwylan' ends with the gradual subsiding of the agitation on the lake's surface, leaving the lake smooth, the water quiet, and the seagull soaring across the sky. At this point there is more than a hint of Bowen's awareness of the great stillness and silence by which all human life is surrounded and to which all will return.

One poem of his is entitled 'Difod' (D, 127). Understood to mean 'Extinction', or more literally and specifically 'Un-being' or 'Non-being', the title is suited to the opening stanza which, in recording Bowen's thoughts as the wind sweeps away the years along the ruts formed by rain, ends with the memorably epigrammatic observation 'Y difod sy'n poeni bod' – this is the extinction that worries existence. But then in the second stanza he imagines the same wind calling the years out of the ruts of the rain, and the sun bringing new days to bud between the silence of yesterday and the speech of today. And this too, he confidently states, is 'y difod sy'n poeni bod', this time contrasting 'difod', in the sense of unbeing, with 'bod', being or existing. He thus encapsulates the strange and puzzling process of the production of the existent out of the non-existent. Then, in the final stanza, Bowen catches in the wind a hint of the scent of years past, and a suggestion of the suns of yesterday brought back to sight today. And this, too, he finally triumphantly asserts, is 'y difod sy'n poeni bod', because it hints at the troubling, insoluble mystery of the progression of time and at Bergson's famous observation that the present is nothing but the past gnawing into the future.

As for Bowen's devotion to metamorphosis, nowhere is it more revealingly apparent than in his poem on the subject, which is one of his finest. A succinct articulation of his poetic credo, it also instances the processes of creation as he understands them. And it makes clear that for him being alive to endless transformation is the key to understanding the modus operandi of the whole universe. The mystery of any poem, he begins by noting, is that it treats the world as malleable wax, thus corresponding to the ocean's age-old habit of decking itself out with the grains and fine pebbles of the sand. The poem, he adds, is the heir to such natural processes of transformation, because but for the restless changefulness of the world it could not dream the dreams essential to its being.

> Cŵyr yw nos a dydd, yn llond lle o sêr yn toddi, yn disgyn, ac yn sefyll ar frigau coeden a fuasai cyn hynny'n rhidyll gwag, megis eirlysiau a briallu'n ymlunio lle bu brethynnau'n llwydo cyhyd. (*D*, 43)

> [Night and day are wax, full of stars melting and falling and studding the branches of trees that previously had been but empty sieves, just as snowdrops and primroses form where for long there had been only the mouldy homespun cloth of earth.]

Then, as this remarkable tour de force of a poem draws to its close Bowen identifies first with Taliesin, ancient magician and prodigious shape-changer of Welsh lore, and then with Ovid who saw land made of sea and anchors on the summits of mountains. A poem's function, Bowen concludes, is to preserve all of this changefulness, rendering it paradoxically permanent. Its operations are a kind of preservative: it is a 'gadwedigaeth o'r serch sy'n trin cŵyr y dydd a'r nos, cŵyr yr afon a'r môr, cŵyr y tywod a'r clai', a safeguarding of the love that moulds the wax of night and day, the wax of river and sea, of sand and clay. The religious overtones of such a claim are unmistakeable.

Bowen is, then, very aware of the substitutive processes that are essential for poems, where tropes regularly replace objects and the lexicon reveals its prodigal and prodigious resource of synonyms, homophones and homonyms as it displays the colourful palette of vocabulary. And in its devotion to the spiritual implications of meta-morphosis, his theology bears some resemblances to what has come to be called the processual theology of today, which holds that God is to be characterised every bit as much by becoming as by being.[11] Processual theology owes much to previous thinkers, such as the British mathematician and philosopher A. N. Whitehead, whose book *Process and Reality* contains several observations useful for bringing the theology of Bowen's poetics into sharp focus.

Whitehead agreed with Henri Bergson that the weakness of the present age was that it was dominated by a spatial sense of exist-ence which ignored its fluency. 'Religion', Whitehead insisted, 'is the vision of something beyond, behind and within, the passing flux of immediate things.' While fully acknowledging (as did Bowen, as we have seen) that the 'Primordial God' exists unchanging to all eternity, Whitehead balanced this with the other aspect of God as the dynamic force everywhere present and active in all creation. 'God's immanence in the world', he wrote, 'in respect to his primordial nature is an urge towards the future based upon an appetite in the present.' He is the principle of creativity itself, since 'becoming is a creative advance into novelty'. What Whitehead repeatedly characterised as the 'ten-derness' of this God 'is directed towards each and actual occasion as it arises'.[12] And it is these occasions that, from the human point of view, are the 'buds or drops of perception which form the extensive continuum' (*PR*, 35). 'God's judgement in the world', he states with reference to such 'occasions', 'is the judgement of a tenderness which loses nothing that can be saved' (*PR*, 347) – an observation strikingly like the one used by Bowen at the conclusion of 'Metamorffosis', where he attributes just such a salvific purpose to a poem.

Bowen's fascination with the mercurial character of the natural world is expressed in a different, lower, key in his beautiful poem about 'Arenig', the majestic mountain – although strictly speaking there are two: Yr Arenig Fawr and Yr Arenig Fach, the Large and the Small – in Eastern Snowdonia that overlooked his parish. At the beginning of the twentieth century it had attracted the attention of two very notable Welsh artists, Augustus John and James Dickson Innes. Bowen's free verse poem pivots around the startling change from mundane to astonishing in the Arenig's appearance during the course of a particular day. Normally, the poem notes, Arenig is content to be humble home to sheep in summer and resting place of snow in winter, which is the kind of thing to be expected of a mountain. It is happy in the homely familiarity of its links with its neighbours, has no wish to 'un-mountain' itself, does not wish to stand out from its relatives. It is content with displaying its unchanging ancient identity from morn to night. But then, one fine summer's evening, it refuses to be a mountain. It becomes strange, even to itself. It turns to flame and flaunts its colours, and it breaks out all over in a collection of green and purple instincts, heaps of blue and pink capacities, craggy mounds of red and black power.

'Arenig' belongs in the company of those poems where Bowen discovered in the ordinariness of experience a capacity for transmutation into wonders. In 'Y Fasged Sbwriel' (*D*, 41) he takes a wastepaper basket in a rural location as theme, crammed as it is with a newspaper, a tin of food, an empty bottle of beer, a banana skin, the wrappings of a chocolate bar and empty packets. These are the relics of the ordinary comforts of life, abandoned here in a setting distant from the city where people can recover their God-given freedom.

Then, in 'Maniach' (*D*, 38) he finds an even more explicit equivalent for the processes of poetry in the discarded scraps that litter the world – the detritus of the wind in the form of the fallen branches that clog the mouth of a stream, and the small twigs scattered across the lawn; the spiders' webs lurking in dark corners in the dying days of autumn, and the seasonal heaps of leaves at the foot of hedges; the committee reports that clutter up the house, along with the clichés of religious publications. These also clog the loft of the mind, he adds, with dust and mess. However, a rag-and-bone man happens by and snaps them all up for smelting in the furnaces of Brymbo steelworks. So why mention such rubbish, he queries at the end, and answers 'Am fod y sgrap yn toddi'n genadwri yn y gerdd'. Because the scrap melts into evangel in a poem.

No wonder, then, that Bowen so often associates the transformative power of nature with those of the poem. 'Pŵer y Gerdd' (*D*, 12) is another lovely poem on this seminal subject for him. In it he notes the quiet, gentle mastery of the sun in its dealings with earth and with shore, where it deigns to touch a grey expanse of beach and sets the mud alight with the ocean's pearls. During daytime the sun presides on high in the heavens where, despite the tumult of clouds, can be heard 'mud sain cymod y sêr', the mute strains of the reconciliation of the stars. Then at night it is indirectly present in the light of the leisurely, restful body now presiding over the earth; a golden moon shines in puddles, and benignly visits the dirt of the roads and the sweepings of the ditch. In all these ways, he concludes, the sun anticipates the power of a poem to purify grief.

His artist's eye, so very evident in such poems as the above, led Bowen to appreciate the visual arts very highly. He travelled restlessly all over the world, visiting most of the countries of Western Europe. He went to Russia (where he was refused a permit to travel to Pasternak's home village), to Greece and Crete (where he lingered at the grave of the novelist Nikos Kazantzakis), and to Palestine and Turkey, and he ventured as far as Australia – in 1980 he entitled one of his collections 'Under the Southern Cross'. His peripatetic adventures provided him with many opportunities to view the great masterpieces of western civilisation, and he addressed poems to several of these and to the artists who created them. He travelled to Istanbul and Anatolia, viewed the site of Troy, trod the banks of the Jordan, paid a visit to Mycenae, ventured into Lebanon, spent time in the garden of Gethsemane, and explored Lascaux.

Yet rarely does his response to such great sights and sites of the world match his response to ordinary subjects much nearer home. His record of his visit to the Cararra marble quarry is not the equal of his poem on humble dust, nor is his praise of Sydney Opera House and the feathered wings of its tiled roof as good as his compelling evocation of a gorse bush in bloom. Yet there are a handful of exceptions where he is at his best when dealing with the exotic. His imagination seems to be most reliably kindled in those places where he finds himself recalling ancient Greek myth, and that perhaps is due not only to his classical education but to an intuition (which he shared with such early Church Fathers as Tertullian) that in their haunting way they intimate some of the spiritual truths of Christianity.

Recalling Jason's legendary sea voyage, he begins 'Y Cnu Aur' (*D*, 156) by reflecting that its image in his mind is that of a golden fleece aboard a ship. He imagines pulling on the oars, salt spray mixing with his sweat, the swell of the sea turning black beneath his boat, eyes fixed in their sockets on the shimmering gold of the wool. All around, dolphins plunge in play, the seagulls' cries ring clear in the stillness, calm settles on the waters at sunset, and the golden fleece shines on board the intrepid vessel as it voyages. In its enchanting power to transport us to a different world the poem is therefore clearly a record of the adventures – spiritual in essence in Bowen's case – of the poetic imagination.

Another fine poem came from Bowen's journey across the Bosphorus from Asia to Europe (D, 188). The first third of the poem describes the ordinary sights he saw during the crossing: the mix of fellow passengers, the mosques and gardens lining the shores, the young fishermen mending their nets. Then the poem begins to move off in a different direction, as Bowen, having landed in Istanbul, pauses to gaze back over the fabled water, and finds himself dreaming of Io, the beloved of Zeus, who turned her into a heifer so that she could escape his wife Hera's vindictive anger. But Hera then deputed a gadfly to harass Io into madness, until she plunged into the Bosphorus for relief and swam the straits to the far shore. Memory of that potent myth leads him next to the sufferings of Prometheus, and he imagines hearing the croak of the eagle as it burrows its cruel beak in the god's liver. Finally, remembering the threat to intrepid adventurers such as Jason and Odysseus from the clashing rocks of the Symplegades he recalls the story of Orpheus, whose lyre had power enough in its music to foil the intentions of the Sirens and their fatally seductive singing. Safely past danger, Orpheus' ship sailed serenely on, just like the modern-day tanker Bowen glimpses directing its course towards the Black Sea.

As a whole, then, the poem 'Y Bosfforos' (D, 186–8) meditates on the magical processes of poetic creation. It celebrates a poem's capacity to enrich ordinary experience by drawing on the resources of the collective unconscious, and to augment its significance by investing it with all the imperious power of myth, legend and symbol. And as we have seen, it was to pagan Classical myth in particular that Bowen sometimes found himself magnetically attracted when wishing to convey his Christian sense of the marvel of life.

The relationship between poetry and the visual arts also entranced him, and in places he deliberately set himself to reproduce some of the artistic techniques he particularly admired. In 'Pwyntilio' (D, 8), a poem about Pointillism, he builds a poem out of words treated

as distinct dots of colour, advertising as much in an endnote. This
reminds us that complementing – or perhaps counterpointing –
Bowen's often consuming passion for the protean creative energies
of the natural world, was his appreciation of life as thickly scattered
with what Henry Vaughan called 'bright shoots of everlastingness'.
A pointillist text – an assemblage of brilliantly succinct phrases such
as the Welsh language in general and *cynghanedd* in particular facili-
tated – was very well suited to capture such a vision.

* * *

Bowen was already forty years of age before he began to write poetry.
More than forty years later he was still going strong. Yet few have
paused to reflect on the extraordinary stamina of both imagination
and spiritual vision that enabled him to continue to write with una-
bated vigour and originality right down to his death at the age of
eighty-four. Such a lapse of critical appreciation may be due in part
to the fact that Bowen's poetry in old age seems not to be marked off
by any clear change of style or of outlook. It is broadly all of a piece
with what has gone before. But then that is achievement remarkable
enough in itself – that the virile energy of affirmation in which Bowen
had exulted when young should somehow be sustained even under all
the no doubt testing stresses and strains of old age. His achievement
in this remarkable respect – the equal, say, of that of the aged Walt
Whitman – deserves to be recognised and celebrated.

But while the late poetry is not distinguished (as was that of W. B.
Yeats, for instance) by any radical new departure it does, I believe,
bear the marks of one or two subtle and noteworthy changes of
emphasis. For one thing a sharper awareness of impending death
is apparent in his interpretation of the Southern Cross, during the
Australian journey he undertook when he was approaching eighty (*D*,
235). In two of the four stars he detects the very eyes of death itself,
visitant to the world ever since creation. In the other two he detects
the triumph of that 'grim spirit' in the form of the two eyes of the
first person to die. Grouped together the stars bear eternal witness
'mai marw sy raid i ni' (that we all have to die).

As ever, however, Bowen instantly insists that existence offers com-
pelling evidence not of the Triumph of Death but of the Triumph of
Life and it is an insistence that seems to take on a new, urgent and
defiant, edge during his final years. One resource on which he now
draws for sustenance is the traces he finds of a past renewed in the

present. In his long poem 'Y Tylwyth Teg', for instance, he places his faith in the secret enduring presence of the 'Little People' in the Welsh land. It is a faith all the more necessary because, following his retirement from the Anglican ministry, he had settled in the Welsh border town of Wrexham, whose anglicised character brought home to him the precarious state of the Welsh language and culture, a condition which was for him yet another disheartening example of a 'pitiful age' (*D*, 252).

Elsewhere, in a rare, considered, confession of the *terribilis* of life, he admitted 'mae na dirstwch sy'n drech/ na thristwch, a'i drefn// yn bwys/ ar ein byd' (there is a sorrow that is deeper than sorrow, its dispensation a weight on the world' [*D*, 251]). It is a sorrow, he sensitively added, that coats the delicate flesh of winberries like fine dust. But the more tempted he was to despair, the more he placed his faith during his final years in the inextinguishable spirit of native life lurking under the very surface of the land of Wales, like the 'tylwyth teg', the fairy folk of old, and like the tap root of a plant. And as his poem on the mysterious disappearance of Owain Glyndŵr at the end of that warrior's life suggests, he saw clear parallels between the persisting dreams of Glyndŵr's return – a stubborn example of belief in resurrection of life from the past – and the Christian story.

For Bowen, both his own lifelong service in the ministry and the poetry that had supplemented it had been true to the spiritual tradition that was a vital part of what was precious and distinctive in the past of Wales. It had perpetuated that tradition under the increasingly difficult circumstances of the present. His last collection of poems appeared in 1983, a year before his death. It included a poem about a visit to the grave of Morgan Llwyd in the old Dissenters' graveyard in Wrexham.[13] A great spiritual writer, the seventeenth-century Puritan Llwyd had lived through the terrible years of the English Civil War and written a series of remarkable books with the aim of bringing the truths of the Gospel to his benighted countrymen and women. His faith, developed under the influence of Jacob Boehme, emphasised the light kindled by the spirit in every person, and it inclined him towards what was at the time beginning to crystallise as Quaker teaching. 'Dos i mewn i'th stafell ddirgel', he had famously advised his reader in his work, 'yr hon yw Duw ynot ti': 'retire into your secret inner chamber, which is God dwelling in you'.

As a radical Puritan, Llwyd was no friend to the Anglicanism of his time, although his naturally eirenic spirit meant he was temperate in his criticism of it. Bowen, nevertheless, implicitly acknowledged him as a great precursor, and felt connected through him with Wales's great tradition of Christian witness. As if to seal this relationship his poem imaged Llwyd's ashes as grains of wheat instinct with spiritual life for the future. Then in conclusion he imagined a choice ear of wheat growing from Llwyd's tomb 'o'r goleuni a egnïai o'i fewn', 'from the energy of light that still radiated from within' (*D*, 267).

To the very end, therefore, Bowen remained constant and indeed buoyant in his faith, insisting that 'Bai yw melltithio bywyd': it is wrong to curse life (*D*, 262). One recurrent motif of his late poetry is that of the dance of life. A holiday in Crete had included a revelatory visit to a dancing floor that had survived from the time of the Mycenean civilisation on the island. The elaborate 'Gloria' included in his penultimate volume even unexpectedly acknowledges, as evidence perhaps of the relaxed catholicity of his vision in old age, a celebration of the dance 'in the hall of the atoms'. And as if in triumphant summation of his lifelong vision, the 'Gloria' specifically connects the holy sacrament of the eucharist to its praise of every aspect of life, now extended to include even the modern machine age:

> Pob gwlad, pob iaith,
> Aent yn fara a gwin:
>
> Pob llafur,
> Gorsafoedd trenau,
> Safleoedd bysiau
> Ar gychwyn teithiau,
> Pob awyrblanio[.] (*D*, 262)

[Every country, every language turns to bread and wine: every work, every train station, every bus depot from which journeys begin, every flight of aircraft.]

All such, he triumphantly concludes, resonate with the one gloria of praise. So had the poems he had produced during his forty-year writing career.

Notes

[1] See Alan Llwyd, *Barddoniaeth Euros Bowen* (Swansea: Christopher Davies, 1977).

2 Euros Bowen, *Oes y Medwsa* (Caernarfon: Cyhoeddiadau Barddas, 1987), p. 73. Hereafter *M*.
3 Euros Bowen, *Lleidr Tân* (Caernarfon: Gwasg Gwynedd, 1989), p. 19. Hereafter *LlT*.
4 Euros Bowen, *Detholion* (Llandysul: Gomer, 1984). Hereafter *D*.
5 Convent website.
6 Alfredo Tradigo (trans.), Stephen Sartorelli, *Icons and Saints of the Eastern Orthodox Church* (Los Angeles: The J. Paul Getty Museum, 2006), p. 242. Hereafter *IC*.
7 Cynthia and Saunders Davies (trans.), *Euros Bowen: priest-poet/bardd-offeiriad* (Cardiff: Church in Wales, 1993), p. 89. Hereafter *EB*.
8 A. S. B. Glover (ed.), *Shelley: Selected Poetry, Prose, and Letters* (London: Nonesuch Press, 1951), p. 29.
9 Euros Bowen, *Buarth Bywyd* (Caernarfon: Gwasg Gwynedd, 1986), p. 68. Hereafter *BB*.
10 Horace Gregory (trans.), *Ovid: The Metamorphoses* (New York: Viking, 1960), p. 31.
11 Interestingly, Canon A. M. Allchin drew attention in his introductory essay to the affinities between Bowen in this respect and the 'creation-centred spirituality of Matthew J. Fox' (*EB*, 24). For a useful introduction to Fox's theology, see his essay 'A Mystical Cosmology: Toward a Postmodern Spirituality', in David Ray Griffin (ed.), *Sacred Interconnections: postmodern spirituality, political economy and art* (New York: State University of New York, 1990), pp. 15–33.
12 A. N. Whitehead, *Poetry and Reality* (first published, 1927–8. Corrected edition, David Ray Griffin and Donald W. Sherburne (New York: New York Free Press, 1985), p. 88).
13 M. Wynn Thomas, *Morgan Llwyd* (Cardiff: University of Wales Press, Writers of Wales Series, 1984); M. Wynn Thomas, 'Seventeenth-Century Puritan Writers: Morgan Llwyd and Charles Edwards', in R. Geraint Gruffydd (ed.), *A Guide to Welsh Literature, c. 1530–1700* (Cardiff: University of Wales Press, 1997), pp. 190–209.

5

GWENALLT:
THE HIERONYMUS BOSCH OF WALES

A former postgraduate student of Gwenallt's captured the volcanic nature of both the man and the poet perfectly in a couple of reminiscences about his behaviour at soccer matches. A demented football supporter, he attended a game in Bangor involving teams to neither of which did he owe the slightest allegiance. Undeterred, Gwenallt (David James Jones, 1899–1968) arbitrarily and peremptorily fixed on one to support and within five minutes was hopping about in his seat bawling obscenities at the 'opposition' and yobbishly swearing at the referee with all the breath in his five-foot-nothing body (when he won the premier poetry competition in Swansea in 1926 he sat touchingly dwarfed in the huge, exotically carved Eisteddfod Chair that had been donated by the Welsh of Shanghai). A passionate viewer of sports (he was brother-in-law to a Welsh rugby international), he was nothing if not aggressive. On another occasion he turned up to watch his student, then the clogger Norman Hunter of local Welsh soccer, play wing-half (in old footballing terms) for the college. Gwenallt later subjected him to a sneering commentary on his ineffectual style, with particular reference to his renowned sliding tackle. 'Why do you spend so much time on your aarse, man', he loudly demanded. 'You're no bloody good to anyone when you're sitting on your aarse.'[1]

Of course, Gwenallt could also be very different. But the gleeful coarseness, the drilling, drawling whine of derision, the fierce disgust, the provocative taunt, and under it all a desperate anger – these are the very tones and accents of Gwenallt's distinctive genius. As his former student gleefully recalled, he could be creatively, comically cruel. This is memorably apparent, for instance, in his Gillray-like caricature of a poor, colonised Wales slung, during the Second World War, between the fat cheeks of a Leviathan's buttocks.[2] At such moments one hears the tones and accents of a culture (as much as a psyche) *in extremis*; which is why they can be heard again in R. S. Thomas, who admired Gwenallt. To the poem Thomas wrote about him he gave a deliberately innocuous title, 'A Lecturer', and opened it disarmingly with an image of 'A little man/ Sallow,/ Keeping close to the wall/ Of life'. But he ends it in a very different key that pays tribute to the cultural and spiritual 'terrorist' in Gwenallt:

> Watch him,
> As with short steps he goes.
> Not dangerous?
> He has been in gaol.[3]

And if R.S. compressed everything he hated about the contemporary world into the single contemptuous term 'The Machine', then Gwenallt likewise anathematised a single, complex, world-encompassing proper noun: 'Mammon'.

Mammon – the greedy pursuit of gain. The term originates with Christ in the New Testament, as Gwenallt well knew. Of his own passionate, restless, troubled and soul-wrenching devotion to the Christian faith there can be no possible doubt, hard-earned in his later years as it was. In his youth he had been attracted to a rational, atheistical Socialism with strong Marxist overtones – an alternative faith he discarded when he realised it involved the worship of a God who had failed. He came to believe that Communism and Capitalism alike were devoted to nothing but the pursuit of self-interest. Yes indeed, he became a Christian poet (sadly to the detriment of his talent in his later years), yet it would in some ways be equally fair to think of him as the poet of Antichrist – a figure who looms terrifyingly large in Gwenallt's apocalyptic collection, *Ysgubau'r Awen* (1939). It is a masterwork of the thirties, so savage in places that it makes most of other Welsh literary products of the decade (including much by Dylan Thomas) look like paper tigers. In it he bitterly notes that the Welsh lack a poet who can give their hopelessness utterance ('a rydd iaith i'w hanobaith hwy').

But Gwenallt himself was exactly that poet. He wrote of a ravaged, colonised, godless land; a land laid waste by the unbridled ferocity of a carelessly callous capitalism; a land whose people had been casually scattered, like billiard balls, to remote pockets of alien re-settlement. He wrote of a Europe that had twice, in his brief lifetime, suffered a much greater devastation. He wrote of a world in which the angels have all been throttled, where the wood of the cross has been rough hewn to make troughs for swine, where mankind is adrift on a vessel whose captain and crew are reeling drunk. Gwenallt's images jolt one like an electric shock, jarring the brain and rearranging the mind; wrenched meanings emerge from the wreck of words catapulted into each other; predictable rhythms serve to evoke the aboriginal power of collective experience; couplets bite into the mind like great circular saws, rasping to the very quick of the reader's imagination. For an intense period, volume after volume reads in places like the Book of Nightmares (to borrow the title of Galway Kinnell's poems about the Vietnam War).

The deep-furrowed face of the elderly Gwenallt, when viewed in photographs, seems to alternate between impish gargoyle and icon of anguish. One who unforgettably figured the human animal as a stoat, whose stinking corpse squats in the sun like an inkblot on a parchment scroll, he had a terrifying imagination whose landscape is mapped out in the story of the Twrch Trwyth (from the *Mabinogion*) upon which he based a magnificent poem. In *Culhwch ac Olwen*, among the many tasks set the hero (Culhwch) by Ysbaddaden Bencawr, the huge unkempt giant whose daughter (Olwen) he wishes to marry, is that of snatching a comb and scissors from between the ears of the ferocious wild boar (Twrch Trwyth) that is given to rampaging through the country, laying it waste. In Gwenallt's poem, the boar figures, as it does in an Alun Lewis poem of the same period, as the embodiment of the crude pagan passion of wild anarchy loosed in Europe and hell bent on creating carnage. That trampling passion is, of course, the mad passion that animates human nature itself in the raw.

In one sense, Gwenallt the poet was playing Culhwch to his age's Twrch Trwyth, finding only in the correspondingly savage saturnalia of the Crucifixion the salvific power sufficient to bridle man's insatiable lusts. Once read, who could ever forget those shockingly indecent lines of his about the raw, desperate human craving for salvation: 'like wolves we lift our nostrils high/ all baying for the blood that did us buy'. But, in another sense, the poet in him was the Twrch Trwyth itself, because, as the almost demonic energy of some of his writing suggests, there was in Gwenallt an unassuageable appetite for a cleansingly annihilating violence. He as good as confesses as much

in his remarkable poem 'Ofnau' (Fears). There he speaks first of the
terror of the possibility that he may forever cease to be, but speaks
secondly of his even greater horror of himself, appalled at the dark
and backward abysm within (*CG*, 134).

* * *

For the source of this, and other, fears, from which Gwenallt's poetry
most irresistibly welled, one can look to his early life and not be disap-
pointed. He was born and raised in Cwm Tawe (the Swansea Valley),
in the chapel-centred communities of Allt-wen and Pontardawe,
where all lived under the paw of the 'leopard of industry', an animal
as unpredictable as it was deadly in its pounce. The music of that
locality was a blend of sorrowfully exultant hymns, the banshee shriek
of hooters, and the ominous groan of cranes. Far from looking at the
world through rose-tinted spectacles, he saw it, all life long, through
the blue protective goggles friendly workmen put over his eyes to pro-
tect them from the furnace's glare when, as a child, he carried lunch
to his father in the steelworks. As he grew, the ruthlessly exploitative
nature of industrial capitalism, provoking an increasingly organised
militancy in the workforce, fired in him a passionate commitment
first to the secular gospel, utopian humanism and devolutionist pol-
itics of Keir Hardie and the Independent Labour Party, and then
to a much harder-line Communism he later came to deplore for its
godlessness. His reaction, when still only a teenager, to the conscrip-
tion introduced during the First World War was to refuse to enlist, on
mingled pacifist and socialist grounds. He was soon hunted down in
rural Carmarthenshire, where he had sought refuge with relatives, and
locked up first in Wormwood Scrubs, and then in Dartmoor. Gwenallt
revisited the experience, in poems, prose and the novel *Plasau'r Brenin*
(1934), although his reporting of it was always carefully selective.

On his release, he resumed his education, and, having studied
at the University College of Wales, Aberystwyth, under the young
T. H. Parry-Williams and the older T. Gwynn Jones (both among
the giants who in the early twentieth century revolutionised, and thus
modernised, Welsh poetry), he was appointed (after a brief interlude
as a schoolmaster in Barry) to the Department of Welsh there, where
he worked for the rest of his life. On those occasions that he had
taken his father lunch at the Gilbertson steelworks (then one of the
largest in the UK), the boy Gwenallt had been terrified by the tremor
in the claw of the crane that suspended a crucible of molten metal

over the heads of the working men. In 1927, it was that molten metal that, splashing over his father from a carelessly prepared ladle, led to his death. It was a gruesome incident vividly described by his friend Albert Davies:

> The white hot liquid spilled from the furnace ladle, too soon, into the pit. The molten metal cascaded like snowflakes on to the body of Thomas Jones, he continued to walk towards his fellow workmen, who were attempting to rescue him. They told me that when the molten metal cooled, his footprints left their imprint in the solid steel that marked his steps to death.[4]

When Gwenallt visited his stricken father on his deathbed in hospital, the older man's primary fear was that he would go blind, because he could not see. To console him, his son told him that was because he had bandages over his eyes. As for Gwenallt himself, that incident reinforced the determination that lasted his whole life, the determination never to close his eyes on the horrors that disfigured the world, many of them, like his father's accident, the barbaric result of human actions.

Gwenallt may have first felt the motions of poetry in the desperate loneliness he had felt when behind bars – it is certainly interesting to note that such loneliness and estrangement finds voice, although in a transposed key, in both of his early poems, the *awdlau* 'Y Mynach' (the Monk) and the controversial 'Y Sant' (the Saint) (the latter notoriously failing to win the chair at the National Eisteddfod at Treorchy, 1928, because it was deemed obscene). But if his poetry had been brought to birth in Dartmoor, it was undoubtedly baptised in that horrifying, searing spillage of liquid over his father. Maybe that incident allowed him to permit himself access to and expression of the rage locked up in him since he had himself been locked up. One of the marvels he had witnessed, as a boy, was that of the great furnaces being tapped – the metal flowing first into the ladle and then into the moulds. It was his father's hideous, outrageous death that allowed Gwenallt to tap the furnace of feeling within him and to pour it into the mould of form – poems of a kind he had not written before; poems that still give off blistering heat; poems that are best read through blue goggles.

Gwenallt is the major poet of the obscenities of industrial 'civilisation', the Hieronymus Bosch of industrial South Wales. In the landscape of his poems, stacks open their umbrellas of flame-handled smoke over the cup of their world; funerals wind their mute way between the thunder of steel mills and the groan of tinplate works: coffins are darkened houses containing cinders of flesh and the ashes of voice; on gravestones are placed silicotic roses and lilies pale as gas (the references are to the deadly 'dust' that accumulated in miners' lungs and the dangerously explosive gas that ambushed them underground); and yet, in this hellish landscape, workers gently shepherd their pigeons by night, releasing their white clouds from the garden hutches to circle around the towering pillars of smoke, where to his eyes they seem like a descent of the Holy Spirit. His is an Expressionist art, so it is no wonder he befriended the refugee German Expressionist artist F. R. Könekamp. Nor is it a wonder that he idolised Dostoevsky (whose 'hallelujahs were born of storms', as noted in *The Brothers Karazamov*) and was fascinated by Rilke, the poet who had produced the Sonnets to Orpheus:

> But you, divine one, unto the last still singing,
> although attacked by the flouted Maenads' throng,
> beautiful god, above the shrieks rose ringing
> among the destroyers your order upbuilding song.[5]

Gwenallt, too, aspired to rise above the shrieks of the Maenads of the inner and the outer world that threatened to tear him to pieces. And he, too, desperately desired to order an upbuilding song. But for one who had seen the pit-cage being drawn up the dark shaft towards heaven by the steel ropes of God's ancient wheels, there could be only one power capable of effecting such a miracle; it is precisely because Gwenallt is the Hieronymus Bosch of industrial Wales that he is also the El Greco of the Welsh religious experience. So many of his images, like those of the Greek, seem to be contorted by both anguish and ecstasy. In his fine elegy to his German Expressionist friend, F. R. Kŏnekamp, he noted that

> El Greco yw ei feistr, artist y santeiddrwydd melyn,
>   Peintiwr wedi meddwi ar Ethsemane, yr hoelion a'r drain;
> Crëwr y Cristiau ystumig a'r seintiau ymestyngar
>   A'u hysbryd fel llafnau Toledo yn torri trwy'r wain. (*CG*, 186)

[El Greco is his master, that artist of the yellow sanctity,/ A painter drunk on Gethsemane, its nails and thorns;/ The creator of the twisted

Christs and the beseeching saints/ their spirit like Toledo blades pierc-
ing their scabbards.]

And what Gwenallt also wrote of Kŏnekamp – 'rheidrwydd ydyw
art fel y fflach yn llygaid Duw' (art is necessary, like the flash in God's
eye) (*CG*, 186) applies equally to his own poetry. But it was only fit-
ting that song, not art, should have been for him the ultimate medium
of spiritual expression because, as he indicated in 'Yr Hen Emynau'
('The Old Hymns'), song had also been intimately attendant upon
his spiritual deliverance, although his return to Christian devotion
had been by degrees rather than through any instant conversion. The
ghostly presence of the hymn can be felt as surely in his best poetry
as in the poetry of Emily Dickinson.

Raised a Calvinistic Methodist, Gwenallt died in the same faith;
but in the interval his restless peregrination had by turns led him to
militant atheism, an extra-institutional Christian faith, the Catholic
Church, the Church in Wales, and in inclination towards Quaker
mysticism. All these were to leave their mark on his religious vision,
which ended up as a kind of synthesis of them all. He charted the
intellectual stages of his early spiritual development in the remark-
able essay he published in 1943 entitled 'Credaf' (I believe). There he
outlined his early progress, aided by a reading of the famous Grand
Inquisitor section in Dostoevsky's *The Brothers Karazamov*, towards
an internationally minded Marxist Communism that viewed the
chapels as tools of the bosses and enemies of the labour movement.
Simultaneously, his materialist philosophy had awakened in him a
deep interest in the hedonistic paganism advocated by Pater and seem-
ingly practised by some of the poets of the nineties, while he was also
in thrall to Nietzsche's contemptuous dismissal of Christianity as the
pallid, anti-life religion of the slave.

But with the coming to power of Labour for the first time in 1924
disillusionment began to set in. The unions, for instance, were patently
at odds with each other and revealed that they were primarily organ-
isations for securing the best possible terms for their members rather
than instruments for revolutionising society. And Labour ministers
proved as disappointingly vigorous in their defence of the Empire
as Liberals and Tories had been. Meanwhile, Russia was making
its increasingly ruthless way towards Stalinism. Gwenallt therefore
began to doubt the perfectionist view of human nature, gradually
reverting to that recognition of original sin that characterised not

only his Calvinist background but also the work of writers – such as Baudelaire – whom he now admired. In 1929 he discovered, in the works of Thomas Aquinas, a Christian humanism, characterised by a perfect balance between the human and the divine, and by the reconciliation of spirit and flesh, of reason with feeling. It was the synthesis for which he had so long yearned, dissatisfied as he had been with the stern anti-humanism of Calvinism, the non-corporeal idealism of Hegelian philosophy, and the secularising tendencies of a Christian Socialism. All his mature poetry, including his visionary indictment of industrialisation, is the outworking of this model of faith. When he came to publish his early poems 'Y Mynach' and 'Y Sant', he prefaced them with a quotation from *Les Nouvelles Littéraires*: 'what one sees in the Neo-Thomist movement is an example of the reaction against German idealism, it is a return to a modern understanding of the realism of Christianity' (*CG*, 2).

*   *   *

'The realism of Christianity': Gwenallt's primary reason for (re)turning to Christianity was his conviction that sin was deeply ingrained in human nature and that fashionable and highly influential modern ideologies naively refused to acknowledge this. So integral to human nature indeed was this sinfulness that it could be redeemed only by the grace of God, operative in the salvific person of the Crucified Christ. This was the subject he addressed directly in his powerful sonnet 'Pechod' (*CG*, 103).

The sonnet is based on a simple, stark contrast between the outward dress of 'civilised' human beings and their primitive inner self, which is associated with primal mud, the slime of primitive beasts, and the bow and arrow that savage early hunters held between finger and thumb. Such vestiges are survivals from the dark forests of prehistoric centuries, and Gwenallt detects contemporary signs of them in modern feet that twitch with the urge to dance. As we humans wander those ancient pathways, he adds, we occasionally glimpse far overhead, through the thick knit of branches, fragments of heaven where the saints chant their anthems of faith and grace and celebrate the *Magnificat* of Christian salvation. And maddened by such glimpses

> Like wolves we lift our nostrils high
> And howl for the blood that ransomed us.

It is a disturbing poem, all the more so for one's suspicion, confirmed by other of Gwenallt's poems, that behind his terror of the primal instincts of humankind lies a revulsion against a primitiveness he specifically associates with black people in general and Africans in particular. Indeed, as 'Y Draenog' (*CG*, 161), another shockingly electrifying poem makes clear, his prejudices against 'foreign', non-Christian peoples extended well beyond the African continent.

The poem opens with a brilliant evocation of a hedgehog rolled tightly into a spiky ball, as if scorning the genial warmth of the sun and despising the friendly chatter of birds overhead. It need not even stir itself and unroll to satisfy its hunger as on its bristles hangs 'a pantry of fleas', as Gwenallt puts it. Then the disgust with which the poem opens deepens and intensifies into visceral revulsion, as he imagines the hedgehog's 'round inner darkness' to contain a whole cosmos of repellent life forms. There leaps the toad, while the songs of frogs and insects ring out clear as a bell, and the old human instincts are given full rein to flow as freely as blood that is red and homosexual. There is no mistaking the thrust of Gwenallt's meaning here. His homophobia is all too clear, and finds expression in a parodic version of the Crucifixion, where Christ's blood flowed for the redemption of all humankind. Gwenallt evidently views homosexuals as vile 'inverts' – the hedgehog's narcissistic turning in on itself, its feeding off its own fleas, its feasting on its own filth, all these characteristics are associated in his disturbed mind with the 'perversions' of gayness, and his revulsion strongly suggests a fear of contamination. Nor does Gwenallt stem his prejudices here. Because he then starts on a sinister riff, associating the hedgehog with the 'primitive cults of the Congo', with the ritual music of the 'idols' worshipped in Malaya and Tahiti, and with the 'cylindrical' gods and goddesses of Japan.

The poem is a disgraceful tour de force of prejudices, all born of a disgust at human nature, and it finds its apocalyptic climax in the final stanza where Gwenallt bitingly hails the hedgehog as 'the prophet on the ruins of Europe', the dark template of all the Continent's vaunted fine arts. It is the creature that has filled the vacuum left by the Trinity, and Gwenallt ends by apotheosing it as an 'immortal ball, the godhead of thorns'. It is an arresting poem, and a forceful reminder of the deplorable aspects of Gwenallt's Christian faith. That it is a poem born of the appalling European crisis of the 1930s, when the carnage of another war loomed ever larger on the horizon and two monstrous dictatorships prepared to lock horns, may to some small degree constitute mitigating circumstances. And there is more than a hint of Spengler's apocalyptic vision of the Decline of the West in its rhetoric.

Fairness requires one to note that while Gwenallt obviously deeply disliked the 'invasion' of white Western culture by jazz, skiffle and the like, he did recognise that these had their origins in 'diwylliant arall' (another culture) (*CG*, 213). He also deplored the *apartheid* regime in the South Africa of his day (*CG*, 231). But when all is said and done, some of his poems undeniably expose a side of Gwenallt that one very much wishes did not exist. It was, moreover, a side sadly implicated in his kind of Christian faith, and not simply a single aberration. In his early controversial poem 'Y Sant' (1926) he associates the carnal pleasures, in which the 'saint' indulges under the seductive spell of a great city, with the ugly teats of a sweet-smelling 'negress' [*sic*] (*CG*, 34); and as for the Temple of Sensual Delights in which the 'saint' sinfully worships, its walls are decorated with alluring images from China, Arabia, 'Moslem India' and Assyria – all representative of decadent pagan forms of worship (*CG*, 36). These are the repellent aspect of a major poet – it places Gwenallt in the company of Yeats, Pound and Eliot, major figures all whose poetry was likewise sullied by such grotesque disfigurements. And they are also the 'necessary' polar opposite of Gwenallt's idealisation of a rural, devoutly Christian, Wales that he came to view as the sanctuary of authentic Welsh identity, as will be seen later.

It would, though, be grossly unfair to Gwenallt's genius, it seems to me, to allow such ugly prejudices (and there are others, including disgraceful intimations of anti-Semitism, albeit by one who was horrified by the Holocaust) not only to overshadow the best of his achievement but to devalue it altogether. His dread of sin, evident in 'The Hedgehog' as in many other poems, owed much to the age through which he lived, an age that saw two cataclysmic World Wars, the death camps of Hitler and Stalin, and the dawn of the Nuclear Age at Hiroshima and Nagasaki. For Gwenallt, the new, Liberal and tolerant form of Nonconformity that had evolved in Wales in the wake of the trauma of the First World War was wholly inadequate to confront and combat that which was appalling in his age. It lacked an acknowledgement of that sinfulness whose inherence in human nature was made abundantly and terrifyingly clear in the world events of the twentieth century.

In 'Y Gristionogaeth', published at the very end of the 1930s under the shadow of another impending war, Gwenallt wondered whether the end of the world might not at long last be nigh and God's return to earth imminent. Could he indeed be experiencing the dread advent of the Last Days, when all would be given over initially to the rule of the Antichrist (*CG*, 73)? If so, then his initial reaction was to pray for the 'hour of the vinegar and the cemetery, the fiery age of the brand and the stake' to pass. Pondering the fate of a humanity sunk deep in self-satisfaction and luxuriating hedonistically in its pleasures, he feared it to be no longer capable of enduring the scourge, blood and myrrh of the Crucifixion story. Abandoned was all spiritual inheritance, dimmed the candle of faith, the paths of old were strewn with thorn and thistle, salt had been sullied. Meanwhile humans pecked fretfully at the earth like starling, thrush and raven and gulped down insects and tiny snails, while the chancels were abandoned to the dogs. The human beast was arrived at the very doors of heaven, with his noise, manure and waste. Bargains were struck even in the manger of the Nativity and financial gain had displaced the Cross of Christ – at this point in the original Gwenallt bitterly rhymes 'llog' (financial interest) with 'crog' (cross) as if his poetry is itself bearing reluctant witness to the corruption of language that accompanies the corruption of values.

Yearning to flee this cursed landscape he imagines soaring to the heights of heaven in the company of the eagles, but instead he bows to his destiny, acknowledges his responsibility, and hopes that humanity may yet be winnowed by bitter experience and fine sifted for the salvation of its soul. It may thus be enabled to heave creation free of its engulfing waves and haul the world out of its shallow nothingness. Finally he wishes on the present corrupt world the finality of destruction and utter obliteration:

> Gwân dy holl epil â'r gynnau, â'r bom maluria di'r byd,
> Poera dân o bob peiriant, a fflam a phlwm o bob fflyd,
> Diwreiddia di dy wareiddiad, a phan fo'r ddaear fel braenar briw
> Down â haul o'r byd anweledig, down â'r gwanwyn o ddwylo Duw.
>
> (*CG*, 74)

[Pierce all your progeny with guns [he mockingly instructs humanity], with the bomb shatter the whole world/ Spit fire from every engine, and pour flame and lead from every fleet,/ Uproot your civilisation, and once the earth is wounded fallow land/ We will fetch a sun from the invisible world, we will fetch the spring from the hands of God.]

It is Gwenallt expressing the same yearning for a cleansing anni-
hilation as had been voiced before him by such great masters of
Modernism as D. H. Lawrence and W. B. Yeats (whom he particu-
larly admired), disillusioned as they all were with what the twentieth
century had made of human civilisation. 'Y Gristionogaeth' sees
Gwenallt adopting a prophetic tone and appropriating the genre of
the Jeremiad so characteristic of much of his greatest poetry. In that
last stanza, the first two lines are end-stopped with the exact mascu-
line rhyme thereby rendered restrictive, as Gwenallt underlines his
wish for finality, an end to the world as it is. But then the final couplet
sees a visionary sentence set free to overflow the line to signify the
birth of a new redemptive order while in rhyming 'briw' with 'Duw'
Gwenallt is emphasising the 'wound' (briw) that is a precondition of
human reconciliation of God (Duw) with His world and His world
with God. Implicit in such an image is the memory of the wound
inflicted upon Christ on the Cross from which flowed the blood that
is the only source of human redemption.

*   *   *

Although unfocused, and therefore unarticulated, the Millennialism
explicitly voiced in 'Y Gristionogaeth' was already incipient in
his early baleful vision of the industrial society of his youth. And
Gwenallt is at his best, and at his most irresistible, when he focuses
his outraged attention on the plight of his native community in the
lower Swansea Valley. During his boyhood, it had been a community
that had found in its Christian faith both the spiritual sustenance
vital for its survival under the harshest of working conditions and a
source of the progressive values, both moral and social, that powered
its impressive will to secure betterment not only for itself but for all
humankind.

In his poems, Gwenallt etches a stark portrait of the devastated
physical and human landscape of this western corner of the South
Wales coalfield. His phrases throb with pain and concentrated fury.
He recalls the 'dusty, suffocating, drunken death' humiliatingly suf-
fered by the workforce; their brave, hopeless struggle against powers
'primitive, catastrophic, and violent'; the 'bucketful of death' deliv-
ered in the condescending form of 'free coal' to miners' doors. He
remembers throats scraped sore by the harsh chemical environment,
the 'blush' of the roaring furnace flames on the faces of the workers,
the 'eloquent rumble of cranes' that was the background music of

their lives, and the silent funeral processions that wound their slow, solemn way between the steelworks and tinplate mills.

Silhouetted against this fiery background are his reminiscences of the remarkable efforts made to maintain a humane life in the midst of this living hell: the children cobbling bicycles together out of bits of old scrap and enthusiastically playing rugby for Wales with a pig's bladder, the stoical widows grimly pocketing the blood money of the paltry 'compo' received in derisory lieu of their husbands' lives, the little back gardens so lovingly planted and tended, the pigsties at gardens' ends providing meat to supplement meagre diets, the dignity of close-knit communities bonded by adversity, evident in the staging of the great ceremonial occasions of life and death. And, of course, he emphasises the extraordinary radical political initiatives proposed by the workers, which were powered by their 'litanies of wrong' and voiced as 'collects of red rebellion'. But most important of all for the middle-aged Gwenallt who produced these poems was the Christian values instilled in the workforce by the chapels that stood at the very heart of community life.

The older Gwenallt who wrote these poems was triply removed from the society he was recalling. First, he had undergone a religious conversion; secondly, he had migrated from the working to the middle class, having settled comfortably into the life of a university academic in distant rural Aberystwyth; and, thirdly, he was aware that the terrible Depression years of the 1920s and 1930s had destroyed the industrial society that had produced him. The first of these removals left their mark in the strongly religious colouring of his recollections. The second in the relative sidelining of the radical political activities of the community of his youth. And the third in the bitter nostalgia of some of the writings.

In speaking of the 'primitive powers' that terrorised the Pontardawe of his boyhood, Gwenallt was translating what precocious early education in the brutal facts of industrial life had taught him about the powerful economic and political forces at work in that world into the moral and religious terms suitable for his older, more religious self. This became a central rhetorical feature of his mature poetry. There he deplored the way in which God had come to be dismissed as a mere fiction and His heaven turned into a nest for fleas. The cross of Calvary had been left to rot on its hill, and scarecrows suspended from its two arms. Meanwhile, the world went its blind way like a malignant engine, puffing through the night with neither a line to follow nor points to guide, while its wheels mangled people and crushed their ideals (*CG*, 112). Elsewhere he raged against the way in which the miners, their faces anonymised by coaldust, had been reduced to cheap tokens for callous barter on the world's Exchange and Mart, and at the way in which they had been savagely punished for their noble dreams of universal social justice by being firmly nailed to a cross, the cement at its base heavily reinforced (*CG*, 113).

In his powerful poems about the disaster of the Depression years, it was in Christian values that he placed his ultimate trust for eventual deliverance from social and economic devastation. A brief flirtation with Catholicism had left an indelible mark on his faith in the form of a devotion to the Virgin Mary, and in 'Ar Gyfeiliorn' ('Astray', *CG*, 72) it was to her guiding star that he looked for escape. It is one of those poems where Gwenallt dons the garb of the Jewish prophets of old thundering against the sinful defections of a once-chosen people who have sold their souls for the coffee and confetti of the world's fair. In consequence, pride of place now lies buried beneath the slag and cinders of hideously disfiguring waste tips, canals are grown stagnant and become breeding grounds for rats bloated from feasting on the corpses of cats and dogs. The land has been abandoned to the alien pagan gods of blind fortune, fate and chance. And the present blighted generation is no better than a wolf bitch howling in the desert for the crazy favours of a prostituted moon.

'Y Dirwasgiad' (*CG*, 141), his second poem about the dreadful years of economic Depression, opens with an electrifying series of tropes capturing the Surrealistic nature of an industrial landscape eerily stilled and listless. So free is the air of umbrellas of smoke that stars shine newly scrubbed. Gone are the palls of murk balefully hovering low over the valley like a latter-day plague of devouring locusts, and gipsy sheep boldly return to trespass and to lick in bins overflowing with empty tins of salmon and sardine. Rivers run clear again, scum scoured from their stones, while lurking trout reappear in waters that have shed their oily film to reveal the squirm of eels weaving nests in the banks. Miners' heels no longer sound an alarm in the mornings and there are no whitened eyes laughing in blackened faces of an afternoon.

But then Gwenallt changes key as he offsets this imagery of a slowly recovered preindustrial idyll with an angry litany of its human cost. Food grows scarce on the tables, and doors and windows are shabby for lack of paint; sour idleness haunts every street corner and miners tramp shadowless from place to place. 'Daeth diwedd ar Eldorado'r trefi' (*CG*, 141), he reports, sardonically noting that the Valley towns no longer entice with their plenty, before concluding that the community has been hollowed out and homes cracked. The very foundations of a once proud and thriving South Wales industrial civilisation have collapsed. For him, this is a society whose spiritual as well as financial bankruptcy has at last been mercilessly exposed.

But even as he increasingly reactivated his earliest spiritual resources and practised a Christian vocabulary, the mature Gwenallt remained wholly alive to the economic and political forces that his poetry tended to occlude. He acknowledged what he had learnt as a youngster at the feet of the workmen of South Wales, that man was a political animal, and he respectfully recalled how he had been thrilled to the core of his young being by the iron of justice palpably coursing through their very blood (*CG*, 134). He remained completely convinced that capitalism was the very image of Antichrist, the root of all social evils, whether manifest in the industrial form he had known as a young man in Allt-wen, or in the form of the new, consumerist, commercial capitalism he shrewdly realised was becoming the curse of the post-war age. Capitalism was, for him, inherently immoral and anti-Christian, an outlook he voiced in several of his later poems. In its industrial phase, it had reduced human beings to mere numbers even in their native environment, treating them as figures to be manipulated in the interests of business and to maximise profit (*CG*, 135). And in the countryside, it had treated land as a mere resource to be exploited, ignoring its historical function of fashioning human place, providing continuity, and sustaining both individual and national identity.

But it was not only over the owners, the financiers, and other controlling and parasitic figures in the world of industrial capitalism that Gwenallt poured the vitriol of his furious outrage, it was also over the workforce itself as he surveyed the bleak, incipiently post-industrial, landscape in the many industrial valleys of South Wales. In his eyes, the bulk of the Welsh proletariat had turned their back on the nation's traditional spiritual and cultural values that had still been vigorously honoured by the working community of the Allt-wen of his childhood and youth. The Welsh were a people gone astray. They had whored after strange gods. Like the people of Israel of old, they had defected from the faith to which their ancestors had remained true for almost two millennia. They had rejected the Welsh language that had been such an important carrier of Christian values virtually throughout its long existence. They had fallen prey to the prophets of Baal.

In poem after poem, he aimed his blistering Jeremiads at his compatriots, the Jeremiad being for him, a boy raised on the language of the Bible, no mere literary genre but a sacred rhetoric associated with the great prophet, and in some of his poetry he consciously drew on the imagery and vocabulary of the Book of Jeremiah. His was the rhetoric of a modern prophet, whose duties were given dramatic currency in 1994 by Don Peppino Diana, a remarkably courageous young priest near Naples, who in defiance of the Camorra published a pamphlet that immediately led to his death in a hail of bullets. 'The Prophet', he wrote, 'is a watchman: he sees injustice and speaks out against it, recalling God's original command (Ezekiel 3: 16–19); The Prophet remembers the past and uses it to gather up new things in the present (Isaiah 43); The Prophet invites us to live, and himself lives in, solidarity and suffering (Genesis 8: 18–22); The Prophet gives priority to the life of justice (Jeremiah 22: 3, Isaiah 58).'6

When, in his poem about Christianity, Gwenallt speaks of 'braenu'r tir', the preparing of fallow land for the sowing of new seed, it is to Jeremiah 4: 3 that he is alluding: 'Break up your fallow ground, and sow not among thorns.' And one of the most celebrated of his poems is a sonnet that opens, 'Er mor annheilwng ydwyt ti o'n search,/ Di, butain fudr y stryd â'r taeog lais', where Wales is accused of having made herself unworthy of her people's affections by prostituting herself on every street corner (*CG*, 98). But next it moves to a confession that nevertheless the country still retains her hold on the Welsh:

> Eto, ni allwn ni, bob mab a merch,
> Ddiffodd y cariad atat tan ein hais:
> Fe'th welwn di â llygaid pŵl ein ffydd
> Gynt yn flodeuog yn dy wyrfdod hardd[.]

[Yet can we, every son and daughter,/ never extinguish the love for you we carry under our breasts:/ We view you with the dimmed sight of our faith,/ As flowering in your beautiful virginity.]

This stubbornly enduring patriotism he attributes to popular memory of Wales as once in her virginal innocence she had been, a country devoted to the values promulgated by deep Christian faith.

Gwenallt takes this image of a nation as a degraded harlot directly from the Book of Jeremiah, as he does the forgiveness he expresses in the lines that follow. The trope is one recurrently used by the Old Testament prophet to describe the plight of the people of Israel following their desertion of the faith of their fathers. 'Thou saidst, I will not transgress', says God in Jeremiah's report, 'when upon every high hill and under every green tree thou wanderest, playing the harlot' (2: 20). But then, like Gwenallt, Jehovah offers to forgive His nation provided she refrain from 'play[ing] the harlot with many lovers' (3: 1) and that she 'return again to me'. For all her defilement of the land by 'committing adultery with rocks and stones', God is willing to receive her back, because He is merciful, and continues to acknow-ledge that 'I am married to you' (3: 14). So Gwenallt ends his sonnet by begging God to be merciful to the Welsh people, trusting they too can be persuaded to recover their ancient faithfulness to the Lord. He follows Jeremiah in believing that his people are among the Chosen Ones of God, a People of the Book still covenanted as of old to the service of the Almighty.

Another theme of Jeremiah's that spoke powerfully to Gwenallt was a concern to find a language adequate for addressing the gravity of his people's spiritual crisis and thus empowered to speak the truth about their parlous condition that the contemporary Welsh needed to hear. 'And the prophets shall become wind, and the word is not in them', laments Jeremiah (5: 13), while Gwenallt opens 'Ar Gyfeiliorn' (*CG*, 72), the poem in which he accuses his people of grievous defec-tions, with the grim warning 'Gwae inni wybod y geiriau heb adnabod y Gair', 'woe unto us if we know the words without knowing the Word'. Of course, he is thinking specifically of the Old Testament equation of Christ with the Logos, a concept unknown to Jeremiah, but he is also articulating a poet's concern that the words he himself uses should be safely grounded in the truths of the Gospel – a con-cern that parallels that of Jeremiah that his words as prophet should be such as faithfully testify to the omnipotence of Jehovah. 'For they bend their tongues like their bow for lies', he proclaims of the Israelites, because 'they are not valiant for the truth upon the earth' (9: 3). 'Their tongue is as an arrow shot out', the prophet mournfully adds, 'it speaketh deceit' (9: 8). As a religious poet devoted above all to the improvement of his nation's condition, Gwenallt likewise aspires to be 'valiant for truth', and to employ a language sanctioned by Grace.

* * *

The idea that one's nation is particularly favoured by God is a very old one, common to most of the nations of both Western and Eastern Christendom. It is an ideology currently favoured by both the USA and Russia, and in both cases is an accessory to their enormous power. In the case of Wales, however, it has always been a function of powerlessness, as became pathetically evident in the late Victorian period. At that time a 'Nonconformist nation' harboured the illusion that it had much to offer Imperial Britain because it supposedly enjoyed a relationship with the Almighty that would allow it to place its unique spiritual gifts at the service of the British Empire worldwide. But a belief that Wales was a country blessed by God was an ancient one, pre-dating the Victorian age by at least half a millennium. It originated partly in the form of myth – the belief that the Gospel had been first brought to Wales by none other than Joseph of Arimathea – and partly in the form of a semi-mythic history. According to this, the Welsh had been converted to Christianity during the final period of Roman occupation (centuries before the conversion of the pagan invading Saxons), and the Celtic Church established in consequence. In due course, every Welsh church and denomination competed for the honour of being accepted as the legitimate heir of those early Celtic Saints. The claims of the Catholic Church in that crucial legitimatising respect were challenged first during the Reformation by the emergent Anglican Church in Wales, before the mantle of a Chosen People was finally appropriated by the loose alliance of sects and denominations that constituted the Nonconformist culture of Victorian Wales.[7]

Chapel-bred, Gwenallt would no doubt have been exposed early to this myth of Welsh religious exceptionalism in its Nonconformist form. But by the time it was making its appearance in his poetry he had become a member of the Anglican communion in Wales, inspired in part by an idealistic and unrealistic view of the C. of E. as 'yr Hen Fam', a church once cherished by the Welsh as mother of their culture. And such indeed it could reasonably claim to have been for the first three hundred or so years of its existence, but by the nineteenth century the Church of England had come to seem an oppressive, alien organ served by clergy who had no knowledge of the Welsh language exclusively spoken by their parishioners and who had no interest in the native culture that had been so enriched by their predecessors.

The Nonconformist sects, increasingly angry at the rights, benefits and privileges granted what was after all a Church that had been designed from the outset to serve the Anglo-British state, and smarting at the humiliating and damaging penalties and restrictions they were forced to endure in consequence, mounted an increasingly determined and bitter campaign in favour of the disestablishment of the Church in Wales. Eagerly championed by such great leaders of late-Victorian Welsh Liberalism as Lloyd George, the campaign eventually met with success. The Anglican Church in Wales was duly disestablished in 1914, under a Parliamentary Act that took effect in 1920 that deprived it of all its lucrative privileges and endowments. It was this step that persuaded leading writers such as Gwenallt and R. S. Thomas (of whom more anon) to hope that the disestablished Church would now reconnect itself with the community of believers in Wales and would thus recommence that distinguished service to native culture that had once been such a boon to the nation. Both, however, were gradually to be disabused of their fond hopes as, despite its disestablishment, the Church in Wales proved as reluctant to devote itself to such national service as had its predecessor, opting instead to remain resolutely anglocentric and statist in its outlook and practices. Consequently R.S. became increasingly disillusioned with the Church he nevertheless continued grudgingly to serve, while an exasperated Gwenallt eventually left the Church altogether to return to the Welsh Calvinistic Methodism of his youth. He had been particularly angered by the election of Alfred Edwin Morris, an Englishman who was not a Welsh speaker, as Archbishop of Wales in 1957. Not only was the Church in Wales no longer the 'Old Mother' of olden times, he railed, it was not even the 'Old Foreigner' that had so outraged nineteenth-century Welsh Nonconformity: it had become 'the Old Traitor' of the nation and its people (*G*, 289ff). The Church, he continued, was the Queen's Church, the Church of the Tories, the Church of Suez, a schismatic Church.

It is, however, Gwenallt the Welsh Anglican who speaks in some of the great poetry of his middle period. Consequently, when in his poem to the proletariat of South Wales he urges them to reject the foreign tools of international socialism it is to the ancient yews growing in Wales's churchyards he advises that they turn instead for wood seasoned and sturdy enough to provide the weapons they need to fight for the justice that can come only through national liberation (*CG*, 134). And it is the long cultural perspective he originally believed he had acquired by joining the Church in Wales that is evident in 'Cymru', a poem that opens by hymning a Welsh soil that has been spiritually enriched and sanctified by the ashes of the countless saints and martyrs buried in it. As Dorian Llywelyn shrewdly points out, 'For Gwenallt ... the past is of itself a value, a type of holy place. The contrast is between a civilized and domesticated past, a *kosmos*, in which life was according to God's commandment, and a present which is moral wilderness' (*CP*, 119). God, Gwenallt resonantly proclaims in the penultimate stanza of 'Cymru' (*CG*, 71), has chosen Wales as His handmaiden, and inscribed His covenant on her gates and pillars. And then in the final stanza he alludes to the celebrated image in Matthew (23: 37), 'how often would I have gathered thy children together, even as a hen gathereth her chickens under her wings, and ye would not', a verse to which Saunders Lewis also turned in one of his late poems.

Dorian Llywelyn has very valuably drawn attention to two variants of Gwenallt's Welsh ecclesiology. The one, whose history and 'cultural pathology' have been traced above, seems to allow for a view of Wales as an especially Chosen Nation, and to entail a distinction between it and supposedly secular, unredeemed, nationalities such as that of the English. This Llywelyn terms the 'Wales–Israel' tradition. The other, however, contrastingly treats the 'sacredness' of Welsh national identity simply as one instant of that sanctifying bond between God and a people that is a potential, and sometimes an actual operative, feature of every national community and its territory across the entire world. This is a vision Llywelyn characterises as a 'Wales as Church' vision, since, according to this version, this particular country simply affords a single, 'local' instance of the universal Church of Christ. In such a context, 'all time becomes, at least potentially, holy time', every territory sacred territory, and 'nationality' and 'nationhood' acquire a sacramental dimension.

The image of a God who seeks everywhere and always to gather a people into the protection of His care like a hen her chicks is particularly apt for Gwenallt, as he was always strongly inclined to consider the rural Carmarthenshire of his forebears, where he had spent many a happy summer in his youth and found sanctuary when trying to avoid conscription, as the *echt* Wales, *pura Wallia*, the spiritual heart of the nation. Such an image had been cultivated by the many in Welsh Wales during the late Victorian and Edwardian eras of his childhood who had retreated psychologically to the country in the face of the alien threat represented by the rapidly anglicising and increasingly immigrant industrial proletariat of the South

Wales coalfield. It had found its apogee in the cult of the 'gwerin',
the ordinary, pious, law-abiding rural *volk* whose way of life had
been influentially and sentimentally valorised by O. M. Edwards in
his popular classic *Cartrefi Cymru*.

Gwenallt was conscious and grateful heir of a Nonconformist
culture that had profoundly affected the Welsh psyche, moulding it
for over a century. Intimate familiarity with the Bible had resulted in
Wales being re-landscaped in the image of the Holy Land, as Bethels
and Bethlehems, Bethesdas and Salems assumed local, contemporary
form as Welsh villages as well as supplying names for the innumerable
chapels. The lexicon of the Bible had melded with vernacular Welsh,
and great Welsh hymn-writers had made of it a people's vocabulary
of the very soul. In the sonnet Gwenallt addressed to Ann Griffiths,
the mystical hymn-writer of late-eighteenth-century Evangelical
Methodism, it was in the terms of her own intimate, Solomonic self-
image as the Bride of Christ that Gwenallt hymned her praise, adding
that she had seen the sun of her nuptial day break over the hills of her
native Montgomeryshire (*CG*, 104). And he concluded the companion
sonnet addressed to the spiritual and literary genius of the restlessly
peripatetic William Williams Pantycelyn – the troubadour of heaven as
Gwenallt memorably termed him, and Griffiths's near contemporary –
by noting how he had translated the exalted language of faith into the
simple, homely vernacular of the labouring and disregarded rural poor.

But in these eloquent tributes to the ardent religiosity, largely past
yet still residually present, of rural Welsh culture, Gwenallt was simply
perpetuating a very well-worn Welsh rhetorical tradition. His original-
ity lay rather in the surprising and imaginatively daring capacity he
showed for interpreting the degraded socio-cultural landscape of the
Welsh industrial South in cognate spiritual terms. In simultaneously
representing that landscape as an infernal region he was in some ways
not only deploying the anti-capitalist, international Socialist, ideol-
ogy he had learnt in his youth but also conforming to the prejudices
of the preindustrial rural Welsh-language culture to which, as we
have seen, he remained deeply attracted. However, when he imaged
the pithead winding gear as an engine of redemption, the cage as a
hoist between sin and salvation, and the homing pigeons as avatars
of the Holy Ghost, then it was his startlingly innovative originality
that was on vivid display.

At this juncture, however, one very important feature of
Gwenallt's religious purview that has been completely overlooked by

his interpreters needs to be emphasised. His unprecedented sacramental vision of the Welsh industrial landscape was almost exclusively limited to that of the lower Swansea Valley – the villages of Allt-wen and Pontardawe of his youth. When later he endeavoured to extend it to encompass the eastern valleys of the South Wales coalfield – including those of the Cynon Valley, the two Rhonddas, the Ebbw, the Sirhowy and the Rhymney – he proved capable of viewing them only as corrupting, alien presences, instances of social and cultural degradation. There was sound sociological ground for this apparent discrepancy. The valleys of the western margins of the coalfield were profoundly different in cultural and social character from those of the east. As Gwenallt's own history illustrated, there were intimate connections and continuities of language, values and culture between such valleys of the South as the Tawe (Swansea Valley), the Amman and the Gwendraeth and their neighbouring rural hinterland. The population of the industrial workforce was fairly homogeneous, recently arrived from nearby rural regions. Consequently, Gwenallt – like some other writers of his generation – could envisage the workforce of such regions as 'gwerin y graith', the coal-scarred equivalents of the rural 'volk' of Rhydcymerau.

By contrast the eastern valleys were the products of traumatic cultural, linguistic and social rupture. They were geographically distant from rural Wales, populated by an alien, heterogeneous population that included a high proportion of immigrants, and home to a society in which the chapels, and the Welsh language with which they were closely associated, had become a marginal and fading phenomenon. There, too, the miners were pigeon-fanciers, like those of Allt-wen, but they were also likely to be greyhound-owners who had thus literally 'gone to the dogs'. The favourite institutions of this 'lumpen proletariat' were the drinking holes of the Working Men's Clubs, and their sporting taste ran to the likes of Tommy Farr of Tonypandy, the erstwhile fairground brawler and legendary opponent of Joe Louis, and the elusive genius of world flyweight champion Jimmy Wilde of Tylorstown, the 'ghost with the hammer in his gloves', as well as to the greats of the rugby field that the young Gwenallt had worshipped.

In these communities, Gwenallt could see only instances of the powerful destructive forces at work that threatened to annihilate the native religious culture that had given him being. And as he grew older, he saw these same alien forces balefully undermining the rural communities that had provided him at a critical time with spiritual sustenance, linguistic gifts and political sanctuary. Despairingly, he composed several resonant elegies for this way of life whose decline during his lifetime had been more precipitous, and little less catastrophic, than the decline of Welsh industrial civilisation – elegy being the dark psycho-social twin of ecstasy in Gwenallt's convulsively bipolar imagination.

One of the most powerful of his lamentations is 'Gwlad Adfeiliedig' (A ruined country), a nostalgic inventory of all that has been lost (*CG*, 67). But the most celebrated is undoubtedly 'Rhydcymerau' (*CG*, 148) – the name of his ancestors' native region – because it points the finger squarely at the most recent cause of this rural devastation of a rich, cultured and civilised society. On the slopes surrounding the village, he shockingly notes, have been planted the seeds of the Third World War. The reference is to the fir plantations that multiplied at an alarming rate in the Welsh uplands following the Second World War as the Forestry Commission and the War Office commandeered large tracts of the countryside.[8] The brazen roots ('gwreiddiau haerllug') of these trees suck all nourishment from the soil and the density of their deadly shade provides a lair for the 'English Minotaur', while from their branches hang the corpses of poets, elders, ministers and Sunday School teachers, their bones bleaching in the sun and steadily washed by the rain in a sinister parody of both baptism and Crucifixion. In this conclusion, Gwenallt revisits his opening nightmare of a Third World War, as he chillingly envisages the beloved meadows of Rhydcymerau turned killing fields, their scarecrows metamorphosing before his horrified eyes into skeletal human figures. It is as if he were conflating the appalling post-nuclear images that had emerged from Hiroshima and Nagasaki with one of Goya's paintings from the Peninsular War.

* * *

One essential feature of Gwenallt's poetry that is routinely overlooked and undervalued is its startling wit, grimly apparent in 'Rhydcymerau', and yet it is a vital component of his religious vision. It is in some ways a variant of the allegorical and domesticating cast of mind typical of such Puritan writers as John Bunyan, but in Gwenallt's case it assumes a positively Baroque extravagance consistent with his permanent astonishment at the outrageous audacity of the Incarnation. Crucifixion and Resurrection – that most unlikely and outlandish sequence of events. So, for instance, he packs his poem about Lazarus with a series of arresting tropes. Man, he announces at the outset, has comfortingly fashioned Death in his own image, treating it as the neat finality of a short story's ending, regarding it as a grand Amen to round off a hymn, carefully tending it as one banks up the fire at midnight to smother its threat. However, the story of Lazarus, he points out, requires a second lock to be added to the door of life, while his resurrection necessitates an Appendix to the human story, which can now be understood only with reference to the great Encyclopaedia of the Resurrection (*CG*, 173).

Likewise, in 'Y Calendr' (*CG*, 170), Gwenallt shows how Christians interrupt the modern, secular sense of the even, undifferentiated flow of time by segmenting it into Feast Days, so that 'Y mae'r Efengyl yn hongian wrth hoel'. The Gospel itself is suspended from a nail in present-day homes in the mundane form of a calendar, as the Saviour was hung on Calvary. Such awareness of sacred time, as qualitatively uneven and non-linear, and pivoting around the scandalously eruptive, transgressive and transfigurative episodes of the Crucifixion and Resurrection, was for Gwenallt the poet undoubtedly one of the most valuable and enduring legacies of the period he spent as a member of the Church in Wales. And in 'Ceiliog y Gwynt', he riffs ingeniously on the image of the cockerel, raised from the dung-hill to grace a church steeple, in honour of the one in the New Testament that had been singled out to play its part in the Providential plan by thrice crowing to break Peter's heart (*CG*, 175). Gwenallt concludes by praying that the modern-day cockerel may perform the very same miracle so as to wring 'violet' tears of repentance – the colour is that of Lent in the Anglican calendar – from the eyes of latter-day believers. 'Y Ceiliog' and 'Y Calendr' are both fine examples of Gwenallt's gift for subverting the routine simple didacticism of pious Welsh Victorian versifying by subjecting it to the mischievous impulses of that little imp of the perverse to which his own unruly religious imagination was so 'devilishly' partial. In his best poetry his vision was never fully domesticated, never obediently house-trained. His wit has been regretted by some as lacking in taste. But then, he might well have countered, what exactly is it that is tasteful about the Christian story, rooted as it is in a recognition of the raw savagery of human nature? When recalling Christ's crucifixion, Gwenallt could not refrain from protesting at 'sgandal ei farwolaeth' (*CG*, 181) (the scandal of his death).

Another interesting aspect of Gwenallt's production tends also to be ignored. Perhaps the most accomplished of all his collections is *Eples*, and as is there made clear in the poem 'Cip' (Glance or Glimpse), by being published in 1951 it appeared at the very time when the exhausted, disillusioned world of post-war Europe was becoming extremely sceptical of all forms of ideology, including that of the Christian faith. As Sartre and others of the time intuited, the prevailing mood among intellectuals was one of spiritual nihilism, a weary acceptance of the absence of any kind of transcendent sanction for human life, a conviction that religious belief could only ever be a self-authenticating act of personal, 'existential' choice, totally arbitrary, contingent and unverifiable. In the religious sphere, the writings of Kierkegaard perfectly articulated this zeitgeist. And in 1952, the year after *Eples* appeared, Paul Tillich published his popular and influential book *The Courage to Be*, which identified the spiritual crisis of the age as one arising from 'the anxiety of meaninglessness'.[9] 'We are', he wrote, 'under the threat of spiritual non-being' (67). One of its aspects, he added, was 'the anxiety of annihilating openness, of infinite, formless space into which one falls without a place to fall upon' (68), and Gwenallt's 'Cip' offers us a Welsh version of that *angst*. Tillich also singled out for praise those few writers of the day who had the courage to own up to, and indeed to face up to, this grave state of existential anxiety, and, as 'Cip' shows, Gwenallt was one who deserved to be numbered among those few. It is a poem in which he directly addresses his own reciprocating misgivings as to the ultimate meaning of existence.

It is occasioned, as the opening stanza admits, by his experience, as a middle-aged university teacher, of seeing a new cohort of students enter college. For him, they signify the remorseless flow of time and the inevitability of permanent change. The question is, whether he can still convincingly view this flux 'sub specie aeternitatis', now that he knows his Darwin and is awed by Einstein? 'Bydd gwacter bywyd, weithiau, ar f'ysbryd yn hunllef', he admits, an admission of his terror at the possible absence from life of any credible sense of ultimate, supernatural purpose. But his anxiety is assuaged by the conviction that 'Y mae rhyw wyneb mawr y tu hwnt i'r wynebau oll' – there is a single great face that underlies this bewildering sea of eager new young faces. He realises that 'Gorllif creadigaeth Duw yw'r wynebau a'r rhosynnau': this proliferation of human features is, like the glorious profusion of summer roses, only the exuberant overflow of God's creation. This leads to the further admission that 'Duw yn unig a edwyn Ei wyneb Ef Ei Hun': it is God alone who is able to recognise

His own countenance. This acknowledgement of the ultimate, pre-Trinitarian, Godhead is rare, if not unique, in Gwenallt's writing. And it seems to proceed from a moment of peculiar psychic and spiritual crisis, consonant with the period. It is this that precipitates a need to trust in the God beyond God, that 'ground of being' which Tillich repeatedly emphasised in his work. 'Cip' is Gwenallt's equivalent to Yeats's 'Sailing to Byzantium', both being poems in which ageing men seek sanctuary from the brash physical and sexual energies, aggressive and threatening, of a new young generation: 'This is no country for old men,/ The young in one another's arms ...'. Both react by escaping to a place of refuge: Byzantium in the case of Yeats, the ground of all being in the case of Gwenallt.

'Cip' suggests that *Eples* derives much of its singular, intense power from the crisis that gave it being, the nexus of anxieties – some acknowledged, others implicit – out of which it grew. It was, after all, a time when Gwenallt's relationship with the Anglican Church was becoming ever more fraught, so that when in 'Y Meirwon', that celebrated poem of recollection with which the collection opens, he recalls the moving pieties of the working community of early century Allt-wen, it is as if he is already anticipating that return to his chapel origins that was soon to happen in his own life adult life. Whatever the special concatenation of circumstances, then, *Eples* was to prove the pinnacle of Gwenallt's poetic career. Two more collections were to follow, but they were of an appreciably lower level of quality. The furious tempest of anger that had propelled his earlier poetry to its heights had blown itself out. His inspired rhetoric began to seem akin to tedious rant. And his Christian faith, while still deep, fixed and sincere, became routinised. No longer was it urgently fashioned out of immediate psychic crisis, nor was it marked by desperate need. The divine afflatus of outrage had subsided. *Gwenallt furioso*, who had once been such a riveting religious poet, was no more.

Notes

1 See the brilliant essay by Hywel Teifi Edwards, 'Asbri Gwenallt', *Lleufer*, 24/4 (1969), 3–6.
2 Christine James (ed.), *Cerddi Gwenallt: Y Casgliad Cyflawn* (Llandysul: Gwasg Gomer, 2001), p. 128. Hereafter *CG*. For an informative English introduction to his work, see Donald Allchin, D. Densil Morgan and Patrick Thomas (eds and trans.), *Sensuous Glory: The Poetic Vision of D. Gwenallt Jones* (Norwich: Canterbury Press, 2000). Translations of some of his poems may be found

in Menna Elfyn and John Rowlands (eds), *The Bloodaxe Book of Modern Welsh Poetry* (Tarset: Bloodaxe, 2003), pp. 93–9 and Joseph P. Clancy (trans.), *Twentieth-Century Welsh Poems* (Llandysul: Gomer, 1982), pp. 94–105.

3 R. S. Thomas, 'A Lecturer', *Collected Poems, 1945–1990* (Tarset: Bloodaxe, 2000), p. 138.

4 Quoted in Alan Llwyd, *Gwenallt* (Talybont: Y Lolfa, 2016), p. 156. This is the definitive biography. Hereafter *C*.

5 C. F. MacIntyre (trans.), *Rilke: Sonnets to Orpheus* (Berkeley and Los Angeles: University of California Press, 1967), p. 53.

6 Don Peppino pamphlet.

7 See Dorian Llywelyn's classic study, *Sacred Place, Chosen People* (Cardiff: University of Wales Press, 1999). A distinction is drawn there between '*a* chosen people' and '*the* chosen people'. A subordinated people like the Welsh tend to adopt the former, powerful, dominant countries such as those of the US and Russia, almost invariably favour the latter. Llywelyn's outstanding study is relevant throughout to the present volume, and includes a valuable chapter on Gwenallt.

8 For an outstanding overview of this development, see Kirsti Bohata, *Postcolonialism Revisited* (Cardiff: University of Wales Press, 2004), Chapter Four, pp. 80–103.

9 Paul Tillich, *The Courage to Be* (London: Collins, Fontana, 1965).

6

WALDO WILLIAMS:
KING IN EXILE

Waldo Williams (1904–71): half a century after his death, the name continues to inspire affection and awe in Welsh Wales. It also triggers a protective instinct, because Waldo (the whole of Wales, it seems, still claims to be on first-name terms with him) was a singular creature; a rare species of human being. He unwittingly captured the essence of his own personality when he singled out for admiration a sentence he had read which said of one individual: '[I]f there was any pride in him, it was simply originality.'[1] A seemingly simple man of unsettlingly radical integrity, almost a Holy Innocent, he was also fiercely intelligent and disturbingly complex, and very widely read, not only in Welsh and English but also (albeit with difficulty) in French, German and Italian.

In some ways a natural loner, in others he was sociable and gregarious, his insatiable curiosity fed alike by his conversations with agricultural workers in the 'local' during his Lyneham period and by the yarns he heard from the old salts who were Cape Horners from the days of sail when he was teaching on the Llŷn peninsula. Deeply attracted to quietism – late in life he felt an affinity for the Quakers (*WWR*, 319–21) – he was nevertheless a stubborn, courageous social activist willing to face imprisonment rather than compromise his beliefs – as indeed happened twice. On both these occasions his refusal to pay his taxes was due to an objection to National Service (intensified by the fact that his nephew was serving in that capacity with the Welch Regiment in Cyprus), but he had earlier come close to suffering the same fate when he withheld his taxes in protest against the use of a portion of them to support British involvement in the

Korean war.[2] So traumatised had he been by that distant war that for some considerable time he had felt totally unable to write, haunted by his hero Gandhi's admonition to Rabindranath Tagore, 'You give us words instead of actions' (*WWR*, 90). His severe crisis of conscience had also occasioned the delay in the publication of the only selection of his poems to appear in print during his lifetime. He could not countenance its appearance, he told his friends who had undertaken to prepare the little book for the press, while his nephew was still riskily patrolling Cyprus. In some respects his case is reminiscent of that of the important radical American poet George Oppen, who around mid-century stopped writing for more than twenty years while committing himself to remedial social and political action.

And of late another important dimension has been added to our apprehension of the complex character of a man who was at once eminently loveable and accessible but also elusive. The author of a handful of luminous poems, of lucid, calm, assured spiritual vision, he has been revealed by recent research to have suffered throughout his life from a wounding trauma that originated in his early childhood.[3] He was chronically restless, both physically and mentally. Apart from the two blissful years of his brief marriage, it seems he experienced 'home' only when visiting the hearths of very close friends or as a utopian state to be desired rather than as a solidly experienced mundane reality. There was something of the tramp about Waldo, despite his long-term periods of teaching, and his excruciatingly brief happy marriage. And analysts would no doubt view his visionary poetry as the defence mechanism he developed to protect himself from the fits of despair to which he was prone and against the all-consuming anxiety that paralysed him periodically, the reason for which will be explored later.

Despite all the efforts of the 'Waldo cult' (or perhaps partly because of them), he remains an enigma. The cult has certainly had its beneficial effects, not least in ensuring that his name and his work remain valued and current in his beloved immediate locality and well beyond the narrow and arid confines of the academy. But it also inhibits just estimation of his achievements. In particular, it foregrounds the transparent goodness of the man at the expense of paying attention to the sometimes dark intricacies of his personality and it gives the impression that he was an original thinker, which he patently was not, any more than was Dante, whose work he devoured in the important Daniel Rees Welsh translation. *Vita Nuova* was an astonishing synthesis of the scholastic and mystical ideologies of his period. The function of poetry is not to serve as a vehicle of original thought. It is quite other, and in Waldo's case it is in significant part to mediate the vision that possessed him.

He unintentionally penetrated to the fundamentals of that vision in a review (1942) of a collection of short stories by his closest friend and kindred spirit, D. J. Williams. Every true author, he there unequivocally states, is one who has had a vision, and it is that vision that moves him or her to create and to give that creation its defining character. He then draws an important distinction between two different types of vision. Some writers, he explains:

> Have to win their vision in reaction against the existent world, by wresting from its indifference that respect for life, and love for every fellow-being, which lies at the root of all great literature. But there are others, more privileged perhaps, who acquire it by deepening that experience they had gained of the world upon first acquaintance with it. They therefore have no need to despair at the chasm between the existent world and the world as it should be. Because they have once been given a glimpse of how there is something of the latter in the former, and something of the former in the latter. And fidelity to that which is eternal is the foundation of their rebellion against the world of time. (*WWR*, 140)

So to which category does Waldo belong? That is a very difficult question to answer. He had indeed been given plenty of reason during the earliest years of his life to mistrust what then must have seemed the established order of times. But the subsequent move to Mynachlog-ddu had partly coincided with a profound change in his experience and partly enabled it. Such divided personal experience may explain why his profound faith in life's essential goodness was susceptible of periods of deep crisis and psychological collapse. But in the end he obviously tended more towards the second type than the first. His greatest poems all seem to presuppose, like the Quakers whose ranks he shyly joined in his last years, the presence of a vital, benign spirit secretly inhabiting the whole of creation and all of its creatures. As he explained in a classic statement of his core beliefs, he trusted 'the direct, intuitive personal appeal of man to man,' but realised that this was being frustrated and perverted by 'the moulds and metrices that shape the ideas that pervade societies' (*WWR*, 268).

'Waldo': the clue to key aspects of his personality and outlook lies in that simple name. It was the name given him by his father probably in honour of Ralph Waldo Emerson, the great nineteenth-century American Transcendentalist, progressive thinker and spiritual universalist. Transcendentalism was an important tributary of the Social Utopianism enthusiastically embraced by Waldo's father, along with a group of similarly progressive friends and relatives, living in Edwardian Pembrokeshire.[4] Other figures of note for the circle included William Morris, Edward Carpenter, John Ruskin, Walt Whitman, Keir Hardie and Tolstoy, and to these Waldo was to add many further names, including Thoreau and Berdyaev. Later, Waldo's education at the University College of Wales, Aberystwyth awakened in him a profound and lifelong devotion to the work of the major figures of English Romanticism, most notably Blake, Wordsworth and Shelley – it was indeed a visit to Nether Stowey that lifted the deep depression that afflicted him during the war. He was inspired by the revolutionary social optimism of some of the Romantics' most famous works. His greatest poem, 'Mewn Dau Gae', opens with a singular personal mystical vision and concludes with the expansion of that vision to embrace the worldwide community of humankind. Those were the twin poles of the vision that governed all of Waldo's most powerful work and activity throughout his life, and that made him at once an introverted mystic and an extroverted social activist. It was all predicated on an enduring, but by no means unshaken, belief – cruelly tested by personal circumstances – in the fundamental goodness of humankind, in the benignity of the universe, and in a spiritual teleology. And time after time he refused to 'exile', as he put it, the spiritual world from the world of social experience and action.

Important to note, too, is that upon moving the short distance from long-anglicised coastal Haverfordwest to the inland rural village of Mynachlog-ddu, nestling in the shadow of the ancient Preseli hills, Waldo was, at the age of seven, moving from 'little England beyond Wales' to a heartland of the Welsh language. He was also relocating to a district already renowned not only for the romance and magic of its ancient landscape but as a hotbed of popular unrest and protest during the first half of the nineteenth century. He had moved into bandit country, a rural land of rebels and staunchly independent-minded thinkers, home to the Rebecca Rioters. These were the jacquerie who, under the colourful leadership of 'Beca', a burly local dressed in woman's clothing, tore down the toll-gates hated by the farmers because they forced them to pay to carry crops and goods to market.

And then, just a few miles north of the Preseli and across the Cardiganshire border, began the region that included the 'smotyn du': the black spot. This area was thus stigmatised by the Nonconformists, who believed it disfigured the fair countenance of Nonconformist Wales, because it was the stronghold of Unitarianism. The hetero-dox sect particularly valued human reason, did not believe in the Incarnation or the Calvinist doctrine of salvation only by divine grace, and encouraged a hardy, rational, independence of mind. Unitarians also shared with Dissenters their hatred of the alien landowning and Church-going class of landlords. These were notorious both for the exorbitant financial demands that some of them made of their Welsh tenantry and for their support of the Tithe system, deeply resented by Nonconformists as an unjust tax. And when the Second Reform Bill of 1867 clearly heralded the defeat of the landlords in the 1868 election, they first threatened tenants with eviction if they dared to vote contrary to their interests, and then proceeded vindictively to eject them once duly ousted from power.

In addition, Waldo identified with the Welsh Baptists, his own close relatives being members of a Baptist chapel, and he took a particular interest in the old chapel of Rhydwilym in his immediate locality that could date its origin back to the seventeenth century. He hugely admired the denomination's traditional unbending opposi-tion to any kind of State interference in an individual's spiritual life, recalling that the sect in Wales had even refused to accept Charles II's Declaration of Indulgence, because that presupposed the right of king and state to grant or deny freedom of worship. And he admired the way this early manifestation of principled individualism continued to find expression in the person of one contemporary Baptist minister whom Waldo characterised as a 'practical visionary' – a term that could also be usefully applied to himself.

Waldo spent much of his life teaching in primary schools, both in Wales and in England, seeming happiest when in the company of little ones. For them he wrote many attractive children's poems, several of them infused with the playful humour for which he was well known and deeply loved. Even the most intense of his adult work was never earnest or solemn; his profundity was wholly unforced, unaffected and totally authentic. And there was an unquenchable glint of mischief in his imagination – from his youth onwards he had been a prolific and adroit manufacturer of limericks. In a review he astutely wrote of 'the seriousness that is the foundation of humour' (*WWR*, 125), and his own quick-witted humour is neatly caught in his humorous recollection of an exchange between him and a warder, during his period of imprisonment in England, when required to dig in intractable, clayey soil:

> 'Tell me, why are you working so hard, Mr Williams?' one of the *screws* said to me when I was digging. 'Making the most of my opportunity.' 'How do you mean?' 'Well, you know, I'm a Welsh Nationalist. I'm getting hold of as much of England as I can with my spade and cutting it up into small pieces.' (*WWR*, 105)

Waldo refused to distinguish between those of his poems that addressed deeply serious issues and experiences, and those – and there were many of them – that were 'occasional' poems, intended purely for friends, neighbours and localities. These were compositions typical of the traditional 'bardd gwlad' or local poet who turned out verses suitable for his or her immediate occasions and surroundings. Such were a service to the local society, and a means of reinforcing the bonds of community – bonds to which Waldo, of course, attached the very greatest importance as they were local instances of that worldwide fellowship that was such a seminal aspect of his vision.

As several commentators have noted, this vision was distinctly apocalyptic in character. Indeed, in referring to the leaves of a tree, *Dail Pren*, the title of Waldo's only volume of poetry, was consciously alluding to a famous passage in Revelation 22: 2. This was hardly surprising given the fraught circumstances of Waldo's early years, that coincided with the First World War, a bloody catastrophe that another poet from his native area, T. E. Nicholas, a noted Welsh Communist as well as Nonconformist minister, addressed in a poem noteworthy for the millennial cast of its rhetoric. *Gweriniaeth a Rhyfel* (*Democracy and War*) was written in free verse – a form alien to Welsh tradition – and modelled on the poetry of Walt Whitman, a poet admired by Waldo's father and uncle who held some interest for Waldo himself. But Whitman's influence was mediated, and filtered, through the less daring poetics of Edward Carpenter, Whitman's English follower. Carpenter's *Towards Democracy* was a Socialist Utopian volume of free verse immensely popular with the intelligentsia of the British proletariat.[5]

An incidental, and no doubt accidental, feature of the title *Dail Pren* is its distant echo of *Leaves of Grass*. The Utopian aspirations of so many of those who were formative influences on Waldo's upbringing were firmly rooted in the prophecies in the Book of Revelation of the imminence of the Second Coming with its promise of a new order of social justice for the whole of humankind. Moreover, being a child of a new century regarded as marking the beginning of a new millennium, Waldo had been born into a world tense with both hope and dread and alive with anticipation. The very year of his birth – 1904 – marked the beginning of the last, and greatest, of the popular religious revivals that had swept through Wales periodically for the previous century. And under its charismatic leader, Evan Roberts, this revival soon took on a millennialist character. In an astute essay on three of the major Methodist hymn-writers of the eighteenth century, Waldo suggested that the fervent atmosphere of such a turbulent period of spiritual revolution found poetic expression in a poetic imagery fresh and unorthodox as that coined in Antiquity (*WWR*, 214). The imagery of his own great poems partakes of exactly such qualities.

In temper as well as in substance, then, Waldo's vision was in some ways the product of his age and background, just as his unshakeable integrity came with the territory, so to speak. It was an aspect of the shaping social and cultural environment of his childhood and youth, an aspect he came to view as already physically laid out in the ancient landscape itself. Later, he was to note appreciatively how the hills of Preseli had supplied him with backbone in every independent stand (they had been an 'asgwrn cefn i mi ym mhob annibyniaeth barn'), and to add that the locality had been a precious redoubt of the Welsh language, a language he loved so deeply not least because he believed it to be instinct with the universal human and humane values to which he was committed.

His special relationship with the language may have stemmed from his coming to it relatively late. He was already seven, and the product of an English-speaking home environment, when he moved to Mynachlog-ddu, and found himself pitched into a largely monoglot Welsh-speaking society. This experience may partly account for his lifelong association of the language with the communal solidarities he so highly valued. But equally significant may have been his delight at discovering in Welsh a world alternative to that he had known at home – a home that, owing to the serious mental breakdown of his father, had at one time been the location of nightmare for a small child. He took to the language as if he had discovered his very own tongue at last. It provided him with a voice for his unique selfhood, and was the facilitator of its development to a unique maturity, as becomes evident when one compares his few English-language compositions in adulthood with his output in Welsh. They are chalk and cheese; the former is never more than competent and invariably derivative, the latter electrifyingly original virtually from the very beginning.

The consequences of writing in a second language was a subject he naturally came to take some interest in (*WWR*, 96). In one interesting letter, he recalled that he had at one time been much drawn to the theory that a writer's exuberant awareness of the rich potential of a language might well be heightened by his or her sense of the ghostly presence of another – Dylan Thomas was one exemplar he specifically mentioned in this connection (*WWR*, 147). He went on, however, to add that he had become less certain of this theory after reading the works of Breton writers, whose use of a second language seemed to be minimalist rather than maximalist. Nevertheless, he remained very aware that the currently perilous condition of the Welsh language had greatly intensified the attachment of writers such as himself to it, and had augmented their awareness of its unique potentialities. This, he explained to a correspondent, had been partly the theme of his important poem 'Yr Heniaith', the old language (*WWR*, 103).

* * *

All his admirers and commentators have been unanimous in regarding 'Mewn Dau Gae' as his masterpiece and in valuing it as the supreme, magnetic expression of his governing vision.[6] It is a retrospective poem, the record of a riveting and transformative vision granted him in his adolescence, when news of the ghastly terrors of the Front, with its deadly maze of muddy trenches, was just beginning to permeate and permanently alter public consciousness during the First World War. The power he encounters is welcomed as 'dihangwr o'r byddinoedd', one who has escaped from the armies, and it is imagined as having dwelt in human bosoms throughout 'oesoedd y gwaed ar y gwellt, a thrwy'r goleuni y galar', the ages of blood on the grass when the light was shot through with mourning. In a revealing aside in one of his review essays, he remarked that an apocalyptic vision is 'hope's unreasonable leap above troubled circumstances' (*WWR*, 177) and 'Mewn Dau Gae' is a poem born of extreme duress. It therefore obviously has its redemptive aspects – there is specific mention early on of how this miraculous manifestation had come to

Waldo, steadily unrolling like a great sea-swell of light through a gap
between two ordinary fields, 'ar ôl imi holi'n hir yn y tir tywyll' (after
I had long been questioning in the dark land). And at the poem's
heart lies the birth of a calming assurance that the whole of life is
underpinned by a 'llonyddwch mawr' (a great stillness) out of which
everything proceeds and to which it will eventually return. The poem
could therefore be accounted what Walt Whitman called a 'retrieval
out of the night'.

'Ymroliai'r môr goleuni': the sea of light unrolled itself. 'Ym':
Waldo loved that little prefix, so much so that he warned against
overusing it (*WWR*, 115). In 'Mewn Dau Gae' especially, it proved
to be a crucial component of his vocabulary, since it is the means by
which a verb assumes reflexive form in Welsh. It therefore offered
him an indispensable means of conveying the universal, indwelling
spirit, the animating principle that lent the propulsion of distinc-
tively individuated life to all things while simultaneously linking them
together. This underlying community of deeply interconnected being
is further suggested textually through extensive exploitation of the
especially rich consonantal and assonantal resources that ensure the
Welsh language has interconnectedness embedded in its very structure
and woven into its texture. 'Daw'r herwr, daw'r heliwr, daw'r haliwr
i'r bwlch' he writes, sonically binding together 'prowler', 'huntsman'
and 'haulier' into a single multifaceted mystical entity.

Waldo believed such sound-patterning (to which he was particu-
larly attuned through his mastery of *cynghanedd*) was part of the
deep structure of the language, and so a 'given', much, he said, as
a scientist accepted the laws of Nature to be. He also believed that
systematic exploitation of this characteristic, as in Welsh strict-metre
poetry, facilitated the mobilisation of the unconscious mind, and
this alone, he added quoting Schelling, could ensure that language
would become enriched and enlivened, as happened in true poetry.
No wonder, then, that at the very heart of the poem Waldo enquires
of his language 'pwy sydd yn ymguddio [that reflexive prefix again]
ynghanol y geiriau?', 'who is it that is hiding itself in the midst of
the words?' It is a recognition that all words proceed from The Word,
the divine originating Logos, and sole author of the deep structure
of language, that alone guarantees that these arbitrary sounds will
harmonise into meaning by underwriting them all. The poem as a
whole is a supreme manifestation of the power of poetic form to
enrich us 'with intimations of life's unsearchable significance' (*WWR*,

156), while also tempering 'our activity with the ennobling calm of contemplation'.

It certainly seems as if language is astir with new life and has been resurrected from the torpor of its everyday (ab)use in 'Mewn Dau Gae', so rivetingly different is the phrasing, so spiritually pitch-perfect is it, and so calibrated to perfection. It perfectly conforms to Waldo's comment elsewhere on 'the living nerve of poetry that runs along the word' (*WWR*, 150). So we encounter 'chwibanwyr gloywbib' (the 'bright-piped whistlers' of the hedgerows), while 'callwib y cornicyllod' likewise captures the sudden flights of the 'wisefleeting plover'. To the attuned ear, the mature gorse clicks in the hedges and the armed vision catches sight of the multitudinous reeds dreaming the blue sky, while rejoicing that the whole of creation is moved to arise, to walk, and to dance in joy at the plenitude of its universe. Overhead the vagrant and peregrine clouds turn red in anticipation of the coming November storms, while human hearts leap up in spontaneous unison, released from their bondage in hard frost.

Epithets are multiplied to capture the quicksilver character of the unmoving mover of this ecstatic scene of extraordinary animation, invoked as 'the hunter of the meadow' (a figure that recurs), 'the archer' and 'the sudden clarifier'. This *primum mobile* is further reverently apostrophised as the witness of every witness, the memory of every memory, the life of every life, and quiet stiller of self's ceaseless turmoil. The poem is full of constructions such as this, phrasing to suggest a penetration to the essence of things. So, the escapee from armies (the 'deserters' of the First World War are also implicated in such phrasing) 'whistles its understanding, understanding until (a new, authentic) understanding is summoned into being': 'chwiban adnabod, adnabod nes bod adnabod'. The word 'adnabod' refers both to the action of an omnipotent Knower and also to the corresponding, and co-responding 'knowing' of the subject who is known. And the mysterious Being is hailed as 'twyllwr pob traha, rhedwr pob trywydd' (the deceiver of every act of oppression, the runner on every trail). Above all, it is apostrophised as 'the exiled king'. Such a multiplying of tropes is consistent with Waldo's remark that 'a piece of literature is a sequence of images and feelings' (*WWR*, 150).

That moving phrase, 'tawel ostegwr helbul hunan' draws our attention to one important feature of this poetry about which Ned Thomas has written very perceptively.[7] Waldo's wonder at the infinity of the universe's wonders, Thomas has noted, is matched by a corresponding awareness – unnerved and unnerving at times – of the unfathomable depths of the human mind. In its second stanza, 'Mewn Dau Gae' makes specific mention of this when it wonders 'Pwy sydd yn galw pan fo'r dychymyg yn dihuno?' 'who is it who calls when the imagination awakens?' At this point attention is pointedly drawn to the fact that the 'vision' being recollected was not only registered by the imagination but may even have emanated from it. Waldo was, after all, very well versed in Coleridge's celebrated theory of the Primary and Secondary Imagination, and he was a devout believer that the imagination was the divine spark in human nature. His protest against the Korean war, he explained, was because he saw in it evidence that 'the old customs and traditions of our civilization have sucked the imagination out of our brains, so that we cannot even conceive of different, alternative conditions' (*WWR*, 369). But Waldo was equally well informed about psychoanalytical models of the generative unconscious. Moreover, he had profound personal experience of psychological trauma and breakdown and therefore experience of the anguish of 'helbul hunan', which means the turmoil of self, or ego – the chronic churn that is its permanent condition. It is an important theme to which we shall eventually return.

What the poem undoubtedly and successfully conveys is the wholly disorientating nature of a revelation that entails a wrenchingly radical alteration of perspective. The experience of reading it is akin to that of entering a maze, the ancient emblem of life's riddle so beloved by Jorge Luis Borges. In places, grammatical structure becomes unclear, referends are unmoored, every new phrase jolts the mind out of the rut of the familiar, and prepositions cluster together to form a veritable thicket of conflicting directions: 'A thrwyddynt, rhyngddynt, amdanynt ymdaenai/ Awen yn codi o'r cudd, yn cydio'r cwbl' (and through them, between them, around and about them an inclusive generative power arose out of hiding, binding them all together). The cumulative effect conveyed by such an inspired 'sacred' rhetoric is one of overwhelmingly multidirectional perception.

And then there is the abrupt change of register as this transcendent experience of mystical union is likened to a mundane experience of human togetherness – Waldo's nostalgic memory of local farmers working in consort, pitchforking hay and building a haystack together. On every such occasion, Waldo wistfully recalls, the 'heliwr distaw', or quiet huntsman, was busily at work 'yn bwrw ei rwyd amdanom', casting his net around us – the image of the divine huntsman being an ancient, revered staple of Christian rhetoric. Most important of all is the conceiving of all these experiences as a manifestation of the return of the king from exile. The apocalyptic reference, as Waldo himself explained, is to a verse by AE: 'Sometimes when alone/ At the dark close of day,/ Men meet an outlawed majesty/ And hasten away' (*WWR*, 319).

Rowan Williams has effectively captured the mysterious power of this poem's conclusion in a version he carefully describes as 'from the Welsh' by way of admitting that his is a free translation:

> Think every day, under the sun,
> under these clouds, think every night of this,
> with every cell of your mind's branching swelling roots;
> but with the quiet, the same quiet, the steady breath,
> the steady gaze across the two fields, holding still
> the vision: fair fields full of folk;
> for it will come, dawn of his longed-for coming,
> and what a dawn to long for. He will arrive, the outlaw,
> the huntsman, the lost heir making good his claim
> for no-man's land, the exiled king
> is coming home one day; the rushes sweep aside
> to let him through.[8]

Williams's choice to translate 'Mewn Dau Gae', which is literally 'In Two Fields', as 'Between Two Fields' seems to suggest that he, too, understands the vision as emerging, so to speak, out of the cracks, or fractures, in the visible universe through which the underlying mystery seeps, and it neatly suggests a vision parallel to that of R. S. Thomas, an admirer of Waldo's, who is repeatedly drawn to the gap in the hedge.

In *Awakened Cosmos: The Mind of Classical Chinese Poetry*, a study of the poetry of the great eighth-century classical Chinese poet Tu Fu, David Hinton writes: 'Poetry is the Cosmos awakened to itself … poetry pares language down to a bare minimum, thereby opening it to silence. And it is there in the margins of silence that poetry finds its deepest possibilities – for there it can render dimensions of consciousness that are much more expansive than that identity-centre, primal dimensions of consciousness as the Cosmos awakened to itself.'[9] The influence of such poetry on the American poetry that derives from Imagism, from that of Ezra Pound to the Objectivism of George Oppen and the Zen Buddhism of Gary Snyder, is obvious enough. But such remarks also illuminate the poetry of Waldo Williams at its greatest, far removed in stylistics though it was from American Imagism. Because that concern of Tu Fu's that Hinton sensitively demonstrates in his analysis, of constant aliveness to the mysterious, anonymous generative energies of a 'Wild Cosmos' of which creation and destruction are but two interfused manifestations, is also adumbrated by different poetic means in 'Mewn Dau Gae' (in two fields). The titular division of lands into doubleness is swallowed up by the great, mysterious cloud of light that slowly erupts as if out of nowhere, obliterating all markers and objects as it rolls ever onwards. The 'bwlch' or gap through which it rolls signifies that rupture of ordinary consciousness that is both cause and effect of this miraculous revelation. Waldo suggestively quoted in a review Heidegger's remark that 'accepting the very essence of the Nothing [that is the source of all Being] is the very heart of experience' (*WWR*, 166), and 'Mewn Dau Gae' is a profound example of such acceptance.

As Hinton explains, the impression given by great Chinese paintings of mountains and rivers materialising out of an empty space suggested by large blank areas in the composition is a symbolic representation of life emerging mysteriously and unpredictably out of the void of unbeing. But while Waldo's poem seems to evoke a very similar vision, it is obviously in no way indebted to Taoist, or Zen Buddhist, thought. Instead, it originates in part in the specific aspects of Christian belief in which Waldo had been schooled by his father and his friends and that found late expression in his attraction to the quietism of Quakerism. And as for possible poetic exemplars, given Williams's intense and abiding interest from his undergraduate days onwards in Wordsworth's poetry, it is surely possible to discern in that mystical experience in 'Mewn Dau Gae' more than a suggestion of that famous moment of dawn revelation on Mount Snowdon that occurs in 'The Prelude':

> At distance not the third part of a mile
> Was a blue chasm, a fracture in the vapour,
> A deep and gloomy breathing-place through which
> Mounted the roar of waters, torrents, streams
> Innumerable, roaring with one voice.
> The universal spectacle throughout
> Was shaped for admiration and delight,

Granted in itself alone, but in that breach
Through which the homeless voice of waters rose,
That dark deep thoroughfare, had Nature lodged
The soul, the imagination of the whole.[10]

Wordsworth later felt that what had appeared to him that special morning was 'The perfect image of a mighty mind,/ Of one that feeds upon infinity,/ That is exalted by an under-presence/ The sense of God, or whatsoe'er is dim/ Or vast in its own being.'

It is, however, from the Book of Revelation that Waldo self-avowedly took the master explanatory narrative of his unique experience, as becomes abundantly clear when the poem moves towards its conclusion: 'Yr oedd rhyw ffynhonnau'n torri tua'r nefoedd/ Ac yn syrthio'n ôl fel dail pren.' 'There were some fountains breaking towards the heavens/ And falling back like the leaves of a tree.' The first verse of the last chapter of Revelation refers to 'the pure river of life, clear as crystal, proceeding out of the throne of God and of the Lamb', while the second refers to the tree of life growing on this river's banks, 'and the leaves of the tree were for the healing of nations'. So, then, at the very time of what Thomas Hardy (a poet well known to Waldo) had powerfully described as 'the breaking of nations', the young Waldo had a counterbalancing, corrective vision of a river and its tree that brought healing. This was the faith that was to sustain Waldo throughout his life, rooted in a trust in the underlying powers silently and everlastingly at work both within human beings and within the universe at large. And so, sustained by this hope, the divine source of which had for him been revealed through vision, Waldo could further assert that those two fields, ordinary yet numinous, had become transfigured under his very eyes into that 'fair field full of folk' famously evoked of old by William Langland in *Piers Ploughman*.

As such lines suggest, Waldo was deeply committed to models of spontaneous human cooperation consistent with a Christian Anarchism and communitarianism. He was also strongly averse to statism of whatever kind, whether capitalist or socialist in character, and regarded the power of centralised modern states as inevitably malign, whether they took the form of Nazi Germany, the Stalinist Soviet Union, or hegemonic Anglo-American capitalism. Some of his poems were written at the very time when President Eisenhower was railing against the 'military-industrial complex', a particularly sinister manifestation of what Tom Paulin was later to term 'the Minotaur' state, and one with which Allen Ginsberg was shortly to wrestle. He summarised the essence of his critique of contemporary society in an important passage from one of the two great statements in which he laid out the grounds of his belief, of his visionary poems, and of his political actions:

> It appears that we are dying, as well as living, in a Mass Society. Our sole escape is to realise that there is not really, and can never be, a human mass ... To some extent, there is a mass mind shaped in the temporal mould ... but there is continuum in which we ourselves merge. The true concretion of society is not the adhesion of the individual to a vague entity that includes all; nor is it a community of interest ... It is the personal, the sum total of the ties that bind us each to each, and this good neighbourhood may be realised by the imagination in the proximity of opportunity that is not spatial. (*WWR*, 268)

He deplored the malign power of 'the Herd mind', adding that 'There is no prison like hypnosis.' And his passionate attachment to the 'good neighbourhood' of the Preseli was greatly intensified by the government reserving many acres after the war to create the tank range at Castle Martin. That, for Waldo, was a gratuitous act of blasphemy.

With a glance at Wallace Stevens, Seamus Heaney has written that 'the nobility of poetry is the imagination pressing back against the pressure of reality'.[11] He had in mind the heroic stand against Stalinism made by the likes of Mandelstam and Akhmatova, by Pasternak and Solzhenitsyn. And he made reference to Simone Weil's remark, made during the Nazi occupation of her native France: 'Obedience to the force of gravity is the greatest sin.' Obviously, by gravity she did not mean the physical force that binds us to this earth. Gravity, for her, was a metaphor for the force of evil oppressive circumstances that all decent human beings were under moral obligation to resist. What poetry does, in the opinion of both Stevens and Weil, is to demonstrate – indeed to insist – not only that a different order of reality is possible but that it is humanly necessary. That reality is a product of the authentic human imagination, rather than the corrupted imagination that has been seduced into obedient conformity with the powers that be. And Waldo inherited from the great English Romantics the belief that this imagination, autochthonous and uncorrupted, was a divine gift inhering in every human being. This meant that his social vision and his religious vision were at root one and the same. 'I believe', he explained, consciously echoing Blake, 'all men to be brothers and to be humble partakers of the Divine Imagination that brought forth the world' (*WWR*, 269).

Turn to almost any page of poetry by any one of the great English Romantics and you will find a variant of Coleridge's lines in 'The Aeolian Harp':

> O! the one Life within us and abroad,
> Which meets all motion and becomes its soul,
> A light in sound, a sound-like power in light,
> Rhythm in all thought, and joyance everywhere –
> Methinks, should have been impossible
> Not to love all things in a world so filled:[12]

But often the link is not made by modern readers, with their set apolitical notions of 'Romanticism', between this belief and the faith shared by most of the great English Romantic poets that the liberation of the human world from the grip of oppression and tyranny was therefore assured in the long term, because that 'one spirit' that was both 'within us' and 'abroad' guaranteed it by making love the 'kelson' (as Walt Whitman was to put it) of creation.

And Whitman reminds us of the important link between English Romanticism and the Romanticism that took a new and distinctly American form in the work of the Transcendentalist Ralph Waldo Emerson and his intellectual followers.[13] If 'Mewn Dau Gae' clearly bears the marks of Waldo's enthusiasm for English Romantic poetry, it also reveals, with equal clarity, the intimate parallels between his vision and that of the great American after whom he had been named. In his celebrated essay on Nature, Emerson alluded to the old division between *natura naturata* and *natura naturans*, giving precedence to the latter, which he memorably described as 'the quick cause' that 'publishes itself in creatures, reaching from particles and spicula, through transformation on transformation to the highest symmetries'.[14] Its *fons et origo* was, of course, the unmoving mover, so that 'motion or change, and identity or rest, are the first and second secrets of nature: Motion and Rest'. So, too, Waldo comprehends that underlying the swift flight of the 'cornicyllod' (plover) and the bright chatter of the myriad hedgerow 'whistlers' lies 'y llonyddwch mawr' (the great stillness).

'The world is mind precipitated', Emerson pithily stated. 'The Universe', he explained in 'The Poet', 'is the externisation of the soul', and in such visionary and ecstatic moments as Waldo recorded in 'Mewn Dau Gae', 'we find ourselves', declared Emerson (*E*, 220), 'in a holy place, and should go warily and reverently. We stand before the secret of the world, there where Being passes into Appearance, and Unity into Variety.' For the American, the Poet is the one gifted with the ability to lift mankind above the lethargy of the commonplace, limited as it is to registering only the customary and imprisoned as it is within a merely utilitarian and material world. The Poet possesses the liberating capacity to refresh humanity's jaded demotic and reductionist vocabulary. In the Poet's hands, the language of the commonplace is revealed to be 'fossil poetry' and his or her 'genius is the activity which repairs the decay of things' (*E*, 225). And so, declares Emerson, 'if the imagination intoxicates the poet, it is not inactive in other men. The metamorphosis excites in the beholder an emotion of joy. The use of symbols has a certain power of emancipation and exhilaration for all men ... Men have really got a new sense, and found within their world another world, or nest of worlds' (*E*, 228). When Waldo therefore enquires 'Pwy sydd yn galw pan fo'r dychymyg yn dihuno' (who is it who calls when the imagination awakens) he may possibly have in mind such passages from Emerson, that conclude with the confident assertion that poets 'are free, and they make free'. Interestingly enough Emerson actually attributes this formulation to 'the ancient British bards [who] had for the title of their order, "Those who are free through the world"' (*E*, 230). This much, and more, we can find in Emerson's writings that are directly relevant to our understanding of Waldo's poetry.

* * *

As we have seen, in 'Mewn Dau Gae' Waldo paid reverend tribute to a divine power he had experienced as 'Tawel ostegwr helbul hunan', the quiet calmer of the turmoil of self. It is a phrase that not only invites glossing, but seems positively to demand it, particularly in light of the revelations that first came to light a few years ago in Alan Llwyd's definitive biography (*CWW*, 44). For the first time, Llwyd paid detailed attention, strongly supported by new original evidence, to the psychic trauma by which Waldo had been haunted throughout his life, the origins of which could clearly be traced back to his earliest years.

It dated from the nightmare childhood experiences that he had confided, with evident reluctance, only to his closest intimates, at the same time confessing their deeply painful and damaging formative influence on his development. When he was about four, he awoke in the dead of night to find he was being glared at by his father's mad eyes just a foot or so away from his face. Hauled from sleep, he was saved from a severe beating for some insanely imaginary transgression only by his mother's intercession. It was the beginning of some three years of domestic hell, during which the little boy not only felt vulnerable but fearful that his father would carry out his threat to abandon the family and leave home. In later life, Waldo confessed he had felt guilt at actually wishing his father *would* leave. He heartbreakingly reports how he and his siblings would tiptoe to their parents' bedroom door and eavesdrop in an attempt to overhear whether there was any chance of domestic peace. He also spent time hanging about the house, just in case he was needed to defend his mother from a physical assault – which, as it happened, never actually came. Gradually, his father recovered his mental balance, and in his later years imbued his son with those values that we have already experienced as operative in his poetry.

Not surprisingly, when his parents passed away some thirty years later, Waldo suffered a major mental breakdown, and underwent extended treatment as an outpatient in Whitchurch mental hospital, Cardiff. There, one of his doctors was actually moved to tears by Waldo's recollections of his traumatic childhood, describing his experiences during that seminal period as 'sheer hell' (*CWW*, 166). Unsurprisingly, the mature Waldo came to realise that an image of God modelled on an image of Him as a loving Heavenly Father was wholly antipathetic to him, admitting that his own childhood experiences had made it forever impossible to imagine God in such terms – interestingly, R. S. Thomas was to admit the same thing, recognising that his father's early deafness had rendered it impossible to form any warm, intimate, relationship with him. As for Calvinism, Waldo pithily remarked that however impressive the grand rational system of theology underpinning it, in the end it was a vain attempt, like trying to wrap a ball in a square piece of paper. This was because it sought to capture a spiritual reality of a totally different kind and order to any the human reason is capable of comprehending (*WWR*, 215). He was equally sceptical of Christian belief in the Resurrection of the body. He found the finality of life evident in a dead body terribly compelling, he explained. The only God in whom he could place his faith was his own God, an 'alternative' God, so to speak, who made Himself known by private, unorthodox, secret, restorative ways and who addressed Himself uniquely and directly to the needs of the individual soul. This, then, was the deeply disturbed ground from which Waldo's mysticism duly grew.

The implications and ramifications of this for Waldo's development as person, as poet, and as believer, seem to be profound. No wonder that he harboured throughout his life a visceral horror of violence that found expression in his crusading pacificism; or that those terrible years of feeling totally helpless resulted in the formation of a personality that was almost pathologically averse to being controlled by others and fiercely determined to defend its individual liberty. Even his great friend D. J. Williams found him to be wilfully principled and exasperatingly obstinate. No wonder, either, that having experienced his mother as his sole protector during those terrible years, he idealised the female principle; or that, having had his own childhood development violently arrested, he retained, in the eyes of his acquaintances, a kind of wistfully childlike quality in his adulthood and that he enjoyed a naturally intimate relationship with small children. Recent research at Harvard into acute cases such as this have interestingly concluded that early trauma of this kind can actually result in the neurological system of the young victim being permanently rewired, so that throughout life such a child suffers a heightened sensitivity to its surroundings – the nervous system standing ever, as it were, on red alert. There seems to be clear evidence that as a person the nervously restless Waldo suffered from this hyper-sensitivity which, paradoxically, actually benefited him as a poet.

And doesn't the early dread of domestic rupture, and his own imagined responsibility for it, a dread that haunted Waldo's early childhood like a dark passion, underlie that rapturous envisioning of 'cyfannu' – integration, healing, wholeness, reconciliation – that is seminal to his poetry? And then there is that aspect of his case on which the psychiatrists who treated him at Whitchurch primarily concentrated: namely his wholly groundless sense of personal guilt, Kafkaesque in character because its cause could never be pinned down. His father, in his mad moods, had accused the little boy of some unspecified 'crime', which he vaguely described as a failure to take responsibility. No wonder that Waldo spent so much of his life desperately making amends for this by willing himself to take personal responsibility – for the Second World War; for the Korean war; for the plight of the Welsh language, for the condition of Wales; for the state of humanity. So prostrated by guilt was he when he discovered that a fraction of the taxes he paid went towards supporting the armed forces during the Korean war, that he could not even bring himself to leave the house for some considerable time because of the intense personal shame he felt. He could not bear to face his neighbours.

The Whitchurch psychiatrists diagnosed Waldo as suffering from an overwhelming, neurotic, Anxiety. Never before in their extensive clinical experience, Waldo ruefully and reluctantly confided to his closest friend, had they come across such an extreme and chronic case of general, unfocused Anxiety as this (*CWW*, 46). And it was that Anxiety, I would venture to suggest, that was his dark Awen, or Muse, and that sought discharge in his visionary poetry. But in thus tracing the psychic roots of some of the leading traits of Waldo's personality and poetry, I do not in any way mean to undermine his spiritual and poetic genius or to impugn either the validity or the spiritual authority of his luminous vision. I mean simply to draw attention to the dark, turbulent sources of the energy that powered all that light and the huge psychic turbines, so to speak, that drove his poetic imagination. Moreover, I would suggest that it is his poetry's periodic readiness to recognise the presence of that darkness that actually underwrites the vision that is affirmed; it vouches for its authority. We are persuaded that Waldo's poetic vision of a world of human mutuality and of divinely inspired creativity, carries weight against all the prevailing appearances to the contrary, because it has been tested against his full recognition of the malign power of the world as it normally exists, and as he himself had known it to be as a child.

Waldo addressed his own darkest experience seemingly 'in passing' in a letter he wrote in 1957. There he mentioned having read Gilbert Ryle's *The Concept of Mind* and of having taking exception to his dismissal of the possibility of any psychological dualism. What had occurred to Waldo as a counter-example, he explained, was a situation (he deliberately treated it as if it were a case with no personal application) in which someone experienced a mental breakdown explicable in terms of a chemical disorder in the brain, and became deeply depressed in consequence. What if such a person subsequently succeeded in recovering his mental equilibrium, Waldo enquired? Did accounting for such an eventuality not inescapably involve the recognition of a duality that at first seemed to involve two experiences that were necessarily totally irreconcilable because they were fundamentally unlike in kind but that turned out in actuality to be a duality that as lived reality were undeniably interlinked (*WWR*, 323)? The implications for his own situation are unmistakeable, although commentators have appeared to overlook them completely. Waldo's conclusion was that the example that had occurred to him was proof that nature could serve spirit, in spite of the two being apparently condemned to be eternal strangers to each other: this in turn was for him proof of the existence of God.

There are several poems written in the immediate aftermath of the Second World War in which Waldo registers the darkness he has known without ever managing – or even trying – to turn it into light. These are his poems of desolation – the equivalent of the great Dejection Odes of the major English Romantic poets whom he so loved. The grimmest, because the most unsparing, of these is 'Y Plant Marw', 'The Dead Children', a poem that frankly confesses its inability to make poetry out of atrocity (*C*, 311). Then there is the first section of 'O Bridd', 'O Earth', a savagely Darwinian account of both the natural world and of human life (*C*, 314–15). As for the second section, it is a desperate *cri de coeur* for escape to the remotest islands of Kerguelen. They are seen as free of the contagion Waldo had, in 'O Bridd', associated with the earth, pristine in their human-less wastes of annihilating iciness. 'Cân Bom', 'the Song of the Bomb', is Waldo's equivalent of a song from Ted Hughes's nihilistic sequence of 'Crow' poems (*C*, 316). A parody of a hymn, it ends in an orgiastic conflation of the human drive to power and to death, as the atom bomb exults in the elimination of the whole human race: 'Mi a'u hysgubaf i dân/ Ecstasi angau' (I will sweep them into the fire of Deathly ecstasy).

A much more complex case is 'Cwmwl Haf', 'Summer Cloud' (*C*, 275–6). It is a great poem whose meaning directly relates to the period in Waldo's young development that it summons to mind. He is recalling an experience that occurred when he was a seven-year-old boy, newly arrived in Mynachlog-ddu, immediately following those dreadful years blighted by his father's mental breakdown. It was therefore a time when the natural world seemed newly blessed, when the stallion's prancing hooves drummed a psalm of praise and the stately cattle ceremonially paraded homewards, their full udders parting the reeds, their horns pillars sustaining the sky. Thus far, the poem might be said to be the Welsh equivalent of Dylan Thomas's 'Fern Hill'.

Waldo movingly sums up the time as one when 'Ym mhob tywydd diogelwch oedd y tywydd,/ Caredigrwydd oedd y tŷ'. Safety – at long last, following long danger – was permanently abroad, present in all weathers; and home, so long the site of unpredictable anger, had at last become a haven of kindness.

But then, the terrible anxiety that had haunted the three previous crucial years of his young life resurfaces, as it was to do throughout his life. It comes suddenly in the form of a summer cloud that, in enveloping him, steadily obliterates all landmarks. It brings with it the desolating terror of complete helplessness, violating the integrity of the fledgling boy's vulnerable personal identity. And it is surely no accident that that cloud is explicitly gendered male – it is the 'spirit of a great giant', that appears totally unexpectedly, just as his seemingly omnipotent father's eruptions had been wholly unpredictable. And just as it is the male principle that is here the destructive force, it is the female principle that is invoked at the poem's end as the healing force. Critics have made much of the return to the house at the end of 'Cwmwl Haf', while failing to notice that the house, the home, is here very specifically – indeed one might say exclusively – the mother's domain. 'Ac o, cyn cyrraedd drws y cefn,/ Sŵn adeiladu daear newydd a nefoedd newydd/ Ar lawr y gegin oedd clocs mam i mi.' 'And oh, before even reaching the back door,/ the sound of the building of a new heaven and a new earth/ reached me in the sound of my mother's clogs on the kitchen floor.' The sense of relief captured in those lines – the relief of having discovered refuge – is palpable, and deeply moving. It is also worth noting that what Waldo remembers is the sound, and implicitly the rhythm, of those clogs – they are beating the time, or measure, so to speak, of his mature poetry.

But the reference to the Book of Revelation transposes the poem into an entirely different key, retrospectively rendering it a poem about a religious experience. In other words, Waldo has drawn upon his memory of early trauma in order to convey a religious sense of the unfathomable, totally unpredictable, visitations of the spirit. The poem shows it manifesting itself in two phases and in two different ways. First, it descends like a 'summer cloud' of unknowing, annihilating selfhood, obliterating all the markers commonly used for orientation, and severing all the crucial, self-confirmatory links that proceed from our customary constant interaction with the external world of sense. It is therefore overwhelmingly disorientating. The second phase involves the recovery of aliveness to self and world but now on an entirely different, more exalted plane, since the ordinary is now instinct with extraordinariness, and the mundane has assumed a numinous significance. The whole process has sound precedent in Christian mystical experience, but it also strikingly resembles that Taoist experience of illumination already referred to.

Such a summary does scant justice, however, to the remarkable strangeness of Waldo's poem that from its very beginning carefully avoids easy interpretation by denying access to any reliable textual markers of place, time or occasion. From the beginning we are mysteriously stranded in a zone of timelessness, which is no-time and all-time, somewhere and nowhere. This Waldo calmly identifies as 'hen le a tharddle araf amser', the old place and slow source of time 'yn yr ogof sy'n oleuach na'r awyr/ Ac yn y tŷ sydd allan ymhob tywydd' (in the cave that is brighter than air,/ and in the house that is out in all weathers). What are we to make of that as a location marker? It is irreducibly enigmatic, while also inexhaustibly evocative. What it seems to gesture towards is an ancient, primal sacred space and sacred time.

'Cwmwl Haf' actually opens with Waldo noticing the names of houses near Lyneham, in Wiltshire, where he spent several years teaching school during the Second World War. He became very aware of living in a heartland of ancient settlement of the British Isles, and began to take an active interest in anthropology. The house names, he reflects, are at once markers of specificity and purely generic in character – names of somewhere but from nowhere. The reflection becomes a springboard into a sense of time as a single, ancient continuum. And so the poem opens at a location geographically distant from that in which it ends, and in a period of time separated by many decades from that it eventually brings to mind. And it is only after such a richly indeterminate opening – he never actually makes clear he is writing from and about Wiltshire – that Waldo begins to supply those details of locality that we have already considered. He thus chooses eventually to 'ground' the poem in his early Mynachlog-ddu experience, a grounding that pointedly includes a mention of the birthing of language that is a crucial distinguishing marker of the human species, that makes even the most ordinary person a 'lord of language'. Folded in such a phrase is both Waldo's special, privileged awareness of being a poet and more than a hint that the common gift of language breeds in human beings an arrogant sense of superiority to all other species and an assumption that the whole of creation is subject to human will. The descent of the cloud puts paid to all such certainties, plunging the boy-come-poet into a 'byd oedd yn rhy fud i fyw', a world that was too dumb to exist and turning him pygmy by making reeds loom large as trees through the mist and stranding him helplessly 'mewn byd sy'n rhy fawr i fod', 'in a world too huge to exist'.

The climax of the crisis takes the form of a crisis of identity, and the bewildered question 'Pwy wyf i' (Who am I), which is thrice repeated, except that at the last it takes the significantly modified form of 'Pwy yw hwn' (Who is this), as Waldo finds he has become 'other' to his very self, radically self-estranged. And with this question comes the corollary recognition of him being terrified of thinking about himself, 'arswydo meddwl amdanaf fy hun'. Particularly arresting because of its violation of grammar, the violent wrenching of it out of joint, is the bewildered exclamation 'Nid oes acw. Dim ond fi yw yma': 'There is no there. Me alone is here'. Recovery, bringing with it a return of/to self and a restoration of the cardinal points necessary for reorientation, comes finally in the form of that homeward journey 'through the bruise' as he puts it. It ends with his tentative lifting of the reassuringly solid latch of the gate and hearing, with huge relief, the familiar sounds of his mother clattering around the kitchen.

'Cwmwl Haf' brings to the fore one important paradoxical feature of Waldo's life and work. On the one hand, he was very deeply devoted to his home 'bro', or locality, the Preseli uplands of North Pembrokeshire to which he addressed several lovely poems. On the other hand, he remained throughout his life something of a 'displaced person', never fully settling in any one place, and appearing to be very much a peregrine soul. These aspects could be said to be the products of the two phases of his early life. His move to Mynachlog-ddu clearly enabled the birth of a new sense of locatedness underpinned by a newly harmonious home environment. But prior to that, and ineradicable, had been that traumatic experience of psychic homelessness consequent upon his father's mental breakdown. This is reflected in several of his major poems, where it is astonishingly transmuted, as in 'Cwmwl Haf', into spiritual insight, and it brings to mind Elizabeth Bishop's poetry, which likewise derived from an irreversible psychic ejection from 'home' at an early age. In her case, too, it was consequent upon mental breakdown – that of her mother, to which the little girl was a paralysed witness. As is apparent in the poems, Bishop was left with a horribly precocious awareness of the impermanence and inauthenticity of what passed for reassuringly trustworthy 'normality', as for all the human arrangements and institutions that sustained it and were sustained by it. Throughout her life she remained at once intrigued and mystified by every manifestation of 'home' that she came across; jealous yet sceptical of it. She felt at home only when experiencing and registering the strangeness of an essentially non-human existence – a chilling strangeness she assumed to be purely secular in character, but which Waldo always rendered in religious terms, albeit terms that also acknowledged its non-human nature. Hers was a materialist's mysticism, his that of a Christian Romantic.

* * *

There is yet one more ingredient to be added to the mix when considering 'Cwmwl Haf'. The poem was completed at war's end when Waldo, still based in Lyneham, was becoming aware of the Labour government's intention to requisition large areas of the Preseli Hills for purposes of military training. As many commentators have noted, most particularly Ned Thomas in his brief masterly study, this event proved to be one that prompted Waldo thereafter to add a political edge to his natural patriotism by aligning himself with Plaid Cymru, the National Party of Wales. One result was committed political activism; another was the appearance, in due course, of a number of powerful poems addressing the cultural crisis faced by Wales in general, and the Preseli area in particular. Both were threatened by an increasingly assertive, and increasingly centralised, Anglo-British state – the Minotaur that was now ominously looming on Waldo's very doorstep. It was a crisis that was for him simultaneously cultural and spiritual, as it involved a malign standardisation that resulted in the devaluation, and hence degradation, of all that was distinctive and individual.

In 'Daw'r Wennol yn ôl i'w nyth', this vision of remorselessly encroaching disaster took the form of bitter elegy, its utterance constrained within the edgy, clipped form of the cywydd metre and etched in biting *cynghanedd* – both instancing, of course, the very best of the rich and ancient cultural tradition that was being eroded (*C*, 251–2). And the tone of the poem is appropriately communal and ageless in timbre, voicing as it does a folk wisdom rather than the protest of a single, isolated voice. The essence of this loss is pithily summarised near the beginning, where Waldo invokes the 'teulu a dry o dref,/ Pobl yn gado bro eu bryd,/ Tyf hi'n wyllt a hwy'n alltud', the family turned out of town, people abandoning their heartland, leaving all to decline into wilderness as they head into exile. For Waldo, it is the end of a special culture of deeply civil and humane community. There are unmistakeable Biblical echoes, reminiscences of the ancient people of God forced to hang their harps on the alien willows. What adds a further frisson is the fact that all this is happening in preparation, in effect, for another war – 'I'w hathrofa daeth rhyfel', Waldo writes: 'to their academy war came'. The allusion overall is to the seizure in 1939 of 6,000 acres of prime grazing land around Castle Martin in west Pembrokeshire by the Ministry of War in order to create a tank-training range. But the poem both begins and ends with the swallow's seasonal return to its nest, even as the people leave their ancestors' traditional home. It is Waldo's brave, but clearly futile, placement of faith in the seasonal renewal of nature, reassuringly immune as that is to the vagaries of the human condition, and thus a guarantee of unbroken continuity at the deepest level of creation.

Waldo's spiritual beliefs therefore had clear cultural, social, and indeed political, ramifications. He put his mystical convictions to work, so to speak, through various kinds of non-violent direct action: civil disobedience, imprisonment on grounds of conscience, and campaigning for Plaid Cymru that even led eventually to his standing for Parliament in the party's name. His was a vision that placed the very highest value on interpersonal relations from the most intimate to the communal. These were for him all sites of sacred experience, and one of his most compelling poems, and undoubtedly his strangest, is an epithalamion, a celebration of his excruciatingly brief, but transfiguringly happy, marriage to his wife Linda. Too rapt and enraptured even to announce itself with a title, it is known to us only by its opening phrase, 'Oherwydd ein dyfod', 'Because of our coming', and reading it is a challenge: we are left to decipher a secret, deeply cryptic lover's code, and one that has moreover been written in shorthand (*C*, 265). One has an overwhelming sense of significance, of bewilderingly multiform and ambiguous signification; of statements that seem to operate simultaneously on an erotic and a spiritual level, as in the Song of Solomon. In modern critical jargon, it might be described as a masterpiece of overdetermination.

It is a poem steeped in a wondering gratitude, and textually it all hinges on, or is made possible by, that remarkable opening: 'Oherwydd ein dyfod'. One would have expected the phrase 'we came to the quiet chamber' but instead what we have is 'It is *because of*

our coming to the quiet chamber'. 'Ein dyfod', 'our coming': it is a
potent formulation because 'dyfod', 'coming', is a fusion of verb and
noun into one. It therefore infuses an established state – in this case
the union of Waldo and Linda – with the dynamism of an unspent
force, a continuing process. This peculiar formulation emphasises that
their union has, so to speak, come to stay; that their marriage is still a
work, or rather an achievement, in progress. It perfectly registers the
risky, ongoing commitment to mutuality that any actively meaningful
marriage never ceases to be.

The magic of what follows – and the poem goes on to radiate a
diffuse sensual and sexual charge unparalleled in Waldo's writing –
stems wholly from that first, fateful, riskily intimate and vulnerable
step. The step the lovers took of setting up house together; that is,
of committing themselves utterly and irrevocably to each other. It
was that ongoing step that took them out of time into the 'timeless
cave' and provided them with passage out into the miraculous fertil-
ity and paradisal bounty of cosmic life. It is, of course, the paradise
of Afallon, the English Avilion that in its Welsh form means 'a place
of apples'. Hence the poem's mention of 'afalau perllannoedd', the
apples of orchards. The poem looks back to wartime, when Waldo
was newly married, and Linda bought a pair of blackout curtains
so thick that he complained they turned the house into a cave. In
the reference to 'yr ogof ddiamser' (the timeless cave), a mundane
domestic actuality is magically transmuted retrospectively – years
after Linda's early death – into a kind of nurturing womb of all exist-
ence, a pure potency. And of course under blackout conditions dark
does assume a new potency, even as light takes on a quality both
precious and perilous.

Linda here becomes Beatrice to Waldo's Dante, his guide and
stay 'trwy'r wythïen dywyll/ I oleuni yr aelwydydd', through the dark
vein, or seam, to the light of hearths. Such a vein suggests the coal
seams of the south Wales from which Linda had come that kindled so
readily into light on hearths across the whole world. Waldo describes
them as branching out into the small twigs of roots, as if thinking
of those underground coal seams mingling with the roots of trees.
But there are also in these images ('vein' obviously brings a human
blood vessel to mind) overtones of sexual congress, a mingling that
reaches down to the most minor of the branching roots of new life,
bringing it to light on domestic hearths. The fact that the whole,
mysterious transfiguring process is dependent on the translation of

dark into light is wonderfully captured, in the Welsh, by the complex interplay of sounds, just like flame racing along a fuse, or the chain reaction of a nuclear explosion. 'Wu … wi … iw … eu … ai … ŵy …' As for the incomplete, and therefore indeterminate structure of the syntax that has baffled so many critics, it seems to me to capture perfectly the sensation of entering a mysterious, disorientating realm of experience totally beyond the familiar, reassuring markers of ordinary, time-bound life. The poetry roams that gloaming realm of passion so brilliantly rendered in paint by Titian in such late paintings as the *Death of Actaeon* and in words in the Ovidian poetry of the Elizabethan age.

The second stanza sees the poem now settle down into a more steady, assured and luminous utterance. Here, a single kiss radiates outwards to touch every star in the deeps of the heavenly archipelago, two breasts nurture the whole earth and two arms protectively embrace the whole locality. And all this, Waldo adds, because of 'our coming to the solid house whose stillness steadies and sustains the joy of our love'. It is a place, and a condition, that allows the whole world to enter that joyous deep opened up in the echoing footsteps of his darling golden girl. It is a love poem of ravishing beauty and of penetrating grief and loss, written as it was after Waldo had lost that love of his life to TB, a mere two years after their wedding. In its way, therefore, it is his Orphic search for his lost Eurydice. There are indeed phrases of mythic resonance, as, for example, when the magical power of Linda's footsteps seems to lead us into the realm of Olwen, in whose wake white clover spontaneously sprang. And it is a revelation of the special, precious place of (an alas vulnerable) love in Waldo's spiritual vision. It blends echoes of ancient fertility myths and rites associating sexual union with the blossoming of life both in nature and in the whole cosmos with a Christian faith in the bounteous benefits that abundantly flow from the sacrament of marriage. The poem's final word is 'eurferch' (goldengirl), a composite term that deliberately echoes the great love poetry of such late medieval masters of strict-metre poetry as Tudur Aled.

This vital process of transmutation of dark into light is again what powers 'Eirlysiau' (Snowdrops), another of Waldo's major poems, which opens on an ecstatic note of acclamation:

> Gwyn, gwyn
> Yw'r gynnar dorf ar lawr y glyn.

> O'r ddaear ddu y nef a'u myn.
> Golau a'u pryn o'u gwely pridd
> A rhed y gwanwyn yn ddi-glwy
> O'u cyffro hwy uwch cae a ffridd. (*C*, 280)

[White, white, is the early host on the valley floor. Heaven has commanded their eruption from the dark earth. Light has redeemed them from their earthy bed, and spring races uninjured from their stirring above field and meadow.]

Black earth is peremptorily commanded here by heaven to yield up the white flowers that signify innocence and purity. The process is an act of redemptive energy – a striking instance of Waldo's obsession with the effortful challenge of turning darkness into light (one recalls that transition of his from the nightmare of early childhood to idyll at Mynachlog-ddu): what could be deathly is forced to become life-bearing. It is this initial, vital, act of transmutation that makes the riot of consequent life that is spring actually possible. The whole process is steeped in the Christian language – the initial 'buying' of salvation, the price paid to enable resurrection into the fullness of redeemed life – except that Waldo deliberately refrains from making that connection with a Calvinist orthodoxy which he viscerally disliked. It is light, and not Christ, that accomplishes this deliverance, effecting a resurrection from the dead, and makes the riot of unscarred life in spring possible. Waldo was clearly no Calvinist, despite Bobi Jones's elaborate attempts to demonstrate that he was, albeit against his rational instincts. As already noted, he commented that trying to reduce the mystery of Being to the measure of reason, however august and imperious that might be as in the case of the systematising Calvinist fathers, was like trying to use a square piece of paper to wrap a ball. His poem is a joyously awed celebration of the sheer, unbridled *recklessness* of a 'God' who risks all, and so to speak risks *His* all on a beauty – and an innocence – as seemingly frail as that of the pure-white snowdrops, backing that beauty to be tough enough to 'godde cur', as the poem later has it; that is to bear all blows of adversity. This, indeed, is true, unparalleled 'courage', as it also exclaims.

Waldo would seem partly to have in mind that other, superior, kind of 'toughness' that a convinced, gentle pacificism, for example, called for. It was in these terms that he movingly commemorated his mother and father in 'Y Tangnefeddwyr' (The Peace-makers). The allusion both there and in 'Eirlysiau', is to the Beatitudes. In Welsh these are

called 'Y Gwynfydau', an abbreviation of their distinctive opening
formula, which in English reads as 'Blessed are they' but in Welsh
reads as 'Gwyn eu byd'. Literally, this is 'White is their world', but of
course 'White' here is a synonym for 'blessed', or 'innocent', or 'pure',
or 'unblemished', and carries in addition overtones of 'beloved'. And
all these layers of the word's meaning are fully and richly explored,
to powerful spiritual effect, in 'Eirlysiau'.

In the final stanza, the snowdrops sing out the purity of what
is called 'the primal whiteness' – a phrase reminiscent of Vernon
Watkins's 'Music of Colours'. Tony Conran's translation conveys
very well the vision of the fracturing of that whiteness to produce
the fiery plenitude of colour as summer blossoms: 'Pure, pure/ Is
their song, the primal white./ When the shards of it scatter/ Like a
myriad fires they'll colour the fields'.[15] Waldo knew his Shelley, and
no doubt was recalling the latter's famous Neo-Platonic phrase about
how 'life, like a dome of many-coloured glass,/ Stains the white radi-
ance of eternity'. In the Welsh, this process is imaged in terms of
the dismemberment of the snowdrop's petals as it ages. And as the
conclusion of the poem notes, for Waldo this whole process is the
work of a Poet God. The trope is worth exploring, because if this
poem reveals to us much about Waldo's conception of God, it also
reveals his seminal belief in the sacred work of the poet. So we can
safely conclude that for Waldo a poet is similarly reckless in the faith
he invests in his power to turn dark into light, similarly forceful in
the uncompromising demands he makes of recalcitrant reality, and
similarly toughly resilient, so that his poetry is capable, to paraphrase
Seamus Heaney, of invincible fidelity to its own alternative reality in
the face of the most brutal actuality.

'Eirlysiau' is therefore about the way in which purity, innocence,
goodness, gentleness, kindness, lovingness – all qualities associated
in Welsh with that word 'gwyn', which also means 'beloved' or 'dear'
– has its own, 'other', power, a power rooted in sacred, rather than
secular, realities. It is therefore a power of an entirely different order
and is such not only because of what it has to encounter, to resist,
to overcome, but also because, by virtue of its 'other', 'otherworldly'
nature, it is inevitably a violation of the established order of things: of
customary norms, conventions, habits, and accepted practices. It is a
violation that can be experienced as violence. It is, as the saying goes,
a 'scandal', an affront, an assault even on the ordinary decencies of
everyday life. It is disturbing, transgressive, disruptive. At the end of

a 1939 letter on the subject of 'Studies in Fascism', Waldo acerbically
pointed out that 'pacifists are people of very aggressive ideas, and
always have been. In fact, the whole case against the early Christians
was put by a Roman statesman who said that their pacifism must not
be allowed to disrupt the Roman Empire' (*WWR*, 282).
   Identifying such a benign, stalwart, version of a potentially
destructive power, and identifying with it, was of the first import-
ance to Waldo, not least because he could not have been unaware of
the dark energy lurking in his own nature, consequent upon those
terrible early years of living in a domestic environment instinct with
violence. Indeed, during the time he taught in the Llŷn peninsula he
was nicknamed 'Waldio' (roughly 'Clouter') by his pupils, because
he could occasionally resort, when provoked in the extreme, to such
actions as banging a child's head in the lid of a desk. As an adult, he
clearly came to realise that such an impulse could never be completely
eliminated, only controlled and transformed into positive, creative
issue. An unreconstructed, crude Freudian would doubtless claim that
all of Waldo's religious poetry is at bottom a 'sublimation' of that
primal violence, and plenty of evidence could readily be found to sup-
port such an assertion. That would, however, seem to me altogether
too reductive and glib an explanation. If a psychoanalytical model is
to be resorted to, that of Jung would seem to offer a more appropri-
ate explanation. Waldo's poetry involved his struggle to come to his
terms with its Self's negative 'Shadow' by accepting it as a destructive
part of his psyche that was susceptible of being put to constructive,
creative use. At the same time, 'Eirlysiau' reveals how very aware
Waldo was of treading as poet along what Graham Greene called
'the dangerous edge of things'.
   Waldo's vision in 'Eirlysiau' is obviously enabled by all the fea-
tures, powers and devices that are gathered in the word 'poetics'. In
the opening stanza, all save one of the rhyming words that conclude
the lines are monosyllabic and thus violently accentuated. So we have
'gwyn ... glyn ... myn ... pridd ... ffridd'. The one exception is in the
penultimate line, where we have 'ddi-glwy', which is also the word
without a partner in rhyme – except that 'ddi' is actually a rever-
sal of the 'idd' there is in 'pridd' and in 'ffridd', the end-words of
the preceding and succeeding lines. And then there is the elaborate
internal rhyming – off-rhyme such as 'gwyn' with '*gyn*nar', then exact
rhyme as in 'myn' with 'pryn' and 'gwanwyn'. The latter, the word for
'spring', actually contains 'gwyn', but couples it with 'gwan', which

when it stands alone means 'weak', as if here to suggest that for all
the glory of its different colours, springtime also entails a gradual
weakening, or attenuation, of its originating source in the whiteness
of the snowdrops.

Why fuss over all these 'devices'? Because it draws attention to
the fact that Waldo has fashioned the textual equivalent of a visual
icon, but by means of sound. 'Eirlysiau' is a verbal icon. The intri-
cate interplay of sounds highlights, in a stylised, hieratic fashion, the
spiritual dynamic with which the whole poem is concerned. It links
'gwyn' directly to power ('myn'), and both of them to the risk of self-
sacrifice ('pryn'), before linking all three to 'gwanwyn' (spring), where
as already seen 'gwyn' is absorbed into the wider process of spreading
the new life which it has enabled to happen. And the heavy end-rhymes
function in a similar fashion. They convey the remorselessness of the
poem, the commitment of the poet and his 'God' to the vision of
the redemptive power of purity; they enact the unstoppable drive to
transmute dark into light which the poem is all about. It is a poem
in which you can feel that alternative kind of 'violence' acclaimed by
Wallace Stevens; the positive energy within that protects us from the
aggressive and destructive pressure from without. It is the power that
protects us from mis-taking established, purely contingent, realities
for immutable truth, from assuming the world is bound to take the
form it currently takes, from treating a hegemonic order as if it were
indeed natural and immutable. And behind all that effortful power
of imaginative assertion, and total commitment to spiritual vision,
lies that anxiety of Kierkegaardian risk which is the signature style
of Waldo's life as well as of his visionary utterances.

Waldo captured the essence of all this with piercing simplicity in a
single phrase: 'y dewrder sy'n dynerwch'. 'The courage that is gentle-
ness.' The hint of internal rhyme between 'dewrder' and 'dynerwch'
lends the phrase a kind of proverbial wisdom. It occurs in a short,
haunting poem whose lack even of a title underscores the impression
that the vision it communicates has materialised spontaneously and
demanded instant articulation (C, 293). It opens with the assertion
'nid oes yng ngwreiddyn Bod un wywedigaeth'; there is in Being's
root no withering or decay. And Waldo next speaks of this root, from
which such gentle courage springs, as the life of every fragile form of
life, 'Bywyd pob bywyd brau.' Then in the brief second stanza, the
root is recognised as the heart's refuge in the face of a disintegrating
world, and as the lowly fortress where 'gwiwer gwynfyd', the squirrel

of blessed existence, makes its little nest. In the Welsh original, there
is a quiet, profoundly suggestive consonance between 'gwiwer', here
the symbol of vitality, and 'gwywedigaeth', which means decay. Once
again, as so often in his poetry, Waldo is insisting on the fundamental,
generative dialogue between light and dark, growth and decay, hope
and hopelessness. The whole poem is a beautiful, grateful tribute to
the spiritual conviction that sustained him throughout all of his life's
trials, private and public, and an affirmation of invincible hope.

As the editors of Waldo's complete poems have usefully noted, it is
modelled in part on Scandinavian myth, and specifically on the tree of
life, the connective between earth and heaven, which is the great ash tree
of Yggdrasil. A little squirrel scampers up the tree in spring and sum-
mer and down in autumn and winter, and acts as messenger between
the eagle that dwells in the highest branches and the dragon that lurks
underground, gnawing everlastingly on the tree's roots without ever
destroying them. 'This tree', Waldo noted in a letter to his close friend
D. J. Williams, 'became woven into the pattern of my writing.'

One of the loveliest, most limpid, articulations both of Waldo's
stand as a spiritual believer and of his singular vision as a poet is
'Caniad Ehedydd', 'A Skylark's Song'.

> Ymrof i'r wybren
> Yn gennad angen
> Fel Drudwy Branwen
> Yn nydd cyfyngder.
> Codaf o'r cyni
> A'm cân yn egni
> Herodr goleuni
> Yn yr ucheldir. (*C*, 324)

It has been neatly translated by Tony Conran, albeit at the price of
making it seem rather Romantic and old-fashioned in English:

> I give myself skyward
> As heartache's envoy
> Like Branwen's starling
> In a day of woe.
> Rising from anguish
> My song's endeavour
> A herald of light
> To the height I go. (*TC*, 115)

It is a poem that invites recall of the famous poem by Shelley – one of Waldo's great favourites – but only so as to mark the profound difference of Waldo's vision of the bird. Far from soaring exultantly into the empyrean at the beginning, this skylark doesn't arise effortlessly from earth, and is certainly no 'blithe spirit'. Instead it takes a risk: 'ymrof i'r wybren', 'I give myself skyward'. It is a perilous act of self-abandonment, and one of profound trust. And it is undertaken because the skylark is a sky-bound messenger of earth's need. The explicit reference is to the story of Branwen's starling from the *Mabinogion*. She was the daughter of King Llŷr (the prototype of 'Lear'), and was married off to Matholwch, king of Ireland, only to find herself skivvying in his kitchen. Having tamed a starling, Branwen taught it, in a twist on the Welsh bardic convention of sending a bird as *llatai*, or messenger of love, to carry a message of her distress back to Wales to summon her giant brother Brân to her rescue.

For Waldo, the story becomes an allegory of the role of the poet in the contemporary world, which is to act, as his poem proceeds to explain, as an empowering messenger of hope to all the countries of the world and as an instigator of rebellion against every kind of oppression. The skylark's song in this opening stanza is instinct with energy and power, as the bird becomes a herald trumpeting the majestic entrance of light into the world.

The poem is, then, one of Waldo's many stirring protests against social injustice whenever and wherever it may be found. But the translation by Conran of 'cennad angen' as 'heartache's envoy' diminishes and distorts the original's force of utterance and range of implication. It is better translated as 'the messenger of need', which indicates the full, generous extent of what Gerard Manley Hopkins's might have described as Waldo's 'parish of care' as a man and as a poet. Yes, the phrase refers to 'people in need' all over the world, but it also refers to what Waldo regarded as the spiritual need for redemption of the whole of contemporary society, alienated as it had become from the world of the spirit, with conscience deadened by custom, and human sympathy in very short supply, and with money, and status and power everywhere in the ascendancy.

And finally, consciously or not, Waldo was referring to his *own* need, the need for psychological sustenance, hope and rescue that had originated in his very early experiences in that nightmare home. Poetry was, after all, the 'cennad angen,/ Fel drudwy Branwen/ Yn nydd cyfyngder' – an envoy of need, like Branwen's starling, in a time of crisis, a messenger, or ambassador that had visited him and that continued to provide him with a means of allaying his permanent insecurities and anxieties. He, like the starling, had so to speak discovered his tongue, been given a language to speak his message. After all, the story of Branwen is a story of domestic abuse; of terror on the domestic hearth. Through that 'wonder tale' Waldo is acknowledging the part that poetry, as the product and messenger of his very deepest inward needs, has played in transfiguring chronic, potentially crippling anxiety, into courageous social action and a mystic faith in the contagion of goodness. Above all, poetry was his precious means of testifying to what he called 'Awen Adnabod'. It is a complex phrase compact of several elusive meanings and prompting many different translations: 'the Muse of mutual recognition', 'the genius of fellowship', 'the gift of empathy', 'the talent of spiritual vision', and so on. But at bottom, all such approximate translations point in the one direction, the direction of Waldo's unshakeable trust in a network secretly binding all people around the globe into single fellowship and harmonious community.

'Gwelaf Duw gweithgar, ymdrechgar, ymladdwr mawr ag anawsterau yn dyfod atom yn unigol i'n cynorthwyo i ni gael ei gynorthwy Ef', wrote Waldo memorably (*WWR*, 322). 'I see an industrious, striving God, a great fighter against difficulties coming to us individually to help us avail ourselves of His help'. And he reinforced this statement with a few lines of his own poetry:

> Ni saif a llunio arfaeth orffenedig
> O'n cystudd ni. Atom y red, a rhoi
> Cymorth ei law yn ddirgel gan ddirgelwch
> Na ellir ei ddatgloi.

'He does not stand and fashion a completed Providence/ Out of our trials and tribulations. He runs to us and extends/ The help of His hand in secret-bound secrecy/ That cannot be unlocked.'

That 'secret bound in a secret' perfectly captures the irreducible mystery of Waldo's own mystic experiences.

Notes

[1]   Damian Walford Davies (ed.), *Waldo Williams: Rhyddiaith* (Cardiff: University of Wales Press, 2001), p. 125. Hereafter *WWR*.

2   For Waldo Williams's fearless committed pacifism, see Alan Llwyd, *Stori Waldo Williams, Bardd Heddwch: The Story of Waldo Williams, Poet of Peace* (Llandybïe: Gwasg Barddas, 2010).

3   Alan Llwyd, *Cofiant Waldo Williams, 1904–1971* (Tal-y-bont: Y Lolfa, 2014). Hereafter *CWW*.

4   See Robert Rhys, *Chwilio am Nodau'r Gân: Astudiaeth o Yrfa Lenyddol Waldo Williams hyd at 1939* (Llandysul: Gwasg Gomer, 1992).

5   For Nicholas, Carpenter et al., see M. Wynn Thomas, 'What a Welshman You would have Made', in *Transatlantic Connections: Whitman US/Whitman UK* (Iowa City: University of Iowa Press, 2005), pp. 227–60.

6   Alan Llwyd and Robert Rhys (eds), *Waldo Williams: Cerddi 1922–1970* (Llandysul: Gomer, 2014), pp. 249–51. Hereafter *C*.

7   Ned Thomas, *Waldo* (Caernarfon: Gwasg Pantycelyn, 1985). See also Robert Rhys, *Chwilio am Nodau'r Gân*; Damian Walford Davies and Jason Walford Davies (eds), *Cof ac Arwydd: Ysgrifau Newydd ar Waldo Williams* (Swansea: Cyhoeddiadau Barddas, 2006). Bobi Jones, who regarded Waldo Williams and R. S. Thomas as the two greatest poets of twentieth-century Wales, and also two of the greatest in Welsh history, goes to painstaking lengths in his long discussions of Waldo's poetry to demonstrate the classical, Calvinistic theology lurking below the surface of the texts. See the essays on 'Waldo and RS' posted on his comprehensive website: *www.rmjones-bobijones.net/llyfrau/Geraint.pdf*. Ever the outlaw, he would have been delighted to see it digitally labelled as an 'unsupported website'.

8   Rowan Williams, 'Between Two Fields', *The Poems of Rowan Williams* (Manchester: Carcanet, 2014), pp. 92–3.

9   David Hinton, *Awakened Cosmos: The Mind of Classical Chinese Poetry* (Berkeley: Shambhala, 2019).

10   William Wordsworth, 'The Prelude', Book 14, in Thomas Hutchinson (ed.), *Wordsworth: Poetical Works* (London: Oxford University Press, 1969), p. 584.

11   Seamus Heaney, 'The Redress of Poetry', in *The Redress of Poetry* (London: Faber, 1995), pp. 1 and 3.

12   Samuel Taylor Coleridge, 'The Aeolian Harp', in E. H. Coleridge (ed.), *Coleridge: The Poetical Works* (London: Oxford University Press, 1974), p. 101.

13   R. M. Jones, *Cyfriniaeth Gymraeg* (Cardiff: University of Wales Press, 1994).

14   Ralph Waldo Emerson, 'The Poet', in *Essays by Emerson: First and Second Series* (New York, 2020), p. 220. Hereafter *E*.

15   Tony Conran (trans.), *Waldo Williams: The Peacemakers* (Llandysul: Gomer, 1997), p. 153. Hereafter *TC*. For other translations, see Menna Elfyn and John Rowlands (eds), *The Bloodaxe Book of Modern Welsh Poetry* (Tarset: Bloodaxe, 2003), pp. 125–33; Joseph P. Clancy (trans.), *Twentieth-Century Welsh Poems* (Llandysul: Gomer, 1982), pp. 127–38.

7

Bobi Jones:
Court Poet to the Almighty

'Enfant terrible': that epithet has stuck like a burr to Bobi Jones (aka
Robert Maynard Jones, 1929–2017) ever since he first erupted on to
the poetic scene in the late 1950s, exuberantly eager to flutter the
dovecotes of Welsh-language literary culture. From the beginning he
was a devotee of irreverence, a fearsome young prodigy whose fearless
assault on so many shibboleths may well have been facilitated by his
'outsider' status – a native of heavily anglicised Cardiff he had opted
to learn Welsh at school during his teens, a highly unfashionable and
unconventional step in itself, and through his long, prodigiously pro-
ductive life he continued to revel in the potentialities of his acquired
tongue with all the gusto of a small child making free with a new box
of paints. His image of the salmon swimming perversely upstream
against the current to spawn is an image of Bobi Jones himself.[1] He
produced whole suites of poems in defiant carnivalesque display of
his adopted language's opulent largesse and savaged those who dared
imperil its existence. Yet a part of him envied the unselfconscious
idiomatic richness of a native Welsh speaker from the very rare rural
areas that had remained relatively monoglot in character. He noted
wistfully of one such character that 'Fe siaradai'n blwyfol-gadarn fel
byd a fu' (He spoke parochially solid like a long-lost world) (*CG*, 16).
    After he had undergone a radical conversion in his twenties to
an evangelical form of Christianity deeply Calvinist in character,
his ecstatic deployment of the full resources of the Welsh language
provided him with ideal means of conveying his unquenchable aston-
ishment at the systematic wonders of the divinely ordained Creation,
including language itself. Simultaneously, the unorthodox version of

French Structuralism to which he was introduced during a period
of study in Quebec in 1964–5 (he would have no truck with post-
structuralism) supplied him with a semiotic Grand Narrative (that
he himself termed a Metanarrative) well suited to his highly rational,
systematising theology. Both accorded with his dominant passion
for fundamental order, deep deterministic structures and totalising
explanations.

For him, Structuralist analysis of linguistic systems produced
conclusive confirmation that all words were securely underpinned
by the revealed Word: every instance of *parole* (to adopt the
Saussurean terminology, as modified in the linguistic theory of
Gustave Guillaume, to which he was much attracted) was but a local
instance of *langue*. *Langue* refers to the closed, self-referential, sys-
tem of signs that is human language, a system that has an internal,
rule-governed structure. Saussure described it as the 'store-house' on
which we all draw whenever we speak or write. *Parole* refers to any
given use of that system, whether oral or written: in short, it stands
for 'utterance'.[2] For Jones, it was vital to emphasise that the plural-
ity of meanings in every instance of *parole* was underpinned by the
constants of grammar and the universals of value that were firmly
embedded in *Langue*. A fierce critic of the relativism he regarded as
inevitably headed for nihilism, he was fond of the old philosophical
argument that in insisting on the mere relativism of meaning one
necessarily self-contradictorily presupposed that the assertion itself
had absolute meaning. He waged a long, increasingly obsessive, war
on post-structuralism in all its forms, and scoffed at what he regarded
as transient linguistic, philosophical and theological fashions. Late
in life he took to dismissing the present as 'the trendy-first century'.
One of the ironies of his case is that historians today tend to treat
the Structuralist Linguistics to which he was devoted as a fashionable
philosophy of the 1950s (which is when he embraced it) that replaced
the post-war fashion for Existentialism.

It has been noted that for Guillaume 'language was an activity
requiring a speaker to create discourse (typically sentences) from a
previously acquired tongue'.[3] This dynamically generative model of
constant language production, contrasting as it did with the static
model of Saussure's original langue-parole distinction, naturally
appealed to Bobi Jones's restlessly creative spirit. Furthermore, in
his version of Guillaume's linguistic structuralism, the science of lan-
guage came to assume a specifically Christian character. It was this

Christian structuralism that underpinned Jones's cultural national-
ism, explained his loyalty to literary tradition, and accounted for his
tendency to equate Welshness exclusively with the Welsh language. It
also meant that all his poetry was at bottom a poetry about language,
and about the specific form of language composition that is termed
a poem. He would have appreciated Joseph Brodsky's celebrated
remark that a poem is a talking back to language. It is clear that his
acquisition of Welsh as a young adult provided him with a degree of
detachment that facilitated appreciation of his second language as a
unique system with its own precious internal 'economy' of rules and
its own range of verbal resources.

Bobi Jones believed that the deep structure of a distinctive Welsh
identity was uniquely inscribed in the Welsh language and transmitted
by it. His own work involved an inspired deployment and explora-
tion of the language's spiritual syntax. And he found metaphysical
significance in the fact that there were several more ways to inflect the
Welsh verb 'bod' than its English equivalent 'to be, or to exist'. The
Welsh literary canon, in turn – which was systemic in character like
the language itself – was for him one of the most effective and power-
ful carriers of a divinely ordained national identity. For him, that
body of literature was inherently religious in character, even though
modern Wales had largely opted for a secularised lifestyle. As for indi-
vidual poems, they were miniature systematic compositions within the
larger systematic structure of a specific literary culture consisting of
distinctive discursive practices and conventions. In its turn, such a lit-
erary culture was one specific sign system within the much larger and
multifaceted sign system that was the system of sounds and related
deep grammar of the Welsh language itself.

For Bobi Jones all these systems, nesting one within the other,
ultimately had their origin in the universal, authoritative religious
truths exclusive to the Christian religion. Infallibly revealed in the
Bible, these were most fully and perfectly apprehended by the divinely
enlightened reason of the elect, individuals mysteriously chosen by
God to be the recipients of His grace. They were the recipients of
'particular grace', humanity at large having being granted only 'gen-
eral grace', in the form of life and all its benefits. General grace, he
believed, manifested itself in three ways in the creation of a poem:
first, in the unavoidable presupposition of values; secondly, through
the drive to discover and celebrate order; and, thirdly, in the certainty
of ultimate purpose.[4]

In his stringent faith, Bobi Jones was influenced by the dogmatic
Calvinist theology of some leading arch-conservative twentieth-
century Christian apologists, such as the Dutch-American Cornelius
van Til, a leading theologian of the Orthodox Presbyterian Church
of the USA. And he was an admirer of Dr Martyn Lloyd-Jones,
last of the great Welsh evangelists, whose charismatic preaching
during thirty years of ministry packed Westminster Chapel, a large
evangelical free church in London capable of holding 1,500. Like
Lloyd-Jones, Bobi Jones was heir to those masters of eloquence of
the nineteenth-century Welsh pulpit who had been famous for their
imaginative expositions of Biblical texts and the galvanising theatri-
cality of their rhetorical conceits. And like them, Jones did not flinch
from emphasising the severely judgemental side of God as well as his
ready love and forgiveness.

Bobi Jones was very aware of how deeply unpopular his Calvinist
faith was likely to be with his contemporaries. It was an awareness
that appealed to the contrariness of his nature. He revelled in con-
frontation, excelling both at sweeping, sarcastic asides and at impishly
provocative statements, while also repeatedly demonstrating a gener-
ous readiness to acknowledge quality wherever he felt he saw it.[5] The
opening poem in a late sequence records his reflections on a typical
Sunday at the seaside at the height of the holiday season. All around
him he finds evidence of contemporary Wales's contempt for the liv-
ing God, who has been driven to seek refuge under the banks of the
Rheidol river at Aberystwyth, with only a dragonfly for servant (*CG*,
342). The hymns of the great eighteenth-century Methodist evangelist
Williams Pantycelyn have, he complains, been flung into the sewer.
Even chapel members seem to lack religious conviction. Soft and
rotten with sentimentality, they deplore the 'sour' and 'stark' teach-
ings of Calvin (*CG*, 344). As for the Welsh Methodists, who once
rejoiced in the description 'Calvinistic', they too have deserted his
faith. Dispirited, Jones ends by beseeching his people to listen once
more for 'y siffrwd tu ôl i'r dweud/ Y daran fain sy'n cripian i galon
grŷn' (the whisper behind speech/ the keen thunder that creeps into
a withered heart).

A figure as important as Calvin in this poem is Saint Thomas the
Apostle, the originally Doubting Thomas who had come to realise
that no individual is sufficient unto him- or herself, and had dared to
take the great leap of faith. Thomas had understood that the towering
mountains of the human mind were fissured by dangerous chasms.

For Jones, Thomas in his original state of doubt was the patron
saint of the sceptical contemporary world. But he had eventually
recognised the truth of Christ's resurrection, and been brought to
the mystical realisation that 'Fy llonydd hun/ Yw Haul ei angor o
hyd. Canol haul yw'r llun./ Roeddwn i'n cylchu'r un a'm cylchai i'
(*CG*, 346) (His anchoring Sun is the stillness of my repose. It rests at
the centre of the picture. I was circling the one who encircles me). In
retrospect, the scepticism on which Saint Thomas had once prided
himself seems to him no more than an adjunct of his self-satisfied
intelligence – a conclusion encapsulating Bobi Jones's verdict on the
prevailing spiritual scepticism of his own age.

His poems are prickly with originality, just like their author, whose
faith, political outlook and temperament all inclined to absolutism
and extremism. A natural Platonist in the form of a dogmatic univer-
salist, he had no patience with the messy Aristotelean empiricism of
his time. With him, it was all or nothing, there was no half measure.
Like Saunders Lewis, whom he admired, he would have no truck
with the tolerant – and from his point of view fatally complaisant
– liberal humanism that was the consensus in Welsh intellectual cir-
cles. In it he saw nothing but the decay of an establishment Welsh
Nonconformity that had strayed far from its origins in the bracingly
'extremist' evangelical Methodism of the late eighteenth century – a
Calvinistic evangelicalism to which he could readily relate. He was
likewise obsessively and militantly opposed to post-modernism, and
to every manifestation of post-structuralist thinking, believing it
fostered a cynical relativism of outlook and led inevitably to nihil-
ism. And he deplored the wry, ironical approach to life favoured by
many contemporary writers and intellectuals, a shilly-shallying atti-
tude, perfectly suited to an awareness of life's surface ambiguities
and ambivalences that overlooked its underlying spiritual coherence.
Waldo Williams was for him a hero, as well as a great poet, precisely
because he had repeatedly recognised and celebrated this unfashion-
able foundational truth.

That strong, stubborn affirmative bent of Jones's faith already
evident in his treatment of St Thomas found further expression in a
poem (*CG*, 152) he addressed to the Canadian pine trees, rebuking
them for their churlish resistance to the benedictions of spring. In
their dark, surly presence he initially detected only a crabbed spirit
and saw nothing but hostile negation in their hard cones. Encased in
their insensible bark, such trees, he prepared to conclude, could never

be poets, exultantly alive to the miracle of a myriad new births. But then, belatedly, he noticed sprigs of new growth on their branches, unexpected proof that the poetry of earth was not after all dead even in these unpromising conifers.

Bobi Jones revealed the social and cultural foreground to his unswerving loyalty to the Welsh praise tradition in a 1983 letter to his devoted American translator Joseph P. Clancy:

> So much of this, I fear, is originally a response to Negation even though it eventually becomes – as I hope it does – something else. Having been brought up in a Wales where bombs were for some time in my childhood my weekly companions, the language denied and betrayed, and hope in 'religion' shattered and replaced by Hegelian contradiction, despair, darkness, ambiguity, lack of direction, the reaction to all this pointlessness was rather violent. Obviously the aimlessness could not just be avoided: one could not flee the wilful incomprehensibility or the brain-washing onslaught on order and significant conceptualising: one could not just dump the ironic destruction of family life, the agnostic hatred of Welsh identity, and the whole artistic attempt to reflect or interpret this absurd world with over-modest fidelity. One could not go back. Indeed, my own work was something of an interpretation, but it was also an attempt to free itself without 'escape.' It was a deliberate re-orientation.
>
> This linked up with blossoming religious interest in adolescent Thomism and sacramentalism which eventually turned to Calvinism though still retaining an Augustinian and sacramentalist position, as well as with linguistic interests – a deepening realisation of the subconscious order in language which I learned from Gustave Guillaume.[6]

'The [Welsh-language] literature I'm bound up with is already well in the middle of a nuclear war', he stated, before adding that 'Praise itself is the negation of nuclear cultural destruction. It is the completest refusal I know of the absurd.' The joy, and humour and affection and fun he saw as characterising his own poetry were all defiant demonstrations of fidelity to people and culture, as were his portraits of individual and of place. And he saw his own 'real, bleeding, concrete community' as a microcosm of culturally threatened peoples worldwide.

This is as revealing, and as moving, a statement as any he ever made. And it provides an interesting context for one of the gentlest and loveliest of his poems: a long sequence recalling his relationship with his beloved grandfather. The old man lived in Merthyr, a cradle of modern industrial culture, and like many from his background placed his trust to the end in a revolutionary Marxist politics, and the young Bobi Jones became fascinated by his invincible commitment to the social uplift of the oppressed masses. He may even have inherited his grandfather's utopian temperament, but in his maturity he chose to throw in his lot with a very different revolutionary philosophy. In a striking poetic celebration of 'Y Bobl a Gerais' (the people I have loved), he writes of his grateful awareness of 'Sudd Duw yn byrlymu drwy ganghennau maddeuol Ei ach/ Y rhain yng ngwallgofrwydd fy ngherddi fydd fy mawl yn dragywydd' ('God's juice bubbling through the forgiving branches of His lineage,/ These will be the eternal subject of praise in the madness of my poems' (*CG*, 91, 83). His poetry is thus the spontaneous outpouring of the divine afflatus of Holy Joy of which he believes himself to be the privileged recipient. But as he aged he began to fear that the original intoxicating spiritual enthusiasm might be on the wane. So, in one sonnet he sadly imagines that the poems that now come to him only occasionally of an evening may be all that is left of the raptures of his youth (*CG*, 87). He is therefore relieved he can still dance along their lines, and revels in the 'chwilfrydedd', the eagerly explorative childlike curiosity, captured in their rhymes. Bobi Jones the Calvinist ecstatic was readily inclined to worship a God who was the Lord of the Dance, and his own poems sometimes approximate to the dithyrambic.

Having yearned long for a child, Jones and his wife were naturally overjoyed at the unexpected late arrival of a baby daughter. Many poems duly followed chronicling a doting father's delight in his baby's growth. One of these concerns early language acquisition, and opens by exclaiming of his little daughter 'Nid wyt ti ond gair' (*CG*, 93) ('You are nothing but a word'). Her efforts to produce meaningful sounds accompany her struggles to walk, and her father dotes on the 'shaky consonants' that dance in her eyes. As yet, she can form the rudiments of only one word at a time, an example for him of the effortfulness of word becoming flesh. And as in the original divine act of creation, her single word summons into being a whole world of response from her adoring parents. As the poem ruefully concludes, 'Mewn ffrog fach a nics triga gair yn ein plith' (In a little frock and knicks a word dwells in our midst).

His little child at play highlights for him the process of gradual unconscious mastery of the pre-existing semiotic code of language. It also brings to his mind the ludic character of art, which he sees as a vital, valid human tribute to the miracle of creation. The poem simply entitled 'Chware' ('Play') came to him, as he wryly observes, while standing 'with one foot in a wheelbarrow and the other in the lap of summer' (*CG*, 79). In it he prays that his little one be allowed to retain throughout life that capacity for unbridled glee that characterises her childhood years, and that as a privileged witness to it he may continue to enjoy its benefits throughout his adult life:

> Ond gweddïaf y caiff banc tragywydd y fraint
>   O storio dy fwrlwm; ac y caf i
>   Ddal y dwli
> Bair i'm cnawd gerdded; byth na'm hiachau o'r haint
>   Sy'n crynu'r croen. Ac na chartho'n lân
>   Ffwlbri 'maban.

[But I pray an eternal bank will have the honour/ of storing your bubbling; and that I may/ Hold on to the folly/ That keeps my flesh going; may I never be healed of the fever/ That shivers the skin. And may it never be purged completely/ An infant's tomfoolery (*SP*, 72).]

There is of course a distinguished genre of poetic prayers by fathers for their children, the most famous perhaps being W. B. Yeats's characteristically magisterial 'Prayer for my Daughter'. But better attuned to the conclusion of 'Chware' is the magical finale of Coleridge's great 'Frost at Midnight', where he promises his infant daughter that 'all seasons shall be sweet to thee', even when

> the eave-drops fall
> Heard only in the trances of the blast,
> Or if the secret ministry of frost
> Shall hang them up in silent icicles,
> Quietly shining to the quiet Moon.[7]

There is one fundamental difference, however. Coleridge is here seeking to protect his baby from his own prostrating glimpse of what it would mean to dwell in a purely material world, devoid of any spiritual presence. He called this dark experience 'dejection', and struggled with it repeatedly throughout his life. Bobi Jones's poetry, by contrast, is so relentlessly affirmative that it is at risk of becoming wearing: its heady certainties can readily grate on a modern reader's sensibilities. There are in his work very few instances of spiritual doubt, although

when he comes to examine Waldo Williams's work it is to precisely
such examples that he pays particular approving attention.

Given his buoyant temperament and boundless delight in the rain-
bow colours of living, it is no surprise to come across him fretting at
his confinement within 'amhurdeb geiriau' (the impurity of words,
CG, 31). Words have no inkling, he complains, 'mor anodd yw gwiri-
oneddau' (how difficult are truths). For release he turns to painting,
and uses words in ways broadly comparable to that of Pointillists and
Impressionists with paint. One poem is devoted to Vermeer; another
pays homage to Cézanne's innovative practice of building his land-
scapes up out of blocks of colour. 'Egyr yr haul bleth/ Hyd y pinwydd
o dasgiadau gwyn' (The sun opens folds of white splashes across the
pinetrees), he writes, adding in parenthesis '(pan fyddaf/ heb sbectol
Cézanne yw Duw)', 'when I have no glasses, God is Cézanne'. And
then he adds 'Roedd Seurat yn iawn: mae pwyntiau ar bobman yn
frith' (Seurat was right: dots are evident everywhere) (*CG*, 32).

*   *   *

Like the masterpieces of Cézanne, Bobi Jones's compositions often
consist of uncompromising blocks of disorientating images and
bald, bold utterances, devoid of the softening of qualification or
the shadow of equivocation. Defiant departures from the rhetorical
conventions that govern the give and take of conversational and rumi-
native writing, they are assertions of a tumultuously affirmative kind.
Inherently theatrical in manner, they seem to some of his critics to
bear the hallmark of their author's wilful, provocative cockiness and
spiritual arrogance. It is after all the misfortune of believers of Bobi
Jones's stamp that their certainties should appear to the sceptical to
smack of superiority and self-satisfaction. He was also criticised for
the exhibitionist streak in his character. As for his manner of writing,
when, as not infrequently is the case, it goes off the rails it can seem
misguided, extravagant and absurd, but when on track it often proves
capable of reaching destinations that are exhilaratingly unexpected.
Bobi Jones is undoubtedly one of the most adventurously original of
late-twentieth-century Welsh poets.

Key to his poetic discourse is his use of conceits. Most poets
deploy similes and metaphors to endorse and augment ordinary
experience, but Bobi Jones belongs to the minority who use the most
extravagant kind of tropes to register an alternative order of exist-
ence. His texts build a kind of parallel universe, offering access to a

reality that is literally other-worldly. Readers are exposed to the shock of the 'real', understood as the transfigured world revealed by grace to members of the Calvinistic elect. The poems are evidence of the imaginative awakening attendant upon a revolutionary conversion experience. They therefore offer a glimpse of the redeemed world, and they act as discursive defibrillators, bringing hearts deadened by the 'normal' back to vivid spiritual life and health. Noteworthy for the galvanising drama of their rhetorical conceits, they are designed for impact and testify to Bobi Jones's holistic vision of both the natural world and the human world as a single unimaginably complex systemic structure. For him the more strained, far-fetched and unlikely his comparisons, the more truly do they testify to the hidden pattern of inter-relatednesses, the secret web of correspondences, in which our lives are suspended. His is therefore a Modernist version of the Metaphysical poetry of Crashaw, Donne and Vaughan.

The virtuosic aspects of Bobi Jones's style are most transparent and most accessible when deployed in celebration of the sacramental potential of ordinary human experiences. Robert Minhinnick's excellent translation of 'Gyrrwr Trên' ('Engine Driver') captures the electric strangeness of that poem's opening:

> Now smoke rivals smoke in its idiots' race
> While fire gnaws the clouds to rags, and soon
> There's a swineyard of blasphemies, a garden of grease.
> But look at the splay-legged driver, singing in his iron cab,
> Of how the lightning vanishes.
> His sweat caresses the plates and gears like some blackbird
> Scattering pollen's perfumes everywhere it steps.[8]

The 'oil-blue soul ghost in this machine' is in fact just an ordinary son and brother, proud father of five children celebrating Christmas day in this seemingly most inappropriate of surroundings. A product of the Welsh chapel, he sings a famous Welsh hymn about redemption to himself – 'how the lightning vanishes' refers to God's anger being extinguished in the blood of Christ. Viewed in this religious light, the 'garden of grease' that is the driver's cab is miraculously changed into a garden of grace. What Minhinnick's translation fails to reproduce, however, is the original's description of the cab as a 'seintwar'; it is a sacred sanctuary, the holy site of a God perfectly at home riding the axle and in the clack of the clinkers. This God is every bit as comfortable amidst the paraphernalia of the modern machine as in His traditional dwelling places of field and hill. Accepting this, the engine-driver experiences God as immanent in metal and coal, as well as in his own brawny, crude, profusely sweaty body.

Like 'Gyrrwr Trên', 'Bwyta'n Te' (Eating our Tea) is a celebration of the sacred dimensions of ordinary experience. But it is entirely different in style, idiom and register from the former, which is consciously modelled on the heroic praise-poetry of bardic tradition, a body of work in which the qualities of a warrior-prince were magnified and extolled. Compared with such an august genre, 'Gyrrwr Trên' cannot but seem mock-heroic, so unsuited at first reading seems its high, proclamatory rhetoric to its 'low' subject. But of course that is Jones's point. We need to adjust our understanding so that the mundane modern reality of the much-despised machine age can reveal its remarkable unsuspected spiritual dimension. His poem translates an aristocratic medieval genre into the startlingly unlikely idiom of contemporary discourse.

Not so 'Bwyta'n Te' (Eating our Tea) (*CG*, 69). Here the high, declamatory style of 'Gyrrwr Trên' is replaced by a relaxed conversational 'low' style, unusual in Jones's oeuvre. The rhetoric is in the key of ordinary family life. And the movement of the text uncharacteristically allows for the gentle give and take of domestic interactions around a tea table. From the beginning there is emphasis on the inherently ritualistic aspects of the mundane, an awareness that a 'love feast' is in progress in this humble family gathering: 'Mae 'na rywbeth crefyddol yn y modd yr eisteddwn/ Wrth y ford de, yn deulu'n cryno dri.' (There is something religious about the way we sit by the tea table, a complete family of three.) The Holy Trinity is adumbrated in that figure, and there are obvious overtones of Holy Communion in the breaking of bread.

But this is a poem written from a radical Evangelical point of view, and so it critiques what to believers of Jones's kind seems to be the glib sacramentalism that characterises the worship of more conventional Christian churches and denominations. Eating tea, it insists, is neither an actual ordination nor an authentic act of worship. But Jones does acknowledge the similarities between the basic elements of this everyday meal and that of the Communion service. This is for him confirmation of how deeply ingrained in the human psyche is the habit of religious observation, and an example of the operations of 'general', as opposed to 'particular' grace.

Many of Jones's poems are conventional in genre. 'Aber-porth (Yn y Gaeaf)' (Aberporth in Winter), for instance, is one of a series in praise of place, and it opens by dismally surveying a seaside town, 'syrffed o dai,/ Hylciau hyll hyd ddistyll' (a surfeit of houses, ugly hulks stretching to ebb-tide (*CG*, 110)). Shabbiness here reigns supreme. But then Jones notices a single round hailstone, which blossoms into a wonder before his eyes: 'Uwch ei ffrwyth teimlais fel edn a ollyngwyd i berllan ber-lau/ Wedi bod noson mewn cysgodle tanddaearol rhag ofn y bomiad/ A'r lle'n llawn dop o smygu i ladd amser' (Above its fruit I felt like a bird released into an orchard of pearls, after having spent the night in some underground shelter to avoid the bombing, the place chock-full of those smoking to pass the time). A simile like this, hyperbolically extended and recklessly mixing its terms until it turns into a conceit, is a staple feature of Jones's writing. Revealed to him in Aber-porth are the features of the One who dwells on land and sea, the sorcerer who can transfigure even the disheartening drabness of a small Welsh sea-side town into a revelation. He has, he feels, been privileged to witness the birth here of a new world, the blinking emergence of a stupefied creature out of the slime of unbeing into the wonder of existence. And the poem neatly concludes by returning to the image of the hailstone image, its whiteness now seen to have come from a black cloud.

Bobi Jones's frequent production of poems on themes typical of Welsh poetic culture, such as this one in praise of place, was no accident. It was consistent with his deep reverence for custom and tradition, all of which he regarded as hallowed. One of his favourite forms, for example, was the sonnet, another was the hymn, while yet others were modern adaptations of strict-metre forms, such as the cywydd or the traethawdl. Appropriately enough, therefore, he chose to describe himself in one poem as a 'Bardd Llys' (Court Poet) to the Almighty (*CG*, 114), whose command 'Bydd di'n brydydd/ I mi' (Be you my poet), he had originally met with a stammered protestation of unworthiness reminiscent of George Herbert.

Very aware of his poetic lineage, Bobi Jones particularly valued the work of the great hymn-writers of the late-eighteenth-century Methodist revival. Ann Griffiths was a predictable favourite, and his tribute to her opens by emphasising the unlikeliness of the trans-formation of a young, carefree, pleasure-loving country girl into an ecstatic, gripped by such a reckless spiritual passion that she became a bush burning, never to be extinguished, and acquired a tongue of flame like those present at the Pentecost. He honours her by adopting her signature practice of raiding the Bible for tropes adequate for expressing her mystical religious experience:

> Ar ôl deifio ei chalon dafotrwm
> A'r berth heb ei difa,
> Fflam-ffrwythodd hi'n dafotrydd
> Dan gawodydd marwol glwy
> A phersawr ei pherson;
> Torrodd ffrydiau lond ei gweled
> A Chanaan oedd ei chân. (*CG*, 101)

[After the scorching of her tongue-tied heart, with the bush still entire, she flame-blossomed into eloquence beneath the showers from the fatal wound [of the crucified Christ], until her person turned fragrant; fountains gushed in abundance, and Canaan became all her song.]

The text is an elaborate exercise in intertextuality: Biblical allusions famously beloved by Ann and forever associated with her hymns are woven into a richly intricate textual celebration of her genius. Tribute is paid in the form of admiring emulation.

Bobi Jones could convincingly ventriloquise Ann Griffiths because he, too, was an ecstatic who, in one unnerving poem, could confess to feeling annihilated at times by the Almighty's overwhelming presence and His relentless demands. 'Gweddi am Gadw'r Traed ar y Ddaear' (A Prayer to Keep my feet on the Earth) (*CG*, 159) opens with the helpless confession, 'Heddiw aeth y Duw byw yn ormod imi', 'Today the living God became too much for me' .'Avalanching' over him from all directions and from every phenomenon, this Presence ruthlessly cancels even the most intimate human bonds, and terrifies him with its awesome manifestation of divine Justice. Recognising its remorseless implacability he resorts to desperate craven pleading for release from his obligations as an obedient believer:

> Fe'm torrir i. Mi wn fod dagr Ei anwyldeb
> Eisoes yn fy nghlustiau, a'i lafnwaith
> Yn estyn at fy nghoes. Mae ar fy mhen ...
> Drugaredd nawr, fy Nghariad, o drugaredd.
> Saf di draw. A gad i mi nawr lithro'n ôl i'r traffig.

[I am broken asunder. I know that the dagger of His lovingness is already in my hearing, its blade reaching down to my leg. He is upon me ... Mercy now, my Beloved, Oh! Mercy. Stand back. And let me slip back into the traffic.]

It is a poem unrivalled in his entire output; a naked confrontation of the *terribilis* of God. Like Kitchener Davies's great 'Sŵn y Gwynt sy'n Chwythu' (considered in the next chapter), it is a gripping example of the existential drama that lies at the very centre of Calvinistic Methodism; the moment of fateful struggle in the soul of one of the elect between the iron requirements of Grace and the 'natural' human instincts of the Sinner. It is a revelation of the terrifying price to be paid for salvation.

* * *

By contrast, the most humanly loving of Bobi Jones's poems are the many he addressed throughout his long, prolific writing career to his wife Beti. He was a strong believer in the central Christian institution of holy matrimony. Recognising in it the highest revelation of 'the holiness of the heart's affections', he never ceased to marvel at the countless blessings that personal experience had proved could follow in its wake. However, his frank admission of the sensuous aspects of this most intimate of human bonds could sometimes occasion disquiet amongst some of his more straight-laced readers. Particularly shocking to them was the affectionately grotesque opening of the poem he addressed to a heavily pregnant Beti. It was a condition all the more to wonder at because the pair had experienced such difficulties in conceiving, and she had suffered several miscarriages along the way.

> Fel hipopotómos ym myllni afon ymdrybaeddi
> Rhwng plyg cynfasau, a finnau'n grocodéil pren
> Yn d'ymyl. Rwyt ti'n myfyrio tu ôl i'th gnawd-fwtresi
> Yn nwfn arafwch lli, gan droi by ben uwchben
> Gan bwyll o du i du, a soddi unwaith eto
> I'r dyfroedd llawn. (*C*, 100)

[Like a hippopotamus in a river's murk you wallow between the folds of your linen, and I a wooden crocodile at your side. You meditate behind your flesh-buttresses in the deep sluggishness of waters, turning your head above them slowly from side to side before sinking once more below the flood.]

His wife's massive clumsy bulk is here verbally sculpted with all the loving tactile attention to every corporeal curve and physical feature visible in Henry Moore's huge sculptural tributes to the fecund

potentialities of the female nude. And like Moore, Bobi Jones sees in
the pregnant Beti the lineaments of an ancient earth mother, a mature
goddess of fertility. To him she seems to have locked out all external
distractions, and to be devotedly listening only to the wordless whis-
per of new life stirring mysteriously within her. She dwells on the
margins of a strange inner world, that of an independent little being
wholly other than herself. The role now allotted her by Providence is
simply to exist 'yn lli llaid amser, hen hipopotómus gariaduslan' (in
the sediment of time's flood, a perfect old lovable hippopotamus). But
this is a poem not only about Beti but also about her husband. It is
his humble confession to a baffled, thwarted maleness overawed by a
condition forever beyond his ken. And it is an intimate revelation of
that special, mysterious, even mystical, power to nurture new life that
is the jealous preserve of the female of the species.

One of the earliest of the Beti poems is guaranteed to bring any
puritan reader up short. Entitled ''Rwyt ti f'anwylyd sanctaidd yn
llawn o ryw' (You my sacred love are full of sex), it proceeds in like
erotic manner: 'Fel tiwlip dwfn yn ffrwydro dan fom yr haul,/ Mae'n
gorwedd ynot fel gwaed' ('like a deep tulip exploding under the bomb
of the sun/ It is bedded in you like blood' (27, 26). It sets out to draw a
distinction between male and female, with the latter seen as inherently
sexual because women are biologically programmed to bring new life to
birth. Indeed, the image of the exploding tulip brings to mind some of
the extraordinary flower images of Georgia O'Keefe. And in the cou-
pling of male and female Jones divines the re-enactment of the original
act of creation itself. So the poem duly concludes with a miniature
psalm of praise, audible in which are echoes of the Song of Solomon:

> I sing you our joy. I sing our being ...
> The perpetual joy of father and mother, into which there crept
> The binder of all that's woven, orange blossoms in His hair
> And pomegranates waving beneath His arms. (C, 27)

The lovingly lingering sensuality in many of Bobi Jones's poems
to Beti confirms his frank appreciation of the sexual dimension of
Christian marriage. His large body of work on this subject is an
undoubted achievement, given a Welsh poetic culture still stuck in
a Puritan time-warp and largely devoid of erotic poetry. Particularly
remarkable are those pieces that resound with a Yeatsian defiance of
the ageing of spirit and flesh in middle age. Then more than ever he

exults in the insatiability of desire and the unseemly intemperateness of passion. So a poem on New Year's Day begins, 'Pardon me for waltzing over the tops of houses,/ Strutting above the parish graves, my skin full/ Of you', and concludes in like extravagant fashion by comparing his wife to a bell ready to ring in a new year in their marriage:

You I am, my bell.
Your grand and Grecian sides are the mixing-bowl
I sound now from the top of tower and roof.
Their turnings answer the lust of each groan,
The sweat of each climb there, each yesterday's craving.
My tongue resounds till the countryside corner's leap
As dawn is proclaimed by an echo from heaven's cave:
Atop the spire a weathercock rises with a tune from the south. (*SP*, 149)

Jones refuses to balk at the use of sexual double entendres and his characterisation of passion's cries as 'an echo from heaven's cave' is a characteristically bold and uncompromising declaration of his belief in the sanctity of a mutually loving sexual congress.

But Bobi Jones was also as aware as D. H. Lawrence of the ambivalent aspects of a human sexuality that could involve the urge to dominate, possess and subjugate, and in 'The Last Moon of the Twentieth Century' he explored this subject in a poem that opened 'The stars have no sex; but the moon, ah the moon/ She too knows terrible yearning between smooth sheets' (*SP*, 133). Familiar with the traditional connection in Western culture between the moon and human love, he affects to disbelieve modern science's discovery that Diana's planet is no more than earth's 'cast-off stone', 'a cold ball' whose 'skin wouldn't shine, and her breezes wouldn't smile'. Instead, he reverts to the ancient image of her as alluringly chaste and remote: her vulnerable nakedness leaves him feeling desolate. But the poem sadly concludes by recognising it is precisely the moon's seductive allure of austere chastity that tempts humans to sully it through the defilement of possession:

But the moon, ah the moon, each night at my window,
Or tormenting me above the river, freezing me in the forest,

She lingers, till some people fly to pollute
Less than human, her lap, making her gem a common. (*SP*, 134)

* * *

The moon poem was one of a suite written by Bobi Jones during a year-long stay in Quebec, an experience he found deeply educative in many ways but that also brought his profound attachment to Wales into focus with a new and painful sharpness. Indeed, one of the strategies he adopted for psychic survival was to seek occasional refuge in the recycling of traditional Welsh bardic forms. One example of this is 'Traethawdl y Gwynt a'r Gân', in which the densely woven text is 'the fort of the song', affording him protection against the 'dragonish foul weather' (C, 139, 126) whose annihilatingly cold wind heralds the approach of the interminable Canadian winter. This produces in Jones a 'mind of winter', a new, stripped-down awareness of the bleak, stark realities of human existence. In the face of this it is his traditional poem that alone can afford him psychological and spiritual sustenance: it is his lifeline to Christian belief.

Other poems of his Canadian experience are likewise a record of his new exposure to the utter inaccessibility of God. After all, he has witnessed the obliteration of the benign summer greenness of the banks of the St Lawrence. All signs of life have been cancelled out by ice and snow, so that 'The lights have been/ Unfastened, and God is muteness' (SP, 135).

> Tears without mourning's warmth, moor of white darkness.
> Flat, carcass-flat without cactus or vine
> Is the current's hardship now.

But even while bleakly admitting that 'What is frightful is how deep life freezes', he gradually learns to adjust his eyes so that they begin to notice the merest stirrings of life in the river's muddy bottom, 'a sort of tiny wriggling like a tongue; no, like a small Nativity' (C, 135). The eventual late arrival of spring brings with it the 'resurrection of the birds', those 'wallgof eithafwyr yr haul' (mad extremists of the sun), that are excitedly urged to 'afradu dros bobman/ Anghymedroldeb eich cân' (liberally squander everywhere/ the intemperateness of your song).

The dark winter in Canada did, however, bring dark nights of the soul. 'Six in the Morning' arrestingly opens with the despairing exclamation 'A tomb, a tomb,/ a tomb, last night', before relief arrives with the arrival of a new day. The ensuing steadying glow of full daylight is 'a candle,/ in the fen of the coffin' (SP, 141). Ordinary life slowly begins to reconstitute itself, and with it 'into the gloom of man's earth' falls 'a shower of doves like litanies'. Yet all this reassuring panoply of the commonplace cannot fully dispel those grim intimations of mortality the previous night had brought with it:

> I will dwell now in the care of the eternal morning;
> and yet
> as though smells of death were still on daybreak's table,
> in the heart of my singing there's a tomb.

Thus the poem ends in blank dispirited cliché, as if Bobi Jones has for once been deserted by the ebullient spirit of belief that is the usual reliable source of his buoyant poetic afflatus.

A more determinedly resilient poem in the face of a bout of dejection is 'Gweddi Nos ar ôl wythnosau o anhunedd' (Night prayer, after weeks of insomnia) (*CP*, 159). Similar in form to a hymn, and with full masculine rhymes throughout, saving one exception, it looks to God's presence for protection from the black dog of depression. The only occasion a reassuringly simple and solid masculine rhyme is not supplied, is when 'Un sy'n cadw'n fyw' (One who remains alive) is followed by 'Dduw ar y croesbren, Groesbren-dduw' (God on the cross, Crucifix-god): there the final element in the composite noun ('dduw'/ God) shares its strong accent with the 'Groes' (cross) in 'Groesbren'. This is a theologically subtle textual device that highlights the fact that Bobi Jones places his faith in a God the assurance of whose saving grace is fully manifest only in the crucifixion. In such a God alone can he continue to believe throughout his long ordeal of sleepless nights.

His most testing experience of physical and spiritual degree zero, however, came when, upon his arrival in Mexico City at the age of thirty-nine in the autumn of 1968, he was so badly affected by altitude sickness that his life was saved only by the prompt action of a young female assistant at his hotel to whom he later gratefully dedicated a series of fifteen poems. The first is written in a strict measure famous in early Welsh poetry and features variations on a set verbal formula:

> Awyren lwyd yn fy nghludo i gôl
> Gofod lle nad oes prinder yr Absennol
> Pan fydd y llen wedi'i thynnu'n ôl. (*C*, 213)

[Grey plane bearing me to the lap/ Of space, where there is no lack of Absence/ When the curtain is pulled back (*SP*, 196).]

From the plane's window he sees a toweringly mountainous land-
scape below, totally devoid of habitation; a 'cold inhuman openness/
And all so watchfully still,/ so spotlessly old' (*SP*, 197). This omi-
nously foreshadows the brusquely peremptory visitation of death,
who 'loves un-friending' and is stone deaf to any pleas for even the
most minor of delays to allow for the final tidying up of the practical,
emotional and spiritual affairs of a life. 'There was no more/ Irony
at last, no ambiguity, no doubts. I entered the facts. The crude event.
History' (*SP*, 199). And it is in this extremity, 'with my head in the
mouth of the beast', that he fully places his trust in Jesus, 'with my
language almost devoured,/ My throat swells in praise' (*SP*, 199).

Having been spared, he ascends to ever higher realms of Hispanic
extravagance, first profusely thanking the unassuming little hotel
receptionist for her cool expertise, and then breaking out into a
diapason of praise for the God of a world the wonder whose every
detail has now been made exhilaratingly evident to him anew: 'Praise,
praise to God for ugly buildings,/ For grimy rain in smoke and for
self-displaying racket,/ Let His crown be exalted for bodily pain and
for sweat on foreheads' (*SP*, 200). It is as if Bobi Jones is intent on
rebuking himself for having previously been so petty and niggardly
in his appreciation of the wonders of life:

> He spread across me all the ease of enjoying clouds,
> Delicately touch the soft white curve of their trembling,
> And lie back to gaze at their existence,
> To look and look and look at the world that is. (*SP*, 201)

There then follows a sequence charting the melodramatic psychodrama
of Bobi Jones's recovery. His wife's impending arrival prompts an out-
burst of unbridled physical, as well as emotional, longing, replete with
the pleasures of sensual anticipation: 'I'll insist, you mischief,/ It's your
body, my little dear, that's filling the room./ All night long I'll swagger
with you without tiring' (*SP*, 201). The images are psychedelic in their
garishness, as if the patient's imagination is still feverish both from the
euphoria of escape and from the effects of medication. He begins to
lose all inhibition and restraint, impatiently bursting out 'Who needs
oxygen now? Take the medicine away!/ Bees don't sting me any more!'
(*SP*, 202). A pang of remorse predictably follows, in which he begs
Christ to forgive him for having opted for 'sin's puny body/ instead of
the royal form you've made there' (*SP*, 202).

A poem on Mexican celebration of the Day of the Dead next serves as the hinge on which the sequence turns and looks homewards to Wales. Well clear of Death's clutches, he can afford to stand back and cut it down to size:

> But you were no wonder, Death,
> Nor in any way uncommon.
> I saw your stereotyped smile. And in peering
> Down your gullet, and examining your teeth,
> I observed your monotony. You're the One;
> But as for me, I'll go to the diverse, the fullness God
> Created through His imagination, the bubbling of passion,
> The various heaps of affection
> Instead of the One grey enemy.

Viewed from Mexico, Wales appears more than ever to be his beloved, 'my-coat-of-many-colours-Wales' as he puts it in an inspired compound coinage, and he prays to Jesus to 'doctor my people/ And bring them by the virtues of Your treatment back to their rightful home' (*SP*, 205).

Bobi Jones was always willing to confront the inescapable prospect of dying, that taboo subject of our age; and he was equally ready to confess frankly to the anxiety and fear it instinctively aroused in him. But however thoroughly he ventilated those concerns, he was always careful to allay them by resorting to his faith in Christ who alone could provide the gateway to everlasting life. To the very end of his long and distinguished career, he continued to many of his readers to seem every bit the cultural outsider he had been at the beginning. He remained an outré extremist in his imagery, while his evangelical faith never ceased to seem 'suspect'. Viewed as a whole, his oeuvre resembles a Bach cantata in its composition, in that a series of majestic pieces of a Baroque richness of subtle complexity is periodically punctuated by affecting confessions of disarmingly simple faith expressed in hymn-like form. One of these opens with a quatrain that may stand as the epitaph of this most singular of twentieth-century writers in Welsh:

> Mae sisial enw Iesu
> Fu'n was i ddynol-ryw
> Yn gyrru arnaf gyffro
> Diwrthdro am fy Nuw. (*C*, 356)

[Whispering the name of Jesus, that servant to humankind, stirs in
me irresistible longing for my God.]

Bobi Jones was acutely appreciative of his relationship to the spiritual
tradition represented by the poets in this volume. He was sweepingly
dismissive, as was his wont, of the major figures of the first half
of the last century. In his opinion they had been fatally corrupted
by the fashion of their age for agnosticism and humanism, and had
all been partial to irony and ambivalence. But in Saunders Lewis,
Euros Bowen and Gwenallt – all of whom he had known person-
ally – he found committed Christians, like himself, whose work was
grounded in a belief in original sin and the overlordship of God. And
he admired Waldo Williams and R. S. Thomas above all, believing
the genius of both to have been firmly rooted, like his own, in the awe
and wonder proper to the creation and its Creator.

Notes

1 Bobi Jones, *Casgliad o Gerddi* (Llandybïe: Gwasg Dinefwr/Cyhoeddiadau
   Barddas, 1989), p. 330. Hereafter *CG*.
2 A short, succinct and admirably clear introduction to the subject can be
   found in Terence Hawkes, *Structuralism and Semiotics* (London: Methuen
   New Accents Series, 1977).
3 John Hewson, 'Rethinking Structuralism: the posthumous publications of
   Gustave Guillaume [1883–1960]', *Langue*, 84/4, 820–44.
4 Bobi Jones website: 'Waldo ac R.S.', 77. Constructed late in life, this elabo-
   rate website became home to a body of late writings, ranging from lengthy
   appreciations of Waldo Williams and R. S. Thomas through meditations on
   the theology of culture to wide-ranging letters addressed to friends and a
   group of unpublished poems.
5 See in particular the debates between Jones and the eminent Wittgensteinian
   philosopher Dewi Z. Phillips, in the latter's *Ffiniau* (Tal-y-bont: Y Lolfa,
   2008).
6 Joseph P. Clancy (trans.), *Bobi Jones: Selected Poems* (Llandybïe: Christopher
   Davies, 1987), p. 14. Hereafter *SP*.
7 Coleridge, 'Frost at Midnight', 240.
8 Robert Minhinnick (trans.), 'Gyrrwr Trên / Engine Driver', in *The Adulterer's
   Tongue: Six Welsh Poets, a Facing-Text Anthology* (Manchester: Carcanet,
   2003), pp. 2–3.

8

THREE POETS

This volume primarily examines the output of religious poets of major cultural impact and consequence. But others of less substantial overall achievement have also produced poems of striking quality and value. And of these, three figures in particular stand out.

The first is William Thomas Davies, Davies Aberpennar, Pennar Davies (1911–86): a single person of multiple, perhaps conflicted, aspects.[1] As his three names suggested, he consisted of a secular trinity of selves, or personae. He was a poet and a preacher, a daring novelist and eminent theologian, a scholar as stringent as he was highly learned, and a humble pastor of his people. He was sociable yet aloof, abstracted yet entirely focused, gentle but adamantine, open and accessible but ultimately impenetrable and unreachable. Deeply private, meditative and bookish, he was also an indefatigable public campaigner who even became a parliamentary candidate for Plaid Cymru, the Party of Wales. The soul of integrity he was nevertheless arrested as a lawbreaker. A pacifist and the most quiet and inoffensive of men, he was accused of being a disturber of the peace. Raised in a monoglot English-speaking family, he unfashionably learnt Welsh and devoted himself to the lifelong service of that language and its culture. In short, he was an enigma – a mystery perhaps even to himself.

His were the most ordinary of beginnings: the only son in a typical working-class mining family in Mountain Ash, or Aberpennar, in the Cynon Valley, one of the fan-shaped arc of mining valleys centred on Cardiff that for half a century had served as the world's powerhouse because it was the premier producer of high-quality steam coal. An exotic, the 'changeling' within his bewildered family, he turned out to have a fantastical imagination and to be blessed with exceptional academic gifts, as became evident once he embarked on an intellectual career that saw him shine first at Cardiff University then at Balliol and Mansfield Colleges at Oxford, and finally at Yale University. But then he abruptly abandoned his stellar academic career to become an ordinary chapel minister, and that at a time when the norm in Wales was not conversion to Nonconformity but rather mass defection from it.[2]

The enigmatic character of Pennar's core personality seems to be parabolically anticipated in the story he used to tell of how, when he was a boy in an ordinary collier's family, a lady had appeared unexpectedly at the door. Dressed in black, her face obscured by a veil, she was, it transpired, a wealthy widow in search of a talented youngster of humble background whom she could assist by providing the educational opportunities best suited to unusual promise. While explaining this, she had briefly removed her veil, allowing Pennar to glimpse her face for the first and last time in his life. The story has to it the ring of a fairy tale and a miraculous, mythic aura such as is associated with the traditional search for the next Dalai Lama amongst the poor of Tibet. Psychologically, it seems to suggest that from an early age Pennar had entertained the not unusual fantasy of being of 'noble' birth, of being special, of not really being the child of his biological parents, of being a kind of foundling. It also has about it more than a hint of that inventive power and taste for the romantic that the adult Pennar was to exhibit in his novels and poetry.

As a young man, his adoption of the nom de plume of Davies Aberpennar (Davies of Mountain Ash) marked his emergence as a promising young experimental Welsh author, one of many who trailed in the wake of Dylan Thomas. He published one of his first poems in *Wales*, the rumbunctious, irreverent ground-breaking literary magazine of the late thirties and early forties edited by the supreme showman and impresario Keidrych Rhys that first showcased the work of Dylan Thomas and his generation. And what was the poem's title? 'Triolet' – Welsh for triplet. A verse trinity, just like its author's clutch of personae. Right from the start, it sounded the shocking note of his own unconventional and challenging authenticity, with its insistence on celebrating a God who had given humankind its coarse, yet glorious, fleshly character: 'Duw a'n gwnaeth, mor frwnt, mor hyblyg' (God fashioned us, so foul, so flexible). A few pages earlier he had published another little poem that ended with a defiant emphasis on 'Cnawdolrwydd y Cariad' (the Fleshliness of the Love) and a confession of seeing in the sunshine of his own day 'Noethni fy Nhad' (My Father's Nakedness).[3]

A couple of pages later (306–8) and the young Davies Aberpennar was reviewing Dylan Thomas's *The Map of Love*, tempering his praise with reservation: 'the typical Dylan Thomas poem', he rather superciliously wrote, 'is a movement of the sensuous imagination built around a slight intellectual theme in associations of colour and sight and sound'. Pennar, as he came to be known, was already proving himself to be a confirmed intellectual, and one who strove, in all his theological and creative writings, to ensure that his frankly 'sensuous imagination' was, unlike that of Thomas, firmly underpinned, but never supplanted, by the steadily focused intellectual vision he had so exactingly trained in Cardiff, Oxford and Yale.

This early, too, he exhibited a precocious desire to bring the two languages and literatures of modern Wales into sympathetic fellowship and cooperation. He published in *Wales* an eloquent, impassioned, prophetic 'open' letter pleading with all Welsh writers of the time to recognise, value, protect and develop their bicultural society.[4] Among those who responded positively to his appeal were Dylan Thomas and Waldo Williams. Meanwhile, the Pennar Davies who had begun as Davies Aberpennar, an English-language Welsh writer, taught himself Welsh and set about fashioning a new cultural identity for himself as Pennar Davies, a writer who wrote almost exclusively in his acquired language. In company with a group of young like-minded friends, pacifists all, who took to meeting during the war years in a house called Cadwgan in the Rhondda Valley, he began to use his creative gifts to explore a number of daring theological issues, to trial a number of different artistic personae, and to experiment with forms of writing new to Welsh tradition. His inclinations towards the spiritual and cultural syncretism which was to become such a feature of his mature writing were greatly reinforced by the active presence of two young German refugees in that group, one of these being Rosemarie Wolff, Pennar's wife.[5]

As early as 1944, he had established his first credentials as an 'Anglo-Welsh' poet through inclusion in Keidrych Rhys's landmark anthology *Modern Welsh Poetry*. This included work by Glyn Jones, Emyr Humphreys, David Jones, R. S. Thomas, Vernon Watkins, Alun Lewis, Lynette Roberts – and Dylan Thomas. But the first seven poems in the anthology were all by Davies Aberpennar, and include the following lines:

> The song of joys of all time
> Is like small coal coming out of a sieve
> On a cold afternoon, unless it sings
> Inside you.[6]

Simple fragment though it is, it could be said to encapsulate the essence of Pennar Davies's vision, as a theologian as much as a writer. His long life was entirely dedicated to the exacting work of extracting, and articulating in deed as much as in word, the 'song of joys' that sang inside him in tune, or so he believed, with the grand diapason of creation itself. What is best about Pennar's vision is first its serene ecstasy of appreciation of the creation in its totality, flesh as much as spirit, pain as well as joy. And, secondly, its generously eirenic spirit. He had the unfailing gift of recognising and synthesising that which was best in a myriad different faiths and spiritual traditions, from ancient to modern times.

On the flyleaf of the copy of *Modern Welsh Poetry* that is in my possession, the author has written, 'Gyda phob dymuniad da a diolch, Mehefin 1949, Pennar Davies' (With every good wish and thanks, June 1949, Pennar Davies). So within five years of the publication of the anthology, the 'Davies Aberpennar' whose poetry had been included there was already choosing to present himself anew to the world as 'Pennar Davies', a Welsh-language poet. It was an identity to which he remained faithful for the rest of a productive life that saw him publish a stream of challenging theological studies and histories, a striking series of novels, and a distinctive body of poetry, while continuing not only to preach but also steadily to advance to an eminent position with the Annibynwyr (Welsh Independents), culminating in his years as Principal of that denomination's leading training institution for ministers.

His poem 'Ave Atque Vale' opens by boldly addressing the reader, in Whitmanian terms: 'I love you/ though, possibly, we haven't met', and, as the title indicates, such familiarity is predicated on a recognition of the shared mortality which is the ground note of all human existence.[7] As for any belief in the 'spirit's' survival of death, Pennar is blunt in his dismissal of any such expectation, viewing it as based on a theological dualism contrary to his own beliefs:

> Somebody's probably told you sometime
> it's the body that dies

and the soul 'escapes'
or 'flies off' or 'moves on'.
Forget it.
The body's not a prison:
and the stuff of the body doesn't die. (*MWP*, 144)

It couldn't have been more plainly put. And it was in this spirit that
Pennar produced a 'praise poem' to the Dung beetle – again recalling
perhaps unconsciously Whitman's great phrase in 'Song of Myself'
in praise of humble 'beetles rolling balls of dung'. 'I marvel at your
tenderness and fidelity', he writes, before expanding on this:

> Is it not the utmost goodness that defecation
> Rouses your humble devotion?
> Is it not supreme wisdom that excretion
> Stirs your awareness? ...
> And though creation's shit is your medium
> What end and purpose is there but the precious love
> That gave the rose
> Its form and colour and fragrance? (*MWP*, 145)

Again like Whitman, Pennar is aware, as he specifically admits in
the poem, that the dung beetle enjoys 'a family connection/ with the
ancient Egyptians' sacred scarab', and he further pays homage to
the dung beetle in Aristophanes' work that elevated a 'patriot peace-
keeper' to heaven to free 'the goddess of peace/ to reign over the
earth'.

However, one poem, 'Cathl i'r Almonwydden' (A hymn to the
almond tree) stands out from the rest of Pennar's work, and per-
fectly crystallises his theology. Pelagius, the early Father of the
Church anathematised by his fellow Christians for preaching a doc-
trine of free will, and duly damned by Welsh Calvinistic Methodists,
was Pennar's hero. Against St Augustine's gloomy condemnation of
nature as utterly depraved, the early Christian theologian argued that
the potential for enhancement by grace was already inherent in all nat-
ural forms, thus asserting a continuity, rather than complete rupture,
between the 'fallen' world and the world as redeemed by Grace. For
Pelagius, as Pennar approvingly put it, 'Grace ... was not merely a
remedial intervention necessitated by the Fall; it danced in the activity
of the creation itself.' 'Not', he added, that Pelagius had ever claimed
'that man could be good without God. What he resisted was not

the doctrine of grace but the growing perversion and mechanization and stultification of it in the world-denying piety of a Jerome or an Augustine.'[8]

This, he further claimed, had been a vision of life particularly attractive to the Cambro-British, the early saints of whose 'Celtic' church were reluctant to follow mainstream Catholic practice and 'institutionalize the life of praise'. Moreover, 'the Brythonic sense of the unity and fluidity of life prevented the Welsh from giving a welcome to the Augustinian emphasis on the moral helplessness of fallen humanity'. This indigenous Pelagian theological strain had been largely driven underground for more than a millennium in Wales, as first the Catholic Church had espoused an Augustinian theology and then Anglicanism had followed suit, adopting an Augustinism filtered through the work of John Calvin. It was only occasionally here and there among the Dissenters who began to appear in seventeenth-century Wales that new versions of the ancient Welsh Pelagian teaching shyly began to reappear. But it was soon swamped by the fervent Calvinism of the Welsh Methodism that, first developing during the last half of the eighteenth-century, went on to dominate nineteenth-century Nonconformist culture in Wales. While admiring what he termed 'the prodigious grace-gifts' of the early leaders of this Welsh Evangelicalism, he regretted that by the nineteenth century its theology had become 'more pietistic and less political, directed rather to the salvation of the trembling soul than to the hastening of the New Jerusalem among men'.

'Cathl i'r Almonwydden' (Hymn to the Almond Tree) is a rapturous Pelagian celebration of the 'dance of creation'. While 'cathl' means 'song', it is a somewhat antique and elevated word deliberately chosen for its spiritual, sacramental associations. The poem is a joyously formal rite of language. Festively ceremonial, it invokes the wondrous blossoming of the tree into its mature flowering beauty, seeing in it the revelatory reawakening of the whole world to the reckless glory of its aliveness. Hence the climactic conclusion of each stanza in an extravagant profusion of adjectives, each crowding hot on the heels of the other to suggest the headlong, heady, yet sober paradox of existence. And while the frame of this refrain remains unaltered, the adjectives are different in each return, thus cumulatively revealing the complex character of the miracle that is the Almond Tree. So 'This bold, brave tree, this gentle, laughing cross' morphs successively into 'This humble, eloquent tree, this merry, mischievous cross', 'This strong and silly tree, this shy and shameless cross', 'This bold, brave, tree, this sweet, proud-laden cross', before the poem triumphantly ends in a blaze of praise for 'This tree which hides her scar, this reckless, living cross'.[9]

In its totality, therefore, 'Cathl i'r Almonwydden' is a meditation on the intoxicating paradox that was for Pennar the humanly insoluble mystery of Christ's sacrifice, to which he looked for clarification of human suffering. But the poem also consciously recalls and celebrates the orgiastic pagan festival of spring renewal because, following Pelagius, Pennar believed that the fleshly, sensuous and sexual human body was as inherently sacred as the natural world. Hence the opening invocation of 'many-breasted nature' is followed by references to Math and Gwydion, the two famous magicians from the *Mabinogion*. This passion for 'paganism' is woven into the fabric of the whole poem through the many references to figures from classical and Welsh myths and legends, all of whom seemed to Pennar to prefigure Christian truths, just as the features of the redeemed world were already adumbrated in unredeemed nature. The poem adopts the Neo-Platonic Christian tradition of reading myths, whether Biblical (Rachel), Classical (Daphne) or Welsh (Heledd) typologically; that is, of viewing them as foreshadowing the Christian truth ultimately revealed only in the figure of Christ and the story of His Passion. And it represents the Christian faith as capable of spanning experiences as diverse as those of 'the widowed and the weak in grief' and those of the young who walk 'hand in hand with summer, drunk with the harvest sun'. With a Baroque daring, it even ventures so far as to speculate that for a believer 'the noisome stench which rose up to [Christ's] nostrils' may seem 'the most glorious incense in the world'.

'The road of excess leads to the palace of wisdom', Blake memorably wrote. Pennar's poem is keyed to this belief. It is significant that its concluding phrase hymns 'this reckless, living cross'. Like Waldo, Pennar responded to the recklessness of God as made manifest in His outrageous self-sacrifice. For him the only appropriate human response to this was one of ecstasy. After all, it is ecstasy alone that allows us to 'stand outside ourselves', as the Latin components of the word (ex-stasis) suggest. When thus 'transported' we are verily carried beyond the realms of the mundane and the banal, and are exalted to an entirely different plane of experience, even though in one sense everything remains exactly as it was before. In its handling of language, image and rhythm, 'Cathl i'r Almonwydden' is consequently ludic, in keeping with the gospel of gaiety that lies at its very core. It is reminiscent of those Hasidic priests of Jewish tradition reputed to have risen from their very deathbeds to dance before the Lord. It is a jubilant poem, if we recall that, as Denise Levertov (whose own father was of Hasidic background) wrote, 'Jubilation … goes back/ to a "cry of joy or woe" or to "echoic/ iu of wonder'. A Christian belief in the transformation of woe into joy is the generative paradox of this altogether 'wonder-full' poem:

> What miracle has transformed a broken body
> Into a milk-white, fertile foam of joy?
> Surely the same as gave the doe her gladness,
> The swallow her ecstasy under an azure sky?
> Surely the miracle which turned the sane to madness?
> Grey disappointment to lovely, living verse?
> Surely the miracle which bewitched ancient temples
> On bright slopes underneath the emerald sea?
> Raise high your blossom to vanquish satire and shame,
> This tree which hides her scar, this reckless, living cross.

Davies was very consciously a poet working within the tradition that is examined in this study. In a fine essay, D. Densil Morgan has compared him with Gwenallt, and reached the following illuminating conclusion:

> The differences between Jones's often granite-like, biblically blatant, and theologically uncompromising muse, which finds a focus in the atonement and the cross, and Davies's more allusive Christian humanism with its emphasis on God's good creation renewed by the Spirit and bound for wholeness and redemption, are more apparent than real. Both take the flesh, and the redemption of the flesh, with the utmost seriousness. For each, the Spirit is not an insubstantial wraith but that power and presence whereby creation is given hope and glory.[10]

* * *

Very different in temperament, as in theological outlook, from Pennar Davies, Roland Mathias (1915–2007) is another striking poet of this Welsh religious tradition.[11] By the time he was embarking on a distinguished career as poet and as a pioneering scholar of 'Anglo-Welsh' literature, the culture with which he identified and which he would so enrich through his researches and publications had for some thirty years been not only prevailingly secular, but aggressively anti-Nonconformist. Undaunted by this, Mathias, the son of a Welsh military chaplain who was to renounce his father's legacy of decorated service to be twice imprisoned during the Second World War as a conscientious objector, nailed his own colours defiantly to the mast in such tart statements as he made about the work of Emyr Humphreys. Humphreys was the premier anglophone novelist of Welsh Nonconformity and, like Mathias, was a Welsh Independent, or Congregationalist, save that he belonged to the Annibynwyr, the Welsh-language branch of the denomination:

> There was something in the community of Wales ... in the past three centuries that made such seriousness about the salvation of the world or of the individual or both a preoccupation – an idea that one would never glean from twentieth-century caricatures of Puritan community, whose chief characteristic was apparently hypocrisy.[12]

As the reference to three centuries of 'Puritan' history in Wales suggests, Mathias followed the common practice of Welsh Congregationalists/Annibynwyr of viewing themselves as the heirs of the seventeenth-century Dissenters, as distinct from the Calvinistic Methodists, the johnny-come-latelies who emerged only in the eighteenth century. He also strongly identified with such defining characteristics of his denomination at its best as its principled individualism, its active social conscience, its respect for reason and its emphasis on personal probity balanced by social responsibility. These qualities, so evident in his own personality and bearing, were of undoubted use to him during his impressive career as a Grammar School Headmaster in both England and Wales.

They were also woven into the texture of his writing, apparent in its style, rhythm, tone, discursive stance, and even its vocabulary. Ever conscious that a person should always strive to be as good as his or her word, in many senses of that phrase, he was meticulous in his choice of words, insisting that they be perfectly suited to their occasion. Consequently, he resorted at times to a vocabulary that could seem pedantic and recondite ('a quirk/ Of reed', 216; 'tarquiniad', 207; *fouilles*, 208; 'setts', 209).[13] His poems seem stiff with backbone, unbending in their witness, demanding of scrupulous attention, their stern syntax sometimes painfully contorted into knots. They are first and foremost challengingly intent on being faithful and true to their source in Mathias's experience, whatever the cost in terms of ready intelligibility or of reader appeal.

They are exemplary, and indeed at times formidable, searches for what Edward Thomas memorably termed 'a language not to be betrayed' – betrayed, that is, by the weakness of the flesh for an easy life and a comfortable sociability, its readiness to rub along through compromise, including verbal compromise – the price of participating in a 'common language'. In these respects, Mathias somewhat resembles the notable Ulster Protestant poet John Hewitt, the opening lines of whose fine poem 'Substance & Shadow' are suggestive of the Welshman's approach to writing: 'There is a bareness in the images I temper time with in my mind's defence;/ They hold their own, their stubborn secrecies'.[14]

Mathias's defiant awareness of his difference, because of his firm religious convictions, from many of the Anglo-Welsh writers of his time is arrestingly expressed in 'Testament'(*CP*, 190), in which he self-deprecatingly portrays himself as 'the child/ Of belief, aching pitifully/ In the unready hours/ At the wounds I must suffer/ When I walked out weaponless/ And grown'. There is scornful dismissal of the fashion, first established by Caradoc Evans in his notorious collection *My People*, for Anglo-Welsh writers to claim that theirs had been 'a heroic escape, a grave/ Hypocrisy strangled'. As he mockingly notes, 'They were all heroes then,/ All bullyboys kicking the pews/ In,' and they all loved to jeer at 'The shabby unmuscled parades/ Of the old Model Army'. In that last phrase Mathias (although a pacifist) enlists metaphorically in the ranks of Cromwell's famous Bible-touting soldiers.

This turn to history to acknowledge his roots, predecessors and antecedents was a constant feature of Mathias who, having been awarded a First in History at Oxford, remained a skilled and ardent researcher throughout his life, developing a particular interest in the history of the Recusants of the Welsh Marches – a revealing example of the ecumenism of his basic outlook. Like the Dissenters from whom he traced his own spiritual descent, the Catholic Recusants had been a principled, persecuted 'remnant'. He was tormented 'in remembering I do not enough/ To integrate the present with the past', and his many poems of commemoration of old-time chapel-goers were an attempt to remedy this perceived deficit.

True to traditional Dissenting practice, Mathias was unsparing in his examination of his own spiritual inadequacies and was particularly prone to compare himself unfavourably with past generations of Welsh Nonconformists. 'Why', he despairingly asks, 'am I unlike/ Them, alive and jack in office/ Shrewd among the plunderers?' (*CP*, 190). He found a Biblical case he believed to be similar to his own in the story of Absalom, the beloved, indulged son of King David, adored by the ordinary people, who turned arrogant upstart and rebel intent on deposing his reverend father. Finally defeated and cornered by the royal forces, he became entangled in the branches of a tree and was duly despatched by one of the officers. Yet, upon hearing of his favourite son's death David, far from rejoicing, fell into an inconsolable lament for the loss of 'Absalom, Absalom, Abasalom my son' that has echoed in Western literature down to the present. In the long poem 'Absalom in the Tree', the renegade recalls that

> There was a kind of glory
> Wasn't there, in breaking up their axioms
> About their prurient heads and one by one
> Bawling out the freedoms not to be kept from us
> In this age we make?
>   Are we not opportunists, you
> And I, life-tasters for a consummate generation? (*CP*, 186)

To a judicious onlooker, Mathias's own life would seem to have been the very antithesis of this, principled as it was from beginning to end, but it did not seem so to him. And he remained uneasily fearful that he had somehow succumbed to the seductive spirit of the age – the permissive zeitgeist of the 1960s which he so deeply abhorred and deplored. The conviction that he was unworthy of his ancestors remained with him throughout his life, and he was particularly aghast at what he, the most painstaking and anguished deployer of words, persisted in viewing as his 'glibness'. This was counterbalanced by his sensitivity to what he termed (*CP*, 215) the 'word-wounds' that could be inflicted through casual talk. Consequently, every poem he wrote was a new struggle – a struggle made palpable in its often arcane vocabulary, its tortuous syntax, its stumbling, searching rhythm and uneasy timbre – against this felt temptation to relax into ease of expression.

Mathias was hardly a Romantic in his relations with the world of nature. His approach to it was not only wary but inclining towards the oppositional, and even to the combative. So, in 'The Mountain', a particularly glum early poem occasioned by feeling culturally isolated

and spiritually lonely when teaching in Carlisle, a fine evening may
have him 'intoning to the height/ "Is not the mountain beautiful
tonight?"' (*CP*, 140). But at a deeper level he reflects that 'in the car-
nival of wrongs/ Those shoulders carry clouds', even though 'this first
disguise/ Of beauty' may be eagerly accepted by self-deceiving human-
ity 'as sufficient prize,/ A florid peak capping all conversation': into
that word 'florid' is packed all of Mathias's disgust at the readiness
of human beings to substitute comforting illusions for harsh truths.

It was his faith that inclined him to this suspicious view of the nat-
ural world, in whose recalcitrance he espied evidence of an ingrained
'fallen-ness'. While by no means immune to its beauty he instinctively
mistrusted it – May blossom he could sceptically regard as a florid
showing-off, and already in June he discerned signs of shortening day,
'kitting out/ Beauty in its own short weave' (*CP*, 219). He felt much
more comfortable with the honest onset of winter, in whose 'slatey
dark what is left/ Of courage is caught as it reels by the arms/ Of the
few and the comely, their storm-roughened bark'.

Mathias was ever mistrustful of his own natural inclinations.
Believing himself to be readily emotional and given to sentimental-
ity he disciplined himself into the sternness everywhere evident in
his poetry. And aware of a sensuousness bordering on sensuality, he
suppressed it as a dangerous threat to his spiritual and moral probity.
A fine poem about this is 'The Path to Fontana Amorosa', in which
he tells of his trek to The Baths of Aphrodite in Cyprus. He begins
by admitting the seductiveness of landscape where all is 'magic' (*CP*,
257), with all the lushness of 'the white goddess's country'. But as
he proceeds on his walk he finds himself to be physically reluctant
to continue through this intoxicatingly sexualised landscape and
turns back, 'def[erring] to reach/ The legendary fountain'. He fears
being morally unmanned, so to speak, by giving in to his inner man.
Such poems as this remind us that Mathias's jeremiads were directed
against himself every bit as much as at his contemporary society. They
were savage self-arraignments.

The theology underlying his mistrust of nature's beguiling wiles
is made explicit in 'Burning Brambles', one of his most accom-
plished pieces. It describes, with physical vividness, the experience,
unintentionally self-flagellating, of tackling a malevolently aggres-
sive bramble patch, growing in a neglected corner of the 'unhealthy'
land. The stoppered old 'black bottles' abandoned there seem to him
ready to disgorge 'a heap of old sins without consequence' (*CP*, 211).

Assembling the pile of cut branches for burning becomes a pain-
fully purgative experience, as he wrestles with 'sullen/ Bramble whips
dragged a while since to their pyramid, crest-fallen/ But free to strike
and trip as they can'. The whole process is a 'slow excoriation' as
'the whips work/ Back on the hand, mindless as snakes but bitter'.
Consigned to the flames they produce an abundance of vile smoke
and 'the smell of a life ill lived as it passes down wind'.

The same misgivings about the natural world surface in 'Porth
Cwyfan'. On the seashore there he notes that 'the morning's cold, the
wind/ Bluffing occasional rain' (*CP*, 204), and he comments on 'the
dried fribbles of seaweed' and 'the black worked into the sandgrains/
By the tide's mouthing', before adding 'I can call nothing my own'
in this 'closed-in, comfortless bay'. Contrasting with this landscape
are the ruined remains of a 'chapel' dating from the long bygone age
of a Celtic saint, 'when the finer/ Passions ruled', Mathias ruefully
recalls, and 'convergent answers belled/ Wetherlike towards God'.
This desolate setting in which faith seems to have been devastated and
rendered irrecoverable prompts him to yearn in implicitly acknow-
ledged impotence for the return of the saint's old power to 'bond men
to single/ Living'.

The disastrous decay of an Age of Faith, and the resulting spir-
itual and moral disorientation, is a constant theme of Mathias's
and one that generates some of his best poetry. For him, as for R. S.
Thomas, Maesyronnen is a site of special significance. There 'the
long white chapel leans, a living pledge/ Left by the men who broke
their Babylon, The staple of the slate' (*CP*, 97). But even as in his
mind's eye he sees 'Jogging evangelists come in aflame', his attention
is inevitably sadly riveted on all the signs of gradual abandonment in
the chapel's austere interior: gaps in the roof 'half blocked up with
boards', piles of dusty hymn-books only ten years old', the 'stiff-
necked family pews' long since unoccupied.

His masterpiece in this mode, and one of the truly significant
poems of post-war Wales, is 'Brechfa Chapel'. Once more the subject
is a comparatively remote upland chapel, and Mathias's approach to
it involves an unexpected exposure to 'the slimed/ Substantiation of
the elements' (*CP*, 222). Behind that word 'substantiation' one senses
the palpable presence of 'transubstantiation', a word rich with sac-
ramental associations. There is an ominousness about every aspect
of the site, from the coot's 'queasy paddle' on the nearby pool to 'the
lowered shoulder/ Of mountain … That shallows and darkens the

eye'. As for the pool itself, it seems to resemble Edgar Allan Poe's sinister tarn, 'as the blackened water treads and nibbles/ The reeds and bushes afloat'.

But what really arrests Mathias's heightened attention is the flock of black-backs that seem to him to 'utter … bankrupt and bully unrest'. Theirs, he adds with distaste, 'Is a militant brabble' – that blunt latter term suggestive of a disgust, positively Cromwellian in its dismissive contempt, at the glib prattle of everyday life. A visit to the adjacent cemetery stirs in him respect for the dead who, though living in times so different from the present, and so much harsher, had stubbornly kept the faith contemporary society has so wantonly abandoned. The respite provided by this turn to the past is soon ended, however, as 'the black half-world comes at it,/ Bleaks by its very door': the startling turn of adjective into verb with that neologism 'bleaks' underlines the desolating nature of Mathias's experience. 'Is the old witness done?' he hopelessly enquires – of himself as much as of any potential reader or witness. A small handful, he notes, continue to worship here, but this wan note of hope is immediately drowned out by the pagan babble from the nearby pond:

> The hellish noise it is appals, the intolerable shilly-
> Shally of birds quitting the nearer mud
> For the farther, harrying the conversation
> Of faith. Each on his own must stand and conjure
> The strong remembered words, the unanswerable
> Texts against chaos.

The line break isolating 'shilly' from 'shally' captures Mathias's visceral response to the arbitrary vacillations of a directionless society. The reference to 'the conversation/ Of faith' articulates his recognition that belief is preciously invested in words, so that the corruption of language, evidence of which Mathias believed he saw and heard all around him, was both sign and cause of the corruption and decay of belief. As for the final lines, they memorably speak to his melancholy awareness of the contemporary dissolution of the bonds of belonging, the dispersal of the community of believers, the severance of all ties of spiritual kinship, and the end of the mutual obligations and solidarities of faith. Salvation is now a matter for the beleaguered isolated individual, who must somehow muster from within the spiritual strength to summon up 'the strong remembered words' that alone can

protect against 'chaos'. It is a classic statement of the fundamental
article of faith of a belated Welsh Congregationalist, who has lived on
into an Age of Disbelief. But it is also a classic statement of Mathias's
whole poetic.

* * *

Universally known as 'Kitch', because his father sported a resplend-
ent moustache like Lord Kitchener's, James Davies (1902–52)
was the author of three works that broke the confining mould of
Welsh-language culture.[15] Later in life, 'Kitch' became a *nom de guerre*
defiantly claimed as his own by an anti-colonial Welsh nationalist and
supporter of the peace movement who hated and despised everything
the imperialist, warmongering Lord Kitchener had stood for, but
who fought as fiercely and fearlessly as the Field Marshall had done
for his beliefs.

Although Cardiganshire-born, he spent much of his life teaching
in the Rhondda Valley, where he excelled as a quick-witted verbal
bruiser in the rough and tumble of the hardest of political arenas,
dominated by the heavyweights of the Labour party. He delighted his
political companions with his quick-wittedness, excelling at repartee.
When taunted by colleagues at school, following the 1936 nationalist
attack on a government aerial bombing school site under construc-
tion at Penyberth, that the arsonists must have used 'England's Glory'
matches, Kitch shot back it was 'Pioneer' matches that had done the
damage. Appropriately enough, his grave in Trealaw cemetery is but a
stone's throw from that of Tommy Farr, the Welsh heavyweight whose
enduring popular fame rests on the gruelling and heroic fifteen-rounds
he fought against Joe Louis in Madison Square Gardens during the
Depression 'thirties', although the short, fiery Kitch was much more
in the mould of the incomparable Jimmy Wilde, the fabled 'ghost with
the hammer in his hand', from the twin valley of the Rhondda Fach.

Kitch's political and religious convictions alike had their roots,
as he very well knew, in his early experience of growing up in a turf-
walled cottage with a tiny plot of land adjoining that his father had
carved out of a corner of the great bog of Caron, in the heart of
Welsh-speaking Cardiganshire. Attendance at the local Calvinist
chapel left an indelible mark on his imagination, and its teaching
continued to be the bedrock of his faith to the end, although modi-
fied in the light of progressive theology and Kitch's ecumenical and
syncretic sympathies. Loss of his mother in painful childbirth when he

was six was undoubtedly the traumatic event that formed his psyche, that loss being cruelly reinforced, a few years later, by his effective 'ejection' from Y Llain (the little cottage) following his father's remarriage to a woman from the coalfield. This necessitated the location of the whole family to 'foreign', heavily anglicised industrial South Wales, where his father had been seasonally working underground as a skilled carpenter.

Late in life Kitch wrote a classic essay that recognised this abrupt 'translation' from one community to another as not only epoch-making for him but also a *rite de passage* re-enacting in microcosm the nineteenth-century mass migration of his people as a whole from their rural homes to a new environment that was both raw and entirely alien.

> And as I look back over the whole journey through the wilderness, I have come to understand that the five years after the First World War changed the course of my life entirely. My youth was spent on the land, on a barren smallholding, in a cottage of one, earthen floor; and then I became a townsman, my feet on paving stones, and the wall of streets pressing in on me. On the way from Llwynpiod to Llwynpia, from Rhydypandy to Tonypandy, I stepped out of yesterday and into today.[16]

In that act of rhyming the placenames of both of his localities is revealed Kitch's lifelong dream (translated into cultural and political action) of reconciling the one with the other. His father's act of selling Y Llain from under him, so to speak, of effectively disinheriting him, and betraying his interests, became for Kitch emblematic of what had happened to Wales as a whole. The country had been robbed of its language and with it its lifeline to both past and future. The Rhondda was the result of this, its proletariat the victims of a colonial act of deracination, dispossession and deliberate disorientation. Passionate and totally unsparing of self, Kitch's commitment to Plaid Cymru, the national party of Wales, was fundamental to his attempt to heal this cultural wound. But that wound was also a spiritual one, and at the very end of his life a great poem issued from it.

Kitch was a lifelong iconoclast, of lasting importance in Welsh literature because during his short lifetime he published three works that outraged public opinion. The first of these was a realistic stage portrayal of one family's life in the industrial valleys. It was entitled *Cwm Glo* (Coal Valley) and it shocked respectability by shattering the sentimental myth of 'Shoni', the Welsh collier, that had depicted him as brave, cultured, generous, noble-spirited and pious. For that plaster image Kitch, intent as ever on mischief in the service of truth, substituted one of an uncouth miner literally 'gone to the dogs', leering and lecherous, fond of drink, given to lying, skilful at blackmail, cunning, and manipulatively devious. Even worse, that miner's daughter (and here the play even cagily hints at incest) is a 'trollop' who readily resorts to prostitution on the streets of booming Cardiff where she knows she can make a good living.

The chapels were outraged, banning performance in several places, and so unwilling were respectable young women to take the part of the prostitute that a typically defiant Kitch ended up casting his sister in the role. His outraged culture failed to recognise that the play, appearing as it did after the great depression had ravaged the valleys for some fifteen years, was in fact an attack on industrial capitalism, demonstrating how thoroughly it had morally degraded as well as savagely exploited its captive workforce. It was also implicitly a challenge to the ineffectual, mealy-mouthed chapels to confront this situation honestly and unflinchingly, and to discover in their faith both the courage and the means to combat it and to remedy it. Like many intellectuals of his generation, Kitch deeply deplored the way in which a Welsh Nonconformity whose dynamic origins he believed to lie in the radical, even revolutionary, evangelicalism of late-eighteenth-century Methodism, had slowly ossified into the moral and spiritual complacency of an increasingly hypocritical theocracy.

Having thus violated one of the most sacred of Welsh cultural norms, the undaunted Kitch, ever forthright and plain-spoken, then proceeded to violate another. This time his demolition job was on an even more revered myth, that of the pious rural 'gwerin', the supposed mainstay of Welsh-language culture. Recalling his own scrapeacre early background, and concentrating on the devastation caused to rural Wales by generations of poverty and depopulation (the population of Cardiganshire dropped by nearly 10 per cent during the first decade Kitch spent in the Rhondda), he produced another play, far less conventional in genre than *Cwm Glo* because it veered towards a hybrid poetic drama. It was evocatively entitled *Meini Gwagedd* (The Stones of Emptiness), the title being taken from Isaiah 34: 11:

From generation to generation it shall lie waste; none shall pass through it for ever and ever. But the cormorant and the bittern shall possess it;

the owl also and raven shall dwell in it; and he shall stretch out upon it the line of confusion and the stones of emptiness.

In this controversial play Kitchener, rather like the 'infamous' Caradoc Evans before him, turns the language of the Bible against the very society that had for so long rather hypocritically preened itself on living by it; and that revenge of language is like the twisting of a knife to disembowel a whole moribund religious culture. In this work the moral despair and helpless degradation of rural late-Nonconformist Wales is exposed in a spirit not dissimilar to that in which Patrick Kavanagh was, at the very same time, exposing the plight of peasant Catholic Ireland. The Irishman bleakly detected there no apocalyptic catastrophe, only 'the weak, washy way of true tragedy –/ No hope. No lust./ The hungry fiend/ Screams the apocalypse of clay/ In every corner of this land'.[17]

Nothing really happens in *Meini Gwagedd*. Everything is over before the play even begins, just as everything was over for the characters before ever their lives began; and all of them are bound together on the wheel of fire of that realisation. It is Michaelmas Eve, and the tormented spirits of the dead revisit the ruins of Glangors-Fach, the farm once carved out of the grudging bog but now reclaimed by it. As immediately becomes clear, these ghosts remain shackled to the spot by passions that are still unspent – passions of revenge and resentment, of frustration and smouldering fury – in a manner reminiscent of Yeats's *Purgatory*.

The early audiences of this strange, unorthodox work were deeply unnerved and unsettled by it, and so were the actors, one of whom succumbed to depression. The work features sterile repetitions of language appropriate to the moral, psychological and spiritual stasis that is its subject. Mesmerised by the text, listeners and readers alike leave behind the daylight world of moral clarity and enter the twilight of the double vision. The poetry is integral to the 'action', not least because *Meini Gwagedd* is at bottom a play about language. In an obvious sense, there are too many words in the work; too much is said, and too little done. Because Kitchener's point is much the same as Samuel Beckett's: that people talk, desperately and incessantly, precisely in order to ensure that nothing is really said, that nothing is done, that nothing happens. Repeated vain attempts, that are in reality no more than empty gestures, are made by the characters to get to the root of the stifling malaise. And it is only with the

understanding that comes from reading Kitchener's subsequent mas-
terpiece, 'Sŵn y Gwynt sy'n Chwythu', that we realise in retrospect
that in so unsparingly anatomising the psychology of evasion, deferral
and displacement Kitchener was not only indicting the society that
had produced him, complete with its moribund Nonconformity, but
also secretly indicting himself.

'Sŵn y Gwynt sy'n Chwythu' (The Sound of the Wind that is
Blowing), is Kitchener's supreme achievement and one of the most
profoundly moving of the Welsh religious poems of the last seventy
years. Commissioned for radio broadcast, the text of this long poem
in free verse was dictated by Kitch (who was too ill to write) while
lying in hospital in the terminal stages of the advanced colon cancer
that was to take his life at the age of 50. He lived just long enough to
listen to the broadcast. As a poem destined for broadcasting, 'Sŵn y
Gwynt' played to Kitch's established strengths. His *Meini Gwagedd*
had been a halfway house between the theatrically orthodox *Cwm Glo*
and the kind of work appropriate for this new medium, for which he
had already written and broadcast several personal essays and remi-
niscences. Radio's privileging of the word suited a Kitch who had
been raised in Tregaron in a rich oral culture. There he had not only
come under the spell of eloquent pulpit oratory but had participated
in the popular culture for which the region was famous, that featured
storytelling, jokes, word-games and rhyming contexts.

But the cultural model upon which the work primarily drew was
that of the Seiat. From the late eighteenth century onwards this spir-
itual group-confessional activity had occupied a seminal place in the
faith and practice of the Welsh Presbyterians, the Welsh Calvinistic
Methodist church of which Kitch was a lifelong member. There was
also a tradition in that sect of keeping an audit of the condition of
one's soul; a minutely detailed and scrupulously honest record of one's
spiritual and psychological struggles. William Williams Pantycelyn,
the evangelist who was one of the greatest of the founding figures of
Welsh Methodism and a gifted writer, had published several remark-
able fictionalised instances of this practice. The most celebrated,
published under the title *Bywyd a Marwolaeth Theomemphus* (1760),
was an astonishing 6,000-line epic of the psycho-spiritual struggle for
salvation, and was greatly admired by Kitchener Davies. One of its
characters is Abasis, an ordinary man who has experienced religious
conversion in his youth, but has since settled down to a happy, com-
fortable family life. Beloved by all, he has a good name, yet Pantycelyn

writes of him that as 'a man's name became his, he lost the name of saint'. Warned by Abasis's example, Theomemphus (the Christian hero of the poem) accepts that he has to undergo the purgatory of putting by Philomela, his wife, and of submitting entirely to the agonisingly absolute demands of God's grace.

Saunders Lewis, another of Kitchener's heroes, had published a daring pioneering study of Pantycelyn in 1927.[18] In it, he had drawn upon contemporary psychoanalytical theories to suggest that the Evangelist had anticipated many of them in his writings, just as in the format of the Welsh Presbyterian Seiat, Lewis further suggested, could be detected the rudiments of twentieth-century sessions of psychoanalysis. The Seiat was 'a clinic of the soul'. Kitch had grasped that radio, as a modern medium perfectly suited to the production of a theatre of the mind for the mind, was also a perfect medium for searching out the deepest secrets of the soul. Saunders Lewis's understanding of Freud was mediated through his reading of Robert H. Thouless's *An Introduction to the Psychology of Religion*, an attempt to reconcile religion and psychoanalysis.[19] *Swn y Gwynt* may be read as an attempt to accomplish a similar synthesis. The phenomenon of (re)conversion in middle age, such as that of Theomemphus and Kitchener Davies, was of particular interest to Thouless, who interpreted the conversion experience as the disintegration and reintegration of the conscious self, the result of the eruption into consciousness of psychic elements previously tensely repressed and relegated to the unconscious. As Saunders Lewis had understood, for Pantycelyn (as for Davies) faith was actually a unique means of exploring the depths of the psyche, and such an exploration was a spiritual imperative, because God was to be genuinely encountered only at the end of this inner journey.

In his own case, Kitchener Davies reflects, as he lies in his hospital bed, damaging passions have been too long repressed, resulting in a distortion to the psyche and a protective development of a false selfhood – an act he now sees as an instance of bad faith and a symptom of inauthenticity. In an autobiographical essay entitled 'Adfyw', he had movingly summarised his condition:

> Only three hurts, which I'll simply mention, have I experienced – the loss of my mother when I was six, the sale of Y Llain when I was eighteen, and minutely witnessing, when I was 27, the malicious cancer, like a convolvulus, choking the life out of the aunt who had raised me. (*DW*, 16)

The primal wound was obviously the loss of his mother (which led indirectly to the loss of Y Llain, and to his dependence on his maternal aunt), but at no time before dictating the poem from his hospital bed had he allowed himself to relive the pain:

> Remember coming back in Tre-wern's trap
> from mother's funeral? You got to sit in the front seat with Ifan,
> and everyone felt sorry for you – a hero, so little, so noble,
> Not everyone gets a chance to lose his mother at six, and learn to
>   act so early.[20]

It is a heartrending passage because, after more than forty years, Kitchener can still approach that moment of loss only obliquely, through the protective device of savagely sarcastic self-accusation. But at least the subject is broached, and as the poem proceeds, it remorselessly explores the lifetime consequences of that initiating moment of suppression of agony. It is to that moment Kitchener attributes his subsequent compulsive passion to act, both on stage and in 'real life'. As the poem proceeds, the masquerade grows ever more elaborate, until it affects every aspect of Kitchener's experience – including, most piteously and terrifyingly, his happy home life with his wife and three lovely daughters.

What it can mean for a small child to be separated from his or her mother first became apparent to psychologists who studied wartime evacuees – and Kitchener was doubly an 'evacuee', in that the loss of his mother had been followed by expulsion to distant foreign Banbury where, a small, Welsh-speaking child, he found himself suddenly adrift in a wholly English-speaking environment. The psychologists found that separation meant 'far more than the actual experience of sadness', it could in fact 'amount to an emotional blackout'. That expressive phrase encapsulates the way in which children who are prevented (like Kitchener) from mourning the loss of their mother, may spontaneously create a psychic defence against their unacknowledged pain by developing a 'false' personality insulated from their very deepest longings. Such a defence may 'successfully' last a lifetime, but it leaves the person feeling inauthentic, a sham, a charlatan, an actor, an imposter – the very feelings to which Kitchener gives powerful voice in 'Sŵn y Gwynt' until, at the very end, his 'conversion' experience results in a breakdown of the constructed self; a crucifyingly painful event that results in liberation and salvation.

Reliving his life, Kitch realises that the fury energising all his political work may have been in part a displaced expression of the anger that was at the heart of the grieving he had never allowed himself to experience for his mother. And his lifelong impulse to challenge, to defy, to shock – this was only a compulsively repeated substitution for that original, primal challenge he had failed to face, and was still terrified of facing; the inner challenge of facing up to the violent pain and anger at the loss of his mother, as well as the other two great losses of his life.

But while the psychological trauma he had suffered as a boy may well have been the generator and driver of the poem, there is no doubt as to the spiritual significance for Kitchener of his late acknowledgement of it, or of the spiritual implications, as he saw it, of the deformation not only of psyche and personality but also of soul that the lifelong trauma had occasioned. The allusion in the title 'Sŵn y Gwynt' to the familiar passage in the Gospels that speaks of the Holy Spirit 'blowing where it listeth' makes its clear that at its deepest level the poem is a personal record of Kitch's encounters with a divine power whose visitations were always unpredictable and sometimes ruthlessly demanding. His failure to prove adequate to those demands is the truth about himself that Kitch forces himself to confront unflinchingly at the very end of his life. At the wounded heart of this poem, therefore, there lies a drama of pitiless self-exposure and self-accusation. It is composed to function as a play for inner voices, at once reminiscent and accusatory, several of which taunt Kitch for the lack of the deepest spiritual courage that underlies all his parade of physical and moral courage that, it is implied, has simply been an act to conceal that fatal deficiency of soul.

At another level, however, the poem conceives of the wind first, and most pressingly, as the ambassador of the imminent death by which Kitch is threatened, and then as a devastating, levelling, destructive social, economic and political power such as effectively destroyed the culture into which Kitch had been born, in which he had been raised, and by which he had been formed. That same wind had proceeded to sweep through the industrial valleys of the South during the Depression of the thirties with catastrophic consequences both for its working-class inhabitants and for the Welsh language and its culture which Kitch regarded as the mainstay and bulwark of Welsh nationhood.

Whether or not Kitchener actually realised he was dying when writing 'Sŵn y Gwynt', it has all the hallmarks of the traditional deathbed poem. Such a speaker's situation is, as Seamus Heaney observed of a poem by Yeats, 'that of somebody *in extremis*, somebody who wants to make his soul, to bring himself into wholeness, to bring his mind and being into congruence with the divine mind and being'. [21] At its outset, the poem delicately acknowledges the medical environment in which it is being composed. It opens by acknowledging the 'breeze thin as a needle of the syringe,/ cold, like ether-meth on the skin' that had come to 'whistle round the other side of the hedge'. That hedge dates back to Kitch's very earliest years, growing up in Y Llain, a homestead on one of the exposed slopes of Cors Caron which was protected from the prevailing south-westerlies only by the thicket planted and lovingly tended by the many generations who had lived there, the last of whom was his father. The dying Kitch is brought to the realisation that he has sought refuge behind such a barrier his entire life, totally contrary to his bold public front, and to his reputation as a fearless campaigner for social, economic and cultural justice in the name of Plaid Cymru on the street corners of a raucous, unruly and sometimes intimidating Rhondda.

The first of his mocking inner voices recalls how, as a very little boy attending his mother's funeral, he had learned to act a part; how he had pretended to grieve in order to avoid really, feelingfully, registering the early deaths in his family and his neighbourhood; and how much he had enjoyed the sympathy and praise that had been heaped on him for his 'bravery'. Then another voice enters the poem to recall, nostalgically, how safe he had felt as a child at the little farm, protected by the surrounding hedges. Next, a temptingly reassuring voice is heard persuading him that he was nevertheless not a coward; instead of cowering in this boyhood refuge, he had courageously confronted and courted the wind by climbing the tall trees. Similarly, later, the voice adds, he had braved the hostile fury of life in a Rhondda hostile to his religion and convictions during the locust years of the 1930s. He had helped in the soup kitchens, joined in the jazz carnivals and the games of football between striking miners and policemen. He had even displayed a kind of reckless courage in taking on all comers by preaching Welsh nationalism on street corners. Briefly persuaded, Kitchener accepts this hymn of (self-) praise, only for another voice to erupt impatiently into the poem, accusing him of vanity, shameless self-display and self-pity. This pitiless voice unmasks the secret satisfaction he had derived from acting the hero; and it rubs his nose in the evident uselessness of all the work he had so manically performed in the Rhondda.

This is the turning point in the poem. The core of Kitchener's selfhood having been completely demolished, he is now able to turn to God in utter weakness, and in complete selflessness. This, of course, is a precondition of the visitation of grace. And God comes calling, bringing to Kitch's mind the episode at the very end of the Gospel according to John when Peter, ever impulsive, decides to forget the crucified Christ and to return to his fishing. All night he and his friends labour in vain, until a mysterious stranger appears and advises them to cast their nets on the other side. Thereupon they catch fish in abundance, and Peter, awakened to the presence of the living Christ, is set on the course that leads to his crucifixion upside down in Rome.

The story he has so often preached from the pulpit now takes on a wholly different and urgently personal significance for Kitch. It is clear to him that he has at last been called to confront the ultimate reality he has spent all his life evading: the reality of God's grace that, like the wind, 'bloweth where it listeth'. It alone can bring salvation, but it does so only by crucifying, through its divine, non-human 'otherness', all that a person humanly cherishes, all that an individual naturally lives by. Hence the great, despairing cry to God, at the conclusion of the poem, a cry *de profundis*, to pity him, to spare him, to refrain from making him a 'saint', in the Calvinistic sense of an elect soul, violently seized and saved by grace.

'Quo vadis, quo vadis,' where are you going?
Stop pursuing me to Rome, to a cross, my head towards the ground.
   O Saviour of the lost,
save me, save me, save me,
from Your baptism that washes the Old Man so clean;
keep me, keep me, keep me,
from the inevitable martyrdom of Your elect.
Save me and keep me
from the wind that is blowing where it will.
So be it, Amen
   and Amen (*TCWP*, 119)

These lines simultaneously cry out for salvation and decry it. They perfectly capture a soul perhaps suspended permanently in spiritual limbo, but also perhaps in transit between what St Paul would call the Old Man and the New Man.

The poem is informed by Kitchener's deep interest in the religious drama of T. S. Eliot, full of the poet's melancholy contempt for modern humanity's attempt to find refuge from spiritual realities in the nullity of frenzied activity. In *The Family Reunion* (1939) conscience is 'the cancer/ that eats away the self', and the work brings the soul to 'the stone passages/ Of an immense and empty hospital/ Pervaded by a smell of disinfectant'.[22] *The Cocktail Party* (1949), specifically mentioned in Kitch's poem, deals with a situation where the self has become 'a set of obsolete responses'; it specifically uses the experience of hospitalisation as metaphor, since 'stretched on the table,/ You are a piece of furniture in a repair shop/ For those who surround you, the masked actors;/ All there is of your body/ And the "you" is withdrawn' (*CPP*, 362–3); and the play balks at trying to understand the process of 'transhumanisation', the suffering on the way to illumination.

There is also *Murder in the Cathedral* (1935), an earlier play but an active influence on Welsh writers in the early 1950s, following a translation of it by Thomas Parry that Kitchener reviewed in 1950, and a broadcast produced by Aneirin Talfan Davies. The morality play format, the anguished prayers, all are important aspects of a religious drama in which a chorus of 'common people' speak to themselves as ones 'Who fear the blessing of God, the loneliness of the night of God, the surrender required, the deprivation inflicted;/ Who find the injustice of men less than the justice of God' (*CPP*, 282) and are therefore content to go on living, 'Living and partly living'. In an essay he wrote on the play, Kitchener commented particularly on 'the terror of the broken souls of a shattered world' that is felt by an Eliot whose tempters in *Murder in the Cathedral* are powerfully real and whose agony of mind is inscribed in the nervous parallelisms of a verse that is always doubling back on itself. Such, too, are the rhythms of Kitchener's writing in 'Sŵn y Gwynt sy'n Chwythu'.

'A curse comes to being/ As a child is formed./ In both, the incredible/ Becomes the actual/ Without our intention' (*CPP*, 336). Agatha's words in Eliot's *Family Reunion* apply, in different yet related ways, both to *Meini Gwagedd* (a play in which the Eumenides are ominously present, as in Eliot's text) and to *Sŵn y Gwynt*. As does her hope that 'The knot shall be unknotted./ And the crooked made straight' (*CPP*, 316). In both works, too, we find 'A misery long forgotten, and

a new torture,/ The shadow of something behind our meagre child-
hood,/ Some origin of wretchedness.' For Kitchener the Calvinist,
that 'origin of wretchedness' could be identified both as Original Sin
and as the knot of experiences following his mother's death. But in
his poem, he comes to the understanding reached by Harry in *The
Family Reunion*:

> And all this year,
> This last year, I have been in flight
> But always in ignorance of invisible pursuers.
> Now I know that all my life has been a flight
> And phantoms fed upon me while I fled. Now I know
> That the last apparent refuge, the safe shelter,
> That is where one meets them. That is the way of spectres.
>
> (*CPP*, 338)

But it was also in that 'last apparent refuge' that Kitchener found the
courage to confront those phantoms. And in so doing he plumbed the
depths of his soul and found his way into his God's presence.

Notes

1 D. Densil Morgan, *Pennar Davies* (Cardiff: University of Wales Press, 2003);
   Dewi Eirug Davies, *Cyfrol Deyrnged Pennar Davies* (Abertawe: Tŷ John Penry,
   1981); Ivor Thomas Rees, *Saintly Enigma: A Biography of Pennar Davies*
   (Talybont: Y Lolfa, 2011).
2 For an interesting autobiographical essay, see 'Pennar Davies', in Meic
   Stephens (ed.), *Artists in Wales* (Llandysul: Gomer, 1971), pp. 119–30.
3 'Trioled' and 'Nawn', *Wales*, 11 (Winter, 1939–40), 303 and 301.
4 Open letter in *Wales*.
5 For a discussion of this group, see M. Wynn Thomas, *Eutopia: Studies in
   Cultural Euro-Welshness* (1850–1980) (Cardiff: University of Wales Press,
   2021), Chapter 7.
6 Keidrych Rhys (ed.), *Modern Welsh Poetry* (London: Faber and Faber, 1944),
   p. 13. Another poem characteristically opens with 'Strew on her bloaters,
   bloaters – for her God/ Won't mind at all – but not a bone of cod' (15), where
   the opening line is a parody of Matthew Arnold's 'Requiescat' but the fol-
   lowing lines are pure Pennar.
7 'Ave atque Vale', trans. Joseph P. Clancy, in Menna Elfyn and John Rowlands
   (eds), *The Bloodaxe Book of Modern Welsh Poetry* (Tarset: Bloodaxe, 2003),
   p. 143. Hereafter *MWP*.
8 All quotations here relating to Davies's discussion of Pelagius come from his
   attractive essay 'The Fire in the Thatch', in R. Brinley Jones (ed.), *Anatomy
   of Wales* (Cowbridge: Gwerin Publications, 1972), pp. 105–16.

9   Quotations are taken from the outstanding translation by Elin ap Hywel, in *Saintly Enigma*, pp. 119–20.

10 D. Densil Morgan, 'Spirit and Flesh in Twentieth-Century Welsh Poetry: A Comparison of the Work of D. Gwenallt Jones and Pennar Davies', *Christianity and Literature*, 56/3 (Spring, 2007), 423–35.

11 See the autobiographical essay in Meic Stephens (ed.), *Artists in Wales*, pp. 159–68.

12 Roland Mathias, *A Ride Through the Wood: Essays on Anglo-Welsh Literature* (Bridgend: Poetry Wales Press, 1985), p. 209.

13 References are to Sam Adams (ed.), *The Collected Poems of Roland Mathias* (Cardiff: University of Wales Press, 2002). Hereafter *CP*.

14 'Substance and Shadow', in John Hewitt, *Collected Poems* (Newtonards: Blackstaff Press, 1991).

15 For fuller information about his life and work, see M. Wynn Thomas, *James Kitchener Davies* (Cardiff: University of Wales, Writers in Wales Series, 2002). Hereafter *JKD*.

16 'Adfyw 1', in Manon Rhys and M. Wynn Thomas (eds), *James Kitchener Davies: detholiad o'i waith* (Cardiff: University of Wales Press, 2002), p. 16. My translation. Hereafter *DW*.

17 'The Great Hunger, XIII', in Patrick Kavanagh, *Collected Poems* (London: Martin Brian and O'Keefe, 1972), p. 53.

18 Densil Morgan (ed.), Saunders Lewis, *Williams Pantycelyn* (Cardiff: University of Wales Press, 2016).

19 Robert H. Thouless, *An Introduction to the Psychology of Religion* (Cambridge: Cambridge University Press, 1923).

20 English quotations of the poem are from Joseph P. Clancy (trans.), 'The Sound of the Wind That Is Blowing', *Twentieth-Century Welsh Poems* (Llandysul: Gomer, 1982), pp. 109–19. Hereafter *TCWP*.

21 'Joy or Night: Last Things in the Poetry of W. B. Yeats and Philip Larkin', in *The Redress of Poetry* (London: Faber and Faber, 1996), p. 160.

22 T. S. Eliot, 'The Cocktail Party', in *The Complete Poems and Plays of* T. S. *Eliot* (London: Faber, 1969), p. 295. Hereafter *CPP*.

9

R. S. THOMAS
AND THE TRADITION

'The Bright Field' is probably the best known of R. S. Thomas's religious poems, and also the best loved, although it is far from being his best. Its attractiveness for general readers of today would seem to lie in the shy, captivating admission by Thomas that he has been 'surprised by joy'; gratuitously rewarded with a divine visitation. What such readers resolutely overlook, however, is the subtext of the poem. That makes it clear that such a transfiguring experience is for him all the more precious for having been so unlooked for, so totally unpredictable, and so fleeting. In Thomas's experience, epiphanies were far from common, and frequently shadowed by misgivings and reservations. As he put it in the much greater, and entirely characteristic, poem 'Sea-Watching':

> Ah, but a rare bird is
> rare.[1]

The line break ironically underlines the tautology of a conclusion that is self-evidently banal and anticlimactic. The portentous pause before the stating of the obvious mocks the naivety of any eager, gullible human expectation of reliable revelation in the face of the overwhelming evidence of implacable divine absence. Thomas's great quarry was ever the *deus absconditus* to whom the mystics of the ages had paid their awed tribute.

Therefore, from the point of view of this present volume, implicit in 'The Bright Field' is a critique of the euphoric tradition of religious praise poetry represented by many of the poets already examined.

Contrast, for example, Thomas's cautious response in that poem to
the circumscribed vision so unexpectedly, ephemerally and condition-
ally afforded him with that recorded in 'Mewn Dau Gae', a work
sufficiently admired by Thomas for him to have taken the trouble to
translate it. In Waldo's poem, a similarly mysterious vision is instantly
accepted, and adopted as foundational, before being confidently aug-
mented into millennialist expectation. Or compare R. S. Thomas's
rueful identification of himself elsewhere with a stubbornly doubting
Thomas with Bobi Jones's concentration instead on the conviction
born in that very same Saint after he had investigated the wound in
the body of the resurrected Christ. Throughout R. S. Thomas's life
(1913–2000), it was with the unconvinced Thomas that he instinctively
continued to identify.

As has already been noted in the chapter on Euros Bowen, R.S.'s
attitude towards his distinguished fellow priest in the Church in Wales
(from whom he had received kindly encouragement and assistance as
an adult Welsh learner) tended to be one of sympathetic amusement
edged with disdain. Compared to that of such an enthusiastic par-
ticipant in the Welsh praise tradition, Thomas's spirit was a tortured
one. He could not but have been very aware of the achievements of
Bowen and fellow Welsh members of his visionary company, but he
studiously refrained from acknowledging any of them except Waldo
Williams, pointedly expressing admiration only for the political stand,
rather than the spiritual standpoint, of two of the most distinguished
and prominent: Saunders Lewis (who was in this political connection
a role model for Thomas) and Gwenallt.

Yet, alongside the striking differences between Thomas's spiritual
outlook and that of those other writers, there are also similarities. His
obsession with the otherness of God, an otherness that inherently pre-
vented human beings from experiencing any direct substantial access
to the *mysterium tremendum* of divinity, and his consequent awareness
of how this left believers bereft and adrift in an irreducibly baffling
world, has its parallels in the awareness of Welsh Calvinists such as
Bobi Jones that behind the inexplicable workings of Grace lay the
eternal inscrutability of a 'Duw absen' – Thomas's absent God, the
deus absconditus that became his lifelong obsession. That is also the
experience of the ultimate Godhead memorably acknowledged by
Saunders Lewis in 'Gweddi'r Terfyn'.

Lewis's deep reverence for liturgy and symbol, and the Welsh
Symbolist Euros Bowen's late attraction to the profoundly hieratic

rituals of a Greek Orthodox church where the priest alone is allowed the privilege of penetrating the inner sanctum, find their parallel in Thomas's deep aversion to the radical reforms in his own Church that degraded such practices. In his jaundiced view, these reforms had resulted in 'bathetic renderings of the scriptures' (*CLP*, 53) and a vulgarised version of the majestic ancient liturgy that he loathed.[2] In his fixed opinion, the solemn, sacred charge of the original text had been entirely lost in the process. And Thomas deplored even more strongly the new version of the Eucharist, which required the priest to turn to face his congregation when ministering Holy Communion rather than to direct his gaze at the altar as previously. The change for him was utterly sacrilegious. Thomas's devotion to image, symbol and ritual as unique sacred mediators of spiritual realities to human beings corresponded closely to the faith of Lewis and Bowen in the same features of worship, while his openness, particularly late in life, not only to alternative versions of the Christian faith but to the spiritual testimony of other, great, non-Christian world religions (most particularly Buddhism) is reminiscent of Vernon Watkins's heterodox and syncretic beliefs and of Pennar Davies's tolerant, liberal ecumenism. He shared Euros Bowen's conviction that 'the celebration of the sacrament saves the word of grace from becoming an ideology of Christ'.[3]

But even after due attention and weight has been given to such traces of continuity, it remains starkly evident that the prevailing temper of Thomas's religious poetry is different in its very essence from that of all other Welsh poets of his time. Not that he was not as fully capable as any of them of responding in an ecstatic, even mystical, manner to the wonders of the natural world. 'May is the white month, whitethorn, daisies and blossom', he wrote in a 1944 Notebook in accents of measured rapture. 'Now comes the yellow month, the meadows plastered with buttercups and the evening light yellow as daffodils. Up in the hills around Adfa and Cefncoch the wild laburnum throngs the hedges, the leaves as yellow as the flowers. The young owls were sitting in the great ash this morning, like mouse grey old men, and just as wheezy. The moon daisies are creeping towards the house.'[4] He continued throughout his life to record in both poetry and prose similar interludes of ecstatic mystical experience, even terming himself a 'nature mystic' during the final years of his life. And as I have elsewhere explained, his dependence on such extra-ecclesiastical experiences deepened as his quarrel with his

Church reached its climax, until by the final decades of his life it was to the world of nature that he primarily looked for spiritual succour, while his poetic imagination became ever more venturesome in searching out alternative religious beliefs.[5] But his temperament also continued to insist on showing its other, dark, face, as he admitted in a Notebook entry as early as 26 February 1945:

> in the heyday of the blood there is nothing I would not tackle, nowhere I would not live, and it be close to the stones and the grasses; but one thing is certain, this is not wholly me, or if it is it demands all my courage to sustain it. Because ever and anon I see it as an unprofitable waste, or as I ask myself am I right to concentrate on the earth and nature as I do? At times it seems so right, and a grim field of battle, all of which suggests that I am sick or abnormal, and there is nothing in Nature for the sick or the abnormal.

As this shows, Thomas was ever helpless to deny his nagging, underlying recognition of the cruelty of the laws governing the world of God's creation. A passage from an unpublished Notebook conveniently captures his bifurcated vision: 'Up beyond the Gweunydd this evening', he writes. 'So happy to be wandering the lanes, the wind, tides of wind in the boughs and the hurrying clouds above. I kneel clasping my staff – and I am. All the universe leads up and centres itself in me. This is not pride but a sweet humility.' (Nbk1, 14 June, 1944.) This is followed directly by a reaction that not only contradicts but undercuts it, as he registers the 'inexorableness of nature's laws'. This in turn leads him to a torturing paradox: 'I say love is one of the highest, if not the highest, things we know – it is creative, it is space-straining, time-mastering, but God is not love. It is a partial truth, or a failure of terminology, or the result of a misconception of the nature of deity. To hold it is to encounter insoluble problems, irreconcilable facts.' (Nbk1, 15 June 1944.)

Tormented as he was by such insoluble conundrums of faith, he was prone to accuse himself of being spiritually diseased, and to regard his soul as having in some way been deformed, as the following searingly confessional passage makes clear:

> Whence comes the furtive love of death within one. The flirtation with destruction, evil, annihilation … At times as I read or think of the future, I realize how little love I have for spiritual health and perfection, as compared with the darker waywardness of the soul. It is only in moments of

weakness or sickness of body that [I] run whimpering to a God created
out of my immediate need. Well, I see God as spirit, moving endless,
impersonal as wind, through the waste places of the world. (Nbk1,
14 March 1945)

A whole lifetime later, Thomas was to confess that 'One is tinged
with the pessimism of poets like A. E. Housman. There is a kind of
life-denying part in one's make-up, a kind of nihilistic approach to
life.'[6] As this suggests, Thomas's vision (not least of his own plight
as both a believer and a priest, and thus as a public professor of
the Christian faith) has its tragic aspects. But these have been deter-
minedly overlooked by his many critics, even though he himself was
not at all shy of using the loaded term 'tragedy' to describe this bent
of his imagination. In an entry in an unpublished Notebook, Thomas
frankly reflected that 'Life is a tragedy ... to those who think, but
whereas none can avoid feeling, most people have long-ago been
taught not to think too much.' (Nbk1, 25 June 1944.) He then pro-
ceeded to identify existential grounds for a tragic vision such as his
own: 'It needs thought and imagination now to realize the full import
of Abel's blood crying from the ground. The average man has neither
– "wise in his own conceit".' Here, the blood crying from the ground is
both the blood of the hare killed by pursuing hounds that he had just
mentioned and the blood of the many that at the time he was writing
were trapped in the carnage of the Second World War.

In another Notebook entry, of 5 January 1945, he mentions how,
when 'reading Hardy (Jude the Obscure) I think that all prose is inad-
equate for dealing with tragedy, indeed with almost any circumstances
of emotions that have the light of eternity or the shadow of annihila-
tion upon them. All such can only be adumbrated in poetry.' Then on
10 February of the same year comes the following passage:

> Is it a God of love that can look on and suffer it all to be? Is it our lack
> of faith that will not turn to him for healing? And what sort of a God is
> it that will let little children suffer for want of our turning to pray?
>
> Is it that with the advance of scientific & medical knowledge we have
> grown too rational in our acceptance of the incurable? Is this the same
> God who disported himself a few weeks back, so heedless of us?
>
> Questions, questions – must they remain unsolved, unanswered? The
> first reaction is saeva indignatio and yet we are weak, we are frail, we
> NEED God. The only satisfactory answer, though essentially tragic, is
> that God too is at war with pain and evil. He, too, suffers as we, only more

so, having the weight of the world's ills upon him. Yet this will not satisfy the philosophers – it is dualistic – it imposes limits on the illimitable.

The problem of accounting for the overwhelming evidence of suffering in a world supposedly created by a God of love: it tormented R. S. Thomas his entire life. And in these early entries may already be embryonically discerned two of the theological strategies he adopted in his poetry in an attempt to cope with it. The first was to detect in Christ's crucifixion an image of a God who Himself suffered with his people. In 'In a Country Church' he speaks of kneeling long in the church porch, vainly seeking a response to his prayers, until he finally sees 'love in a dark crown/ of thorns blazing' (*CP*, 67). But then, such a vision of an empathetic God, adopted particularly in the poetry of his late-middle period, led only to a myriad theological objections, including that such an image of divinity inevitably involved a denial of God's awesome omnipotence and overlooked His wholly transcendent aspects.

While of course aware of the theology of *kenosis*, according to which God opted to set aside his full divinity in order to assume the form of Christ, Thomas seems never to have been satisfied by it. Instead, he turned to another explanation, and one that came to loom large in his late work when death was ever impending. His strategy now was to foreground that very transcendent otherness of God, and to emphasise that when thus coolly viewed *sub specie aeternitatis* the otherwise vivid world of human experience faded into ephemeral, illusory importance. Along with this latter perspective went Thomas's lifelong interest in the inevitably limiting and distorting medium of language, which he came to regard as a merely human construct, fatally flawed by the limiting and distorting capacities of human faculties. Language could at best be but a darkling glass that inevitably muddled understanding. And the older he got, the more Thomas seems to have been attracted to the wholly super-human dimension of ultimate spiritual reality that was emphasised by Eastern faiths such as Taoism and Buddhism. In the process, Christ, in His role as the unique mediator of the divine to human beings, largely vanished from his picture. Content even with accepting that all individuality would be entirely annihilated at the end, Thomas settled for cremation.

The early Notebooks also confirm how cunningly equivocating was the title of Thomas's first published volume, *The Stones of the Field*. That very phrase, taken from the Book of Job, is first mentioned in the context of Thomas's harsh criticism of the life of modernity and signifies his profound desire for a return to a simpler form of living, rural in character, and attuned to the wonder and mystery of God's world. In this connection, therefore, the title is consistent with Thomas at his most affirmative and mystical. But that same Book of Job is also referred to in the Notebooks in an entirely different context, and one that lends it a wholly different character.[7] The theme of the Book, Thomas now asserts, is the unimportance of human existence when viewed against the background of a supreme Godhead of 'superlative' power, an impersonal power that is revealed impartially in 'winter and summer ... lightnings and clouds'. When set in that context, preoccupation with human suffering seems symptomatic of the inadequacy of human understanding and of the limitations of language. But then, one might add, in the Book of Job the existential implications of these two contradictory aspects of human relationship to the divine are given unforgettably tragic expression, and indeed some modern interpreters have foregrounded this and argued that Job's capitulation to an Almighty who has simply demonstrated His crass overwhelming power is intended as an ironic comment on its divine 'legitimacy'.[8]

There are, then, several sources for Thomas's chronically tragic sensibility, and yet another of these becomes apparent when one recalls his largely overlooked interest in Miguel de Unamuno's classic study of the 1920s, *The Tragic Sense of Life in Men and in Peoples*. One comment in particular of Unamuno's seems particularly pertinent:

> There is [a] tragic Inquisition which the modern man, the man of culture, the European – and such am I – carries within him. There is a more terrible ridicule, and that is the ridicule with which a man contemplates his own self. It is my reason that laughs at my faith, and despises it. And it is here that I must betake me to my Lord Don Quixote in order that I may learn of him how to confront ridicule and overcome it.[9]

Elsewhere the Spaniard talks of the attempt of Pilate, the sceptical man of culture, to turn the crucifixion into a mockery, a comedy. And he adds that the true heroism of a modern believer is to face and overcome such ridicule, a ridicule to which the rational part of his own self exposes him. He is doomed to be a Don Quixote of the spirit, a believer permanently trapped between doubt and conviction, and uncomfortably alive, always, to the ridiculous aspects of his faith, as supremely symbolised in the enigma of the cross. Alone among the twentieth-century religious poets of Wales, R. S. Thomas was such a Don Quixote.

* * *

In general, Thomas was a more convincing and compelling poet when, as usually was the case, being tormented by God's absence than when he had fitful occasion for affirming His presence. It was the publication of *H'm* in 1972 that saw him unveil the major preoccupation that was to sustain him for the rest of his life and to result in a great body of religious poetry. Recently settled in Aberdaron, despairing of both culture and politics, returning to the comforting vastness of ocean, awed by the vaulting sky-scape of a peninsula composed of ancient rocks and crossed by legendary pilgrim paths marking it as sacred space destined to become a 'laboratory of the spirit', he began to send out his distinctive verse probes into inner space. Seamus Heaney characterises the Thomas of this, late, period brilliantly in *Stepping Stones*. Having discussed his interest in the early Thomas and his Prytherch poems, Heaney goes on to say that

> when I came back to him, it was in the 1980s and I was lecturing on contemporary British poetry at Harvard. What I loved then were those later poems about language, about God withdrawn and consciousness like a tilted satellite dish – full of potential to broadcast and receive, but still not quite operating. He got very far as a poet, a loner taking on the universe, a kind of Clint Eastwood of the spirit. Every bit as unsmiling as Clint, but in either case you couldn't be sure there wasn't a truly wild comedian lurking in there somewhere.[10]

That 'comedian' duly put in his appearance in volumes like *H'm*.

The omnipresence of a God who remained tantalisingly absent; the haunting otherness ('the seal's eye-/ball is cold') of a natural world glorious and murderous by turn; the irreducible mysteriousness of a relativistic, post-Einsteinean universe; the necessity and futility of prayer; these and like themes gave rise, over some half-dozen volumes, to a quietly intense experimental poetry of incomparable spiritual consequence. Pun, irony and ambiguity perfectly encapsulated the double-think of a faith that nevertheless remained stubbornly persistent. He generated lapidary epigrams, Gnostic parable, Borgean fantasies, scientific tropes, meditative exercises, a modern *Mass for Hard Times* (1992), and a spiritual *Counterpoint* (1990), in an attempt to develop, with the assistance of a post-modern theology informed by an eirenic sympathy with some of the world's great non-Christian faiths, a subtle new religious vocabulary that would be truly answerable to the scientific outlook, and that was empowered to speak to the dis-enchanted and largely post-Christian sensibility of the modern world.

But much has already been written (not least by myself) about the subtleties, complexities and labyrinthine perplexities of Thomas's poetry of chronically distempered and compromised faith. It would therefore be superfluous to add to that voluminous body of discussion here. What may reward some further exploration, however, is Thomas's awareness of his position within an ancient Welsh tradition both of worship and of poetic religious expression. And the very first important fact to register in this vital connection is that Thomas was not an 'Anglican priest', another of the 'country priests' of English literary tradition, as has been almost universally assumed by his many commentators. Rather, he was most emphatically and pointedly a priest of the (Anglican) Church in Wales, which was an entirely different matter, and a deeply consequential one. It was, indeed, a distinction to which he felt a militant attachment throughout his life. After all, his own decision to enter the priesthood had been significantly influenced by it.

Thomas was actually older than the Church into whose service he entered, the latter[11] having finally legally uncoupled from the state in Wales as late as 1920, following a century of fierce, and increasingly bitter, campaigning by the 'alliance' of Welsh Nonconformist denominations that had de facto become the nation's 'church' of choice. It was precisely this historic act of ecclesiastical disestablishment that had helped persuade the young Thomas that this 'new' church could and would become the national church of his nation. After all, he knew that the Church of England had fulfilled that very role for many of the previous centuries, during which time the Welsh people had taken to affectionately referring to it as 'yr Hen Fam' (the Old Mother). But then the nineteenth-century Church had become thoroughly Anglicised, and so completely alienated from the Welsh people as to seem a foreign, colonial intruder.

In its disestablished form, the Church in Wales, or so the young Thomas had ardently believed, would forsake its traditional commitment to statism, imperialistic militarism and arrogant English nationalism and recover its ancient mission of national service. But as I have endeavoured to show in some detail elsewhere, his whole career in the priesthood was destined to be an increasingly bitter disappointment in these respects. By the time of his departure from it, so disillusioned and embittered had he become that he had begun to turn his back on 'his' Church. Having taken, not entirely voluntarily, an early retirement under circumstances that had left him permanently resentful, he increasingly turned for spiritual solace to the landscape of the Llŷn peninsula where he had settled. There he related primarily to the sea that roared into the dangerous bay immediately below his very door, to the birds whose freedom from boundaries and constraints he so envied, to the particularly ancient Cambrian rocks of this elongated bough of land, and to the scatter of simple churches (originally Celtic foundations) that (like his own church of St Hywyn in Aberdaron) stood as a reminder that this locality had for many centuries been traversed by pilgrims on their way to the holy island of Enlli (Bardsey). 'There were other churches', he recalled in *The Echoes Return Slow*, 'from which the population had withdrawn, Celtic foundations down lanes that one entered with a lifting of the spirit', not least because they stood for a God so different from 'the God worshipped only in cathedrals, where blood drips from regimental standards as from the crucified body of love' (*CLP*, 53).

Cloistered within the boulder walls of his small, ancient (and antiquated) cottage, he settled for living a largely sequestered life, ranging abroad freely to explore the surrounding countryside he so loved and busying himself with various local campaigns to defend what was left of the rich cultural life of this distinctive district but otherwise choosing a hermit-like existence. At least until his wife's passing and his eventually turbulent second marriage, this late Thomas found it so painful an experience to attend Eucharist that he sought out alternative liturgies in the natural world, as his poetry demonstrates. He increasingly devoted himself to his poetry, as that enabled him to connect with the *fons et origo* of the sacred experience that his Church had expelled. He had, in any case, long established to his own satisfaction the solid theological grounds for precisely such a retreat to the text:

Well, word is metaphor, language is sacrament, sacrament is language, the combination is perfectly simple. In presenting the Bible to my congregation I am presenting imaginative interpretation of reality. In presenting the sacrament, administering the sacrament of bread and wine to the congregation I am again conveying, I'm using a means, a medium of contact with reality (in a slightly different medium from language). (Quoted in *SO*, 193)

'Christ was a poet,' Thomas bluntly asserted, 'poetry is religion, religion is poetry ... the New Testament is a metaphor, the Resurrection is a metaphor.'

As I have tried to show at length elsewhere, the history of this long experience of disillusionment and consequent reorientation is inscribed in Thomas's religious poetry, and it is important evidence of the centrality, for him, of his relationship both to Welsh spiritual tradition and to the body of poetry that had for a millennium and a half issued from that source. There is a typically wry acknowledgement of this indebtedness, as of his own ambivalent feelings about prominent aspects of the Welsh religious tradition, in one of the many poems in which he paid tribute to the spiritual genius of Ann Griffiths:

> If there was a campaign
>
> for her countrymen, it was one
> against sin. Musically
> they were conscripted to proclaim
>
> Sunday after Sunday the year
> round they were on God's side. England
> meanwhile detected its enemies
>
> from afar.[12]

Here he is satirising both nineteenth-century English imperialism, and the entrenched Welsh Nonconformity of the same period, increasingly obsessed as it had become with social conformity and respectability, and given to intoxicating orgies of communal hymn-singing.

It is interesting that the first individual to recognise and appreciate the indebtedness of Thomas to Welsh religious culture was Saunders Lewis, another maverick product of the same culture and another who notoriously distanced himself from it in its ossified nineteenth-century Nonconformist manifestation.[13] The work of all the important poets of twentieth-century Wales, whether they were ostensibly religious or not, Lewis observed in a private letter of 1953 to Kate Roberts, rested on the inherited body of Christian belief.[14] Regardless of whether they themselves were believers or not, they all drew on that Christian store of imagery and symbolism. The only contemporary practitioner who was ready to acknowledge this however, he added, was R. S. Thomas. It remains to add that Thomas favoured two ways in particular of advertising and maintaining his own special relationship to Welsh Christian tradition: by addressing poems to sacred sites, and to representative individuals. In both cases, the texts discharged ultrasonic waves whose return to sender reliably enabled him to check his own spiritual bearings.

Undoubtedly the most prominent of the religious sites addressed in his poetry was St David's cathedral, a national institution that Thomas regarded with the deepest suspicion and disapproval, as 'A Line from St David's', his poem on the subject, confirmed (*CP*, 123). He deplored the alien character of an ecclesiastical edifice that continued to flaunt its military banners and refused to acknowledge the Welsh language. For him, this all testified to the unreconstructed nature of the disestablished Church in Wales, which stubbornly remained anything but the Church of Wales. This was all the more galling because not only did the cathedral purport to commemorate the patron saint of Wales, Dewi Sant, and claim to be the spiritual heir to his native Celtic church, but it was situated in a district whose indigenous, Welsh character had found expression in the incomparable richness of language found in the poetry of that native of Pembrokeshire, Waldo Williams, whose genius Thomas deeply admired. In the poem, the Welshness banished from the cathedral is found lying low in the humble, green 'wall lettuce' that hides in the crevices of its stonework. Thomas associates that lettuce with the medieval Giraldus Cambrensis, the churchman who had taken a stand, stirring but futile, against Norman insistence that Canterbury replace St David's to become the seat of ecclesiastical power in Wales as in England.

Thomas's insistence on mentioning in his poem that he had arrived at St David's 'by way of Plwmp', seems puzzlingly gratuitous until one recalls that, as Jason Walford Davies has illuminatingly pointed out, the name of the village of Plwmp probably derived from the English for 'pump'. It may therefore have originally signified the presence in the village of a well. A source of water sacred in Celtic tradition, a well was also very relevant to the figure of Dewi, who was popularly known as 'Dewi Dyfrwr', or 'Dewi/ the water-drinker' as Thomas has it. In the poem, therefore, 'Plwmp' functions as a secret spiritual and cultural cipher. It acts as a textual divining rod, indicating exactly where in this colonised landscape authentic spiritual power actually rests.

Far more appropriate as a site for commemorating St David than the cathedral erected in his name, in the opinion of Thomas as of Saunders Lewis, was the smaller church at Llanddewi-brefi, the village in rural Cardiganshire marking the site of the sermon the humble saint famously delivered when the ground rose into a hill beneath his feet, allowing him to address the gathered multitude. Tellingly, though, in Thomas's early poem to 'Llanddewi' the church puts in no more than a token appearance. The focus is instead entirely on the tranquil country setting, 'where the sheep pasture and the shadows fall/ Thick as swathes under the sun's blade'.[15] There Thomas imagines himself viewing 'the moles lifting the ground,/ And think[ing] of the saint's cunning and how he stood/ Preaching to the people from his secret mound'. In the work of the moles, it is as if the very earth still recalls the way it made itself available as both pulpit and altar to Dewi Sant in recognition of him as truly native of its soil.

By contrast, the cathedral at St David's is regarded in 'A Line from St David's' as little better than a vulgar intruder in the Welsh landscape and an impudent imposition upon it. The beauty of the Pembrokeshire countryside in high summer is lyrically acknowledged – the golden 'hawksweeds in the hedges', the 'larks ... like a fresh chorus/ Of dew', the 'blue lining' of an incomparable day is made 'Partly of sky, partly of sea', and Thomas finds the ageless sight of a plough becalmed by rust and a man sharpening a scythe beguiling. But the whole point of summoning up such a rural idyll is so that Thomas can end by abruptly banishing the stone cathedral from sight and from mind: 'this is of more/ Importance than all the visitors keeping/ A spry saint asleep in his tomb' (*CP*, 123).

It is significant, too, that Thomas should specifically situate himself in 'Llanddewi' ('St David's church') as looking out 'beyond the wall of the old church'. He is clearly thinking not of the church building itself but of the stone enclosure within which it sits. At many of the sites of old churches in Wales such a wall faithfully continues to trace an ancient sacred boundary, that of the *clas*. The *clas* was the building seminal to Celtic monasticism. Unlike later Norman monasteries, which typically consisted of a whole complex of buildings, it was a single building that housed an independent community of monks headed by an 'abad'. It has been estimated that between the seventh and ninth centuries Wales may have contained as many as 150–200 *clasau* scattered across the length and breadth of the country. After the Norman conquest, some of these Celtic foundations were attached to Benedictine or Augustinian religious orders, while others were replaced by Norman churches. Thomas therefore valued every trace of a *clas* as a reminder of the Church in Wales's long-standing claim (legitimate in his opinion) to be the true heir of native Celtic Christianity. This was a claim that had originally been famously advanced by renowned Welsh Tudor scholars and Protestant churchmen in an attempt to persuade their people to abandon their traditional deep devotion to the Church of Rome and to accept instead as their very own the upstart new Church of England, a church they would otherwise have been instinctively inclined to reject as foreign to themselves.

The very name 'clas' remains buried to this very day in the name Glasbury, a hamlet situated in Powys, in the Welsh Marches, a region which was the seedbed of early Welsh Dissent in the mid-seventeenth century. Nearby stands Maes-yr-Onnen, a simple chapel of that period converted from a medieval long-house. It is one of the most important sites in the history of Welsh Dissent, since the foundation of the 'cause' dates back to the period of the ministry of the famous Vavasour Powell in the 1640s and of his subsequent missionary work during the 1650s when he was one of those authorised by Cromwell's government to approve or eject Anglican incumbents. However, the present building dates back to the 1690s, when a farmhouse originally converted for the purposes of worship during the 1660s, after a series of Acts had condemned Dissenters to a marginal existence, was modernised.

Thomas valued this 'chapel/ Left stranded in the hurrying grass' not because of what he termed 'the stale piety' imprisoned within its modern walls but for 'that rarer air,/ Blue as a flower and heady with the scent/ Of the years past and others yet to be' (*CP*, 24). In mentioning the 'blue flower', Thomas has specifically in mind its profound importance for Romantic poets, following Novalis's celebrated valorisation of it in his unfinished story *Heinrich von Ofterdingen*. For Novalis, as for E. T. Hoffmann and later German Romantics, it signified not only youthful love but also the metaphysical yearning for the infinite and unreachable. Thomas Carlyle went further and saw in the

blue flower an image of poetry itself, and of the Romantics' venera-
tion of its sacred power. There is therefore a quiet subversive wit in
the way that Thomas here associates the exotic flower cultivated in the
hothouse climate of high German Romanticism with the humble trad-
ition of plain Welsh Dissent, and uses it as a trope for the intoxicating
smell of ordinary fresh air that 'brushed each window/ and outsoared
the clouds'/ Far foliage with its own high canopy'.

But then the poem concludes with a quiet modulation of key that
attunes it to the high Romantic tradition after all, as Thomas reports
having heard, 'incredulous .../ Up in the rafters, where the bell should
ring,/ The wild, sweet singing of Rhiannon's birds'. Chapels do not, of
course, possess either a belfry or bells, and so are free, or so Thomas
here implies, to offer home to a far superior form of heavenly music.
He is alluding to the famous passage in the Second Branch of the
Mabinogion where the otherworldly birds are said to sing over the sea
at Harlech, and to the other reference in *Culhwch ac Olwen* when they
wake the dead and send the living to sleep. In the Second Branch, the
seven survivors of carnage feast, and 'as soon as they began to eat
and drink, three birds came and sang them a song, and all the songs
they had heard before were harsh compared to that one. They had
to gaze far out over the sea to catch sight of the birds, yet their song
was as clear as if the birds were there with them.'[16] A lifelong bird-
watcher, Thomas was enchanted by birds, envying them their literally
transcendent freedom.

*   *   *

R. S. Thomas had the soul of a solitary, and so he found the com-
bination of quiet and simplicity deeply conducive to the inwardness
of spiritual meditation, particularly when experienced within the
ancient walls of a Welsh religious building, whether chapel or church,
marinated long in time. These humble buildings provided him with
a sustaining sense of cultural, as well as spiritual, continuity. They
marked the ley-lines, so to speak, of a spiritual tradition native to
his land. They enabled him to feel reassuringly grounded in Welsh
religious tradition, particularly when the sites were relatively isolated
and thus insulated from all casual human traffic and intercourse, to
which he was notoriously allergic.

An intriguing early confession of the lure for him of religious
buildings in 'lonely out-of-the-way' places is found in his 1948 essay
'Dau Gapel'/ Two chapels.[17] It provides valuable insight into the

fusion of religious and nationalist views in his outlook when he was in his mid thirties. In it he outlines the competing, and contrasting, claims of Maes-yr-Onnen and Soar-y-Mynydd on his affections, beginning by inadvertently revealing his ignorance at that stage of the history of early Dissent in Wales when he speculates that the scatter of 'small chapels in wild romantic settings' was 'a sign ... of the adventurous spirit of the early nonconformists' (*SP*, 43). Not so, of course. The origin of that practice was the notorious Five-Mile Act of 1665 that decreed all places of worship that were served by former priests who had left their parishes to turn Dissenting ministers must be removed by at least five miles from the parish from which they had been 'expelled'. Be that as it may, Thomas confessed it was the remoteness of some of these old buildings that continued to fascinate him.

His essay pivots around a contrast between a 'chapel of the spirit' and a 'chapel of the soul'. Maes-yr-Onnen is for him the former, and there he speaks of having found himself 'in the Spirit' with St John the Divine on the island of Patmos, and of having been granted a vision of 'the breadth and height of the mystery of the creation', an experience that eluded capture in language. Revealingly it is to the (rather trite) Welsh, Victorian religious poetry of Gwili that he turns in order to express his young man's experience of the eternal youthfulness of God. It is an early example of Thomas tentatively learning to align himself with the Welsh-language poets of native religious tradition. And this association provides him with a springboard to the great myths and tales of medieval Wales, prompting the same leap of imagination as is accomplished in his poem about the same chapel.

But then he turns his attention to Soar-y-Mynydd, which he designates 'the chapel of the soul'. Situated deep in the upland country beyond Tregaron, this hauntingly situated chapel was built to serve the scattered community of farmers and shepherds of the Welsh hills. There, too, he experiences a vision, but this time one of 'the soul of a special type of man, the Cymro or Welshman. For the very source of Welsh life as it is today is here in the middle of these remote moorlands of Ceredigion. And it is in places of this sort that the soul of the true Welshman is formed' (*SP*, 46). This offers us a glimpse of the disconcerting naivety of Thomas's concept of Welsh nationhood at this early juncture in his development and of his jejune readiness to entrust the future of Wales to such a vision.

But from the point of view of the present discussion, it is the spiritual conclusion he reaches on the strength of this national vision that should cause us pause. If he had to choose between the two chapels, and his respective visions, he explains, he would unhesitatingly opt for Soar-y-Mynydd, despite his readiness 'to admit the value of the spirit'. This is because

> the truth is that a nation that is fighting for survival cannot afford to change its soul for some obscure spirituality no matter how excellent that may be from the individual's point of view. Anyone who can feel for the life of the Welsh countryside has experienced something too strong and too profound to be ascribed to another world, or another life. Here, in the soil and the dirt and the peat do we find life and heaven and hell, and it is in these surroundings that a Welshman should forge his soul (*SP*, 47).

It is a stunning assertion of a challenging credo that was to be heavily revised, although never totally abandoned, by Thomas throughout the many remaining decades of his life. By the end, it had modulated into a belief that the spiritual experience he had experienced at Maes-yr-Onnen, and that had proved after all to be deeply ingrained in his own nature, was in itself that precious aspect of his Welshness that allowed him to keep house in a cloud of witnesses, as Waldo Williams had so memorably put it.

Thomas responded to the appeal of old chapels, associating them with the era of pre-Nonconformist Dissent. It was the chapels of the nineteenth century, and the form of worship they practised, that were anathema to him. In them, he believed, religion had become vulgarised and cheapened, hymns were embarrassing expressions of Victorian sentimentality at its worst, God was spoken of in demeaningly familiar terms, and congregations were controlled by a patriarchy of deacons who had 'crease[s] in their soul[s]', as he vividly put it. This is the intolerant, bigoted, chapel culture, puritanically repressed and correspondingly hypocritical, that the poor, innocent, well-meaning 'Morgans' is doomed to serve in Thomas's powerful tragic portrait of the life of an upland preacher in 'The Minister'. This long poem is a kind of short-story in verse in the notorious tradition of Caradoc Evans. But it is complicated by the fact that Thomas clearly sympathises with Morgans' plight because it resembles his own, condemned as he too was to serve what he came to believe was a mercenary, hard-bitten rural community in Manafon.

Yet Thomas could on occasion be moved by recollections of the periodic revivalist fever and fervour that could possess even the congregation in a grey, drab nineteenth-century Nonconformist chapel. So, it is in 'The Chapel' (*CP*, 276), a plain, unostentatious building 'a little aside from the main road' and ignored by the roaring traffic, that he found himself imagining how

> here once on an evening like this,
> in the darkness that was about
> his hearers, a preacher caught fire
> and burned steadily before them
> with a strange light, so that they saw
> the splendour of the barren mountains
> about them, and sang their amens
> fiercely, narrow but saved
> in a way that men are not now.

It is a poem poised beautifully and movingly between a wistfulness for a supposedly uncomplicated, simpler age of belief and an irony laced with distaste at not only the 'ferocity' but the 'narrowness' of that age's conception of 'salvation'. Noteworthy, too, is Thomas's uncharacteristic imagining in this poem of Nonconformity's spiritual consonance with the landscape within which it had flourished. So, in their transport, these ecstatic worshippers look with fresh eyes at the grandeur of the 'barren mountains' within which their familiar chapel nestles.

Thomas was magnetically attracted to religious buildings away from the main roads, regardless of whether they were church or chapel. So, 'Llananno' begins with a stanza to that effect before it proceeds to record Thomas's spiritual journey into the church's quiet, deserted, uncanny interior, where 'the screen has nothing,/ to hide'. This seemingly innocent remark becomes intriguing when one learns that the great glory of Llananno church to this day is 'one of the great treasures of Welsh craftsmanship', as the authoritative building conservation website has it (*buildingconservation.com*), 'a late medieval rood screen and rood loft of *c*.1500, trimmed with some of the finest carved decoration to survive anywhere in Wales'. This screen was a feature of the old church that originally stood on the site of the present, unremarkable nineteenth-century church. Thomas was very partial indeed to all such religious artwork, and would undoubtedly have been doubly so in the case of this exceedingly rare relic at Llananno (situated alongside the River Ithon and dedicated to St Anno) because it was deemed to be the work of the esteemed Newtown, or Montgomeryshire, school of wood-carvers. A rood screen perfectly accorded with his conservative emphasis on respecting the mystery befitting the altar, while an additional attraction would undoubtedly have been that the screen at Llananno bursts with plant life:

> The bressummer trails with vines, pomegranates and water-plant issuing from the mouth of a wyvern. The vines symbolise Christ. The popular pomegranate motif represents eternal life. (*friendsoffriendlesschurches. org.uk*)

And to further attract Thomas, some believe there is good reason to suspect that the screen may have been connected to the nearby Abbey Cwm Hir, that resting place of the corpse of Llywelyn ein Llyw Olaf, the last native Prince of Wales, a site to which Thomas actually dedicated one of his poems.

Given all this, Thomas's mere glancing, desultory mention of that remarkable screen suddenly becomes infused with significance. It lends arresting power to the observation that for once 'the screen has nothing to hide', an observation immediately glossed in the lines that follow:

> Face to face
> with no intermediary
> between me and God, and only the water's
> quiet insistence on a time
> older than man. (*CP*, 304)

The majestic screen, erected to separate the nave from the focal point of holiness, which is traditionally the chancel, has been by-passed, so to speak. It has been rendered totally superfluous. Because here Thomas has been afforded the rare privilege of direct and naked admission to Godhead itself, such as Moses had been granted in his 'audience' with the burning bush. Also unusual is Thomas's describing of this encounter as 'serene' and his description of its consequence: the walls of the church are seemingly dissolved, as his heightened hearing registers the sound of the waters of the River Ithon running nearby. It is an uncanny experience, as the inside becomes the outside, and the church merges into the countryside within which it is located. It is a rare perfect fusion of Thomas's experiences as priest and as nature mystic.

'Llananno' also alerts us to one further important feature of Thomas's religious experience: that it has a specifically local habitation and name. It is an experience that for him was actually dependent on his relationship to Wales. Even more limiting, it was largely dependent on his relationship to North Wales. His own guilty realisation of this was recorded in an important passage in his early Notebook:

> What strange spell is this upon me, that if I go anywhere in North Wales, Talyllyn, Lleyn, Anglesey, Llangurig, I feel at home. Whereas nowhere in the wide world else will I have that feeling. Is it that my mind has been formed out of things which are essentially North-Welsh? I know that when I hear or read the word water I see a 'pistyll' somewhere in Merioneth, or if valley a 'glyn,' and pass a bwlch such as around Llangywer. It is no use – I am powerless against it. I have tried to be noble and to say 'Wherever God calls me, there I will go,' but if He called to the South or to England, I could not obey. It seems awful that soul should be stronger than spirit in me, but thus it seems. I am hearing ever the strange accent or inflection of a pennillion [sic] singer, and seeing with most pleasure the keen dark face of a Merioneth shepherd.

True, Llananno is not in North Wales, but it was local to Thomas's parish at Manafon, and thus clearly for him fell within the parish of his spiritual experience. His appreciation of it confirms the point he made in *Neb*, that the end of wartime petrol rationing had allowed Elsi and himself to take off in their car and to get to know areas of Wales that had been unknown to them both previously.

Thomas could all the more readily relate to his own church at Manafon, because the modern building, basically Victorian, had been built on the site of an old *clas*. Acknowledgement of that is implicitly made in his beautiful early poem 'Country Church (Manafon)'. The feature of the building that for Thomas was most precious, because so pregnant with significance, is mentioned at the very beginning: 'The church stands, built from the river stone' (*CP*, 11). For him it is as if the very water itself had solidified into the form of the church. Thus envisaged it exemplifies for Thomas the flow of Celtic spirituality from its source in the sacred wells through the early British Church, hence into Welsh Catholicism and finally into the Church in Wales. As

in the case of Llananno, the presence of water in the vicinity of the
church at Manafon was of the utmost importance for Thomas. As for
the rectory there, so close was it to the stream, that its cellars season-
ally fell victim to its flooding. Thus the river Rhiw, sometimes quiet,
at other times in the fury of fully spate, became very much part of
their lives, as he explained in his singular autobiography *Neb*, tellingly
recalling that its sound at night 'was like that of the blood coursing
through their veins'.[18] He added that this setting perfectly suited his
father, the old sea-captain, whose beloved hobby was fly-fishing.

Two advantages flowed from Thomas's persistent association of
water with the continuity of the Welsh spiritual tradition. It allowed
him to treat that tradition as 'given', as going with the very grain of
the land, and therefore as impossible to destroy, however adverse and
hostile the human circumstances. And it enabled him to separate the
tradition from the fraught issue of language, which might otherwise
have called into question the legitimacy of Thomas's claim, as an
English-language poet of Wales, to being heir to a tradition that had
after all been fashioned and transmitted by Welsh-language writers.

Recalling Manafon forty years and more after he had left the
parish, Thomas would nostalgically recall 'this village and a church
built with stones from the river, where the rectory stood, plangent as
a mahogany piano. The stream was a bright tuning-fork in the moon-
light. The hay-fields ran with a dark current' (*CLP*, 23). Much the
same image for the little river Rhiw occurred again to him later still,
when in 'Manafon' (*CLP*, 323) he recalled 'that rectory,/ mahogany of
a piano/ the light played on', a place where 'the river's/ teeth chattered
but not/ with cold'. And his fascination with the Celtic association
of water with spirituality made it natural for him, when recalling his
period of priestly service at Manafon, to speak instinctively in related
terms when describing his callow unease at ministering there to rural
people of such an alien, illegible character:

> Small-minded
> I will not say; there were depths
> in some of them I shrank back
> from, wells that the word 'God'
> fell into and died away,
> and for all I know is still
> falling. Who goes for water
> to such must prepare for a long
> wait. (*CLP*, 23)

The emphasis here, of course, is as much on his own immaturity, inexperience and inadequacy as on his parishioners' indifference to his own conception of the spiritual.

So important to Thomas was 'Afon Rhiw', that in his old age he devoted a whole poem to it, in which, no doubt recalling his father's passion but also Yeats's famous poem about the mythical Connemara fisherman, he wrote of his own experience of fishing in its water (*CLP*, 203). 'Its methods', he wrote of the river, 'were not sweeping/ away, but by a continual plucking/ to make one lose one's hold on its stones'. It was therefore necessary to master the skill 'of standing patiently for a while/ amid flux'. And throughout the poem he worked a parallel between his cunning angling for trout and the equally patient process of teasing out God, a process involving his learning that, like the elusive fish, his search for Him prospered better when his thoughts dwelt in the shadows and depths than when loftily scanning the heavens, where they, too, would be 'drawn into the light's/ dryness to perish of too much air'.

As for wells, he wrote a poem having undertaken the rather perilous adventure of visiting Ffynnon Fair (St Mary's Well) (*CP*, 292). Situated at the base of Aberdaron mountain, it is a site of legend because its water remains forever miraculously fresh, though the well has for long been mistakenly believed to be flooded with sea water at every tide. Suggesting that the well has reasonable claim to be 'the holiest of Welsh religious sites', the noted mountaineer and nature writer Jim Perrin has memorably described the spot:

> The lower of two ancient paths scored across the green southern slope of Trwyn Maen Melyn will, in its 'circuitous and most hazardous' way, lead you there. The path is worn down to gravel in places and lichens that had spread across steps carved in the rock have likewise been scuffed away by the passage of modern pilgrim feet. At sea-level you must traverse right, facing out, then cross a runnel up which waves rush powerfully when a sea is running, before gaining an ascending flake on the back of the rocky cove to reach a niche perhaps 10 feet above high water. It is adventurous, dangerous at times.

Perrin points out that the reverence for the well long pre-dates Christian history, before he concludes by lyrically recalling how

> To sit on the cliff ledge by this Virgin's well at sunset, with the island of Enlli glowing before you, the tide-race roaring between, and the black

cross/white cross flicker of a shearwater careening among the waves, is to know something of the sense of tragedy that haunts the loveliest places. And to feel gratitude that this one, protected by its perilous access, remains undefiled.[19]

In his poem, too, Thomas finds consolation in the feeling that, so old is this well and its situation so remote, it has managed to avoid being defiled, despite the best efforts of some of those who have visited it. So he magnanimously overlooks the unsightliness and inappropriateness of the coins that are beginning to gather in heaps in the well's depths, 'the tarnished offerings/ of the people to the pure spirit/ that lives there', imagining instead the eternally virginal well 'giving itself up to the thirsty', while 'withholding/ itself from the superstition/ of others, who ask for more'. And the opening lines succinctly capture in a multiple pun the complexity of Thomas's understanding of his relationship, as a Welsh person of the twentieth century, to his nation's spiritual heritage: 'They did not divine it, but they/bequeathed it to us'. 'Divine', as in discovering water underground through the use of a divining road; 'divine' as in 'imagine' or 'foresee' – a meaning folded, of course, into the noun 'divination'; and 'divine' as in pertaining to the deity: Thomas deploys the word in full knowledge of the interweave of these three meanings, and in full appreciation of its consequent knot of implications. The ancient Celts did not discover the sacredness of the well, since it was never hidden and secret like the sources of the Eleusinian Mysteries, but manifest and readily available like the later Christianity; they did not foresee its continuing significance right down to modern times; nor did they divinise it, since it was already instinct with the presence of divinity. But they did respect it, and they thus ensured that its power would remain, available and undiminished, down the long millennia.

As for 'bequeathed,' it has its roots in the Old English for 'utterance' (cf. 'quoth'), and so carries within it a suggestion of a sacred spoken wish and instruction. As used in the present context, therefore, it implies that language has been used to convey an awareness of a sacred trust of precious national inheritance. And it therefore further implies that by 'voicing' his awareness of that trust in his own time Thomas intends his poem to transmit it to future generations.

* * *

Running water: it is associated again with the living continuity and ready availability of the Welsh spiritual tradition in 'Llanrhaeadr-ym-Mochnant', a topographical placename associating the church with the waterfall nearby, just as 'Manafon' means 'place by the river'. But in this poem in honour of the birthplace of Bishop William Morgan, the renowned Tudor ecclesiastic and Renaissance Humanist scholar responsible for the majestic translation of the Bible into Welsh in 1588, centuries before most of the other peoples of Europe were enabled to read the Scriptures in the vernacular, the water is also specifically associated with the vital part played by the Welsh language and its authors in the maintenance of that tradition. Thomas was naturally particularly appreciative of this connection. He rejoices in the way 'the smooth words/ Over which his mind flowed/ Have become an heirloom', adding that

> Beauty
> Is how you say it, and the truth,
> Like this mountain-born torrent,
> Is content to hurry
> Not too furiously by. (*CP*, 192)

But as a fellow writer, he is also particularly aware of how deceptive such 'serene prose' actually is; how it offers not the slightest hint of the 'intolerable wrestle with language', as T. S. Eliot memorably put it, that had effortfully produced such an achievement. So he imagines Bishop Morgan's mouth as filled with 'rows of teeth/ Broken on the unmanageable bone//Of language'. And he also imagines that in undertaking such a Herculean challenge, the Bishop, working in his 'small room/ By the river', had been driven to 'expiat[e] the sin/ Of his namesake'. The cryptic reference is to the 'heretical' Pelagius (renegade apostle of the theology of Free Will), traditionally known in Wales by the name of Morgan. Such a speculation, unsupported though it may be by modern scholarship, seems to arise spontaneously out of Thomas's awareness of how much of his own religious poetry had been the product of a spirit similarly tortured by misgivings, anxieties, and guilt; a spirit haunted by 'heretical' inclinations.

Nor was this the only poem he dedicated to Bishop Morgan. Another was 'R.I.P. 1588–1988', a poem marking the quatercentenary of the translation of the Bible into Welsh – a seminal religious and cultural event the adequate celebration of which Thomas felt was being scandalously neglected by a Church reluctant to acknowledge the Welsh language. His outrage at a cultural slight that he attributed to the anglicisation of the Church in Wales finds indirect expression in the poem's opening bitter reference to the condescension of an imaginary Englishman upon hearing the outlandish and unpronounceable name of the remotely situated Llanrhaeadr-ym-Mochnant. At the heart of the poem, however, lies an extended comparison of the effect of Morgan's great achievement to the revivifying power of water. The arrival of the Welsh Scriptures was a 'tumbling/ of water out of the sky/ copiously as grace pouring// to irrigate the hearts/ of a people that had grown arid' (*CLP*, 159).

So fixated, however, is Thomas on the comparison between the Welsh spiritual tradition and water that he overplays his hand. The metaphor is extended to breaking point and beyond. It starts promisingly enough with him identifying the river as 'the mill/-water turning [Morgan's] pen/ to the grinding of Hebrew/ to Welsh corn'. But then it grows ever more laboured, as he also imagines the stream as 'flooding/ him with vocabulary,/ now smooth enough for the dancing// of his mind's fly time/and again on its surface,/ angling for the right word'.

Much more interesting is the shift at the poem's centre to questioning the wisdom of an over-reliance on the undoubtedly inspired language of Morgan's translation. Because 'language can be/ like iron. Are we sure we can bend/ the Absolute to our meaning?' This, of course, is a question that troubled Thomas throughout his long writing life, and one he returned to time and again in his poems. Unfortunately, though, in this poem his worrying away at it becomes as tediously predicable, and as poetically fruitless, as his fixation on water, except when it modulates into a sad wondering whether 'an obsession' with the Welsh language may be 'an acknowledgement we are too late/ to save it'.

It was with pleasure that Thomas learnt, shortly after settling in Manafon, that his predecessors as Rector included three who were noted for their contributions to Welsh literature: Evan Evans (Ieuan Brydydd Hir), the eighteenth-century figure renowned for having saved the precious manuscript record of medieval Welsh Poetry mouldering in the attics of Welsh country houses; Walter Davies (Gwallter Mechain), an early nineteenth-century man-of-letters; and the much more obscure William Morgan (Penfro), a copious early twentieth-century producer of undistinguished verse. These were of the first importance to him, because they provided a direct link to

'Yr Hen Bersoniaid Llengar', the group of Anglican clergymen who, in defiance of their Church, had made an immense contribution to Welsh letters and culture between 1818 and 1858. For Thomas, they were the harbingers of the 'alternative' Church in Wales that he continued stubbornly but fruitlessly to hope might eventually emerge following disestablishment. They had endeavoured 'to light Welsh/ confidently on its way backward/ to an impending future' (*UP*, 139). The Manafon trio were also for Thomas a rueful, painful reminder that, until as recently as the early twentieth century, his parish, now so depressingly anglicised, had been thoroughly Welsh-speaking.

Awed by Gwallter Mechain's intellectualism, his superstitious rural parishioners came to fear him as a magician, endowed with supernatural powers. And from the poem, undistinguished but heartfelt, that Thomas devoted to his forerunner late in his career, it is obvious that he believed the 'poor priest/ of a dispensable parish' to have been an *alter ego*. A portrait of his spiritually perplexed self is clearly discernible in the following:

> The weekly climb
> Into the crow's nest of his pulpit,
> Telling them of the glimpsed land,
>
> Trying to believe in it
> Himself. The words digested
> The bell's notes more easily
> Than his intellect his doctrine. (*UP*, 133–34)

And as if in defiance of his parishioners, Thomas incorporates an accomplished *englyn* by Gwallter Mechain into his poem. Not only is it a cultural Trojan Horse – a dangerous insinuation into the midst of the anglicised parishioners of the culturally proscribed native language that is no longer intelligible to them – but it speaks of the treacherous killing of Llywelyn the Last Prince of Wales by the English, and is thus a synecdoche for the betrayal of the language by the border parish of Manafon.

Even more important an *alter ego* for Thomas was Ann Griffiths, the young fun-loving country girl so dramatically transfigured, following her conversion to Methodism, into an ecstatic, loved by the Welsh for the remarkable hymns she dictated to her maid. Although Griffiths's home at Dolwar Fach was not far to the north of Thomas's

Manafon, he seems not to have become deeply interested in her until much later. But eventually she, too, came to represent for him his church's potential for serving the Welsh nation, since throughout Ann's lifetime Methodism had remained a dramatic movement for reform within the Church of England. But once the Welsh Calvinistic Methodists had broken with the mother church, she had been enthusiastically adopted by them, and thus served as a bridge between Welsh Anglicanism and Welsh Nonconformity. She also excited Thomas's interest because she represented an age of faith untroubled by the kinds of unavoidable doubts that assailed him and his increasingly sceptical and secular age.

In 'Ann Griffith' (*CP*, 281) he testifies to his joyful possession by Ann's spirit, not only by recording that her baptismal surname had been Thomas, like his own, but by weaving a whole poem out of the Biblical images made so familiar by her remarkable hymns that they had entered popular Welsh vernacular. He adopts the same inter-textual practice in the opening stanza of his ambitious 'Fugue for Ann Griffiths' (*CP*, 470–5), only to change tack abruptly in the second stanza by translating her images into terms that a modern, uncomprehending, English-speaking readership might be expected to understand. Consistent with the musical analogy in the poem's title, this signals a change to a much lower, contemporary 'key', beginning with a lexical concession signalled by a condescending direct address to the modern reader. This prepares the way for a parodic instance of the vulgar blasphemy typical, in Thomas's opinion, of the reductive modern mind's approach to the mystery of belief. So, in Ann's repeated celebration in her hymns of her wedding to the divine Bridegroom (an echo, of course, of the Song of Solomon), Thomas pretends to detect an admission that she has 'cuckolded' her husband – a familiar old accusation traditionally levelled against the Virgin Mary that crops up at the beginning of Joyce's *Ulysses*.

At the heart of the poem, however, lies Thomas's awed acknowledgement of the mystery of an ordinary untutored country girl's mastery of the grammar of the spirit. His poem opens by textually carving her face into 'the figure-head of a ship/ outward bound' and it records the astonishment of her confessor at 'the fathoms/ of anguish over which she had/ attained to the calmness of her harbours'. From here, he proceeds to mild self-accusation for having so long been blind to her spiritual genius, and so far forgets himself as to use familiar terms of endearment while tacitly admitting to having previously succumbed to the cynicism of an age when Christianity has become a 'myth shifting/ its place to the wrong end/ of the spectrum under the Doppler/ effect of the recession of belief'. As it nears its conclusion, the poem becomes so feverishly clotted with extravagant images that it risks imploding into incomprehension. But its many egregious failures prove that so desperately important was Ann Griffiths to Thomas that, in his determination to articulate it, he ended up working beyond the limits of his gifts. The resulting failure of his attempt to translate her simple, pure and piercing faith into the incompatible terms required by his resolutely scientific age, movingly exposes for us the tragic magnitude of the challenge with which Thomas the poet wrestled all his life.

In his outstanding study *Gororau'r Iaith* (one of the most important of all studies of Thomas), Jason Walford Davies has drawn attention to the wealth of allusion to Welsh-language literature secretly inscribed in the poetry. This private, privileged insider-talk was yet another of his devices of self-legitimisation; another important way for him to make sure that his work in English retained its integrity by fully and faithfully aligning it not only with Welsh-language culture in general but with Welsh spiritual tradition in particular.

He was an ardent admirer of the celebrated masters of the strict-metre poetry of the late medieval period, and he loved the epigrammatic brevity of their poems. Two poets in particular whose output was avowedly religious appealed very deeply to him. Between them they instanced in their work some of the most important and characteristic topoi of the period. One of these was Gruffudd Llwyd, who regarded himself as the court poet of God, and believed the Almighty had graced him with the poetic talent he felt called to dedicate to His service. He was also the author of a poem patriotically claiming that the overlooking of the young Owain Glyndŵr for knighthood at that early point in his young career when it seemed well deserved typified England's scornful mistreatment of the Welsh.[20] But it was Siôn Cent whom Thomas loved above all, many of the fifteenth-century poet's themes and urgent concerns having anticipated his own.

Siôn Cent remains a shadowy figure, elusive to modern scholarship: very little is known, and much has been accordingly speculated, about his origins, life and output, with some scholars even doubting whether such an individual may even be said with any certainty ever to have existed.[21] The consensus, however, is that he may have been a native of the Welsh Marches active between 1400 and 1430. An outsider alike to the Welsh bardic and the Welsh ecclesiastical establishments, he was very likely a layman heavily influenced by the preaching friars, the Franciscans and Dominicans. His dissenting outlook found expression in a scorn for the tradition of praise poetry that had long provided the backbone of Welsh bardic poetry and in the reforming passion of the fierce, sermonic poems in which he attacked the corruption of the contemporary world. This was the world whose vacuousness Siôn Cent, adopting the *vanitas* and *ubi sunt* conventions the Middle Ages had borrowed from *Ecclesiastes*, memorably excoriated in his greatest poem 'I Wagedd ac Oferedd y Byd' (To the Nullity and Vanity of the World). So fond was R. S. Thomas of this poem that he chose it as one of his very particular favourites when interviewed for the Welsh version of Desert Island Discs.

Thomas frequently quoted Siôn Cent's aphorism 'ystad bardd astudio byd', the poet's responsibility is to study the state of the world. It is a pithy summary of the trademark realism of outlook that scholars believe may show Siôn Cent's familiarity with the novel philosophy of the Oxford school of his age, whose luminaries included William of Ockham and Roger Bacon, the remarkable friar who was one of the earliest advocates of the scientific method. They sought to replace the Platonism traditional to classic medieval theology with an outlook grounded in experiential practice, and Ockham championed a philosophical nominalism that, in prioritising the singularity of individuality, undermined the Platonic devotion to the Ideal.[22] Since the praise tradition of Welsh bardic tradition had long been based on that Platonic Idealism, it attracted the particular scorn of Siôn Cent the Ockhamist, who dismissed it as an anachronism.

Contempt for the trashy values of the contemporary world; anger at its endemic corruption; an unflinchingly realistic assessment of human existence; a confirmed anti-clericalism; a rejection of the suspect hyperbole and euphoria of the praise tradition; an attraction to sermonising; a mistrust of glibness; a determined commitment to a language concise enough 'not to be betrayed', as Edward Thomas put it, by seductive rhetoric; and a grim, implacable acknowledgement of the inescapability of mortality: R. S. Thomas shared all of these features with Siôn Cent. In addition, both were capable of fusing patriotism with piety. In an important essay with which R. S. Thomas may well have been familiar, Saunders Lewis, his role model, suggested that a poem which he described as the finest written about the calamitous cultural as well as political consequences for the Welsh of the eventual failure of Glyndŵr's rebellion, was probably written by Siôn Cent.[23] Scholars have recently suggested that he may probably have participated in that uprising, and that he had lost his lands in consequence. No wonder, therefore, that this important early-fifteenth-century poet should have been so important a figure for R. S. Thomas. In him he found yet another important *alter ego* in the Welsh spiritual tradition to which he strongly believed his own religious poetry belonged, a maverick whose relationship to it was as important, but also as complex and conflicted, as his own.

Notes

[1]   R. S. *Thomas: Collected Poems, 1945–1990* (London: Orion, Phoenix, 2000), p. 306. Hereafter *CP*.

[2]   R. S. *Thomas: Collected Later Poems, 1988–2000* (Tarset: Bloodaxe, 2004), p. 53. Hereafter *CLP*.

[3]   Donald Allchin's summary of Bowen's poem 'Y Gair' (The Word), in Cynthia and Saunders Davies (eds), *Euros Bowen: Priest-Poet/Bardd-Offeiriad* (Penarth: Church in Wales Publications, 1993), p. 24.

[4]   All such entries are taken from the recently discovered Notebooks that came into my possession in 2018 and copies of which I have retained, after depositing the originals in the R. S. Thomas Research Centre, Bangor University. For an overview of the Notebooks, see my article that was published in the Christmas issue of *PNReview*.

[5]   See 'R. S. Thomas: "A Retired Christian"', in M. Wynn Thomas, *All That is Wales: Collected Essays* (Cardiff: University of Wales Press, 2017), pp. 185–212. Hereafter *ATW*.

[6]   'The Oldie Interview: R. S. Thomas', *The Oldie*, 79 (1995), 15.

[7]   For a fuller discussion of the importance of the Book of Job for Thomas, and its relevance to *Stones of the Field*, see 'War Poet', in M. Wynn Thomas, R. S. *Thomas: Serial Obsessive* (Cardiff: University of Wales Press, 2013), pp. 13–36. Hereafter *SO*.

[8]   See, for example, the essay by the Norwegian-Canadian philosopher Herman Tennesen, 'A Masterpiece of Existential Blasphemy: The Book of Job', *The Human World*, 13 (November 1973), 1–10.

[9]   See J. E. Crawford Flitch, trans. Miguel de Unamuno, *The Tragic Sense of Life in Men and in Peoples* (London: Macmillan, 1921).

[10]   Seamus Heaney, *Stepping Stones: Interviews by Dennis O'Driscoll* (London: Faber, 2008), Chapter Four.

[11]   For fuller discussion of Thomas's quarrel with his Church, see *ATW*, 165–84.

[12]   'Fugue for Ann Griffiths', in *Welsh Airs* (Bridgend: Seren, 52).

[13]   For a fuller discussion of Thomas's important relationship to Saunders Lewis, see 'Son of Saunders', *SO*, 93–106.

14 Jason Walford Davies, *Gororau'r Iath:* R. S. *Thomas a'r Traddodiad Llenyddol Cymraeg* (Cardiff: University of Wales Press, 2003), p. 80. This is a brilliant and comprehensive study of Thomas's important relationship to Welsh-language literature.

15 Tony Brown and Jason Walford Davies (eds), R. S. *Thomas: Uncollected Poems* (Tarset: Bloodaxe, 2013), p. 27. Hereafter *UP*.

16 Sioned Davies (trans.), *The Mabinogion* (Oxford and New York: Oxford University Press, 2007), p. 32.

17 Sandra Anstey (ed.), R. S. *Thomas: Selected Prose* (Bridgend: Poetry Wales Press, 1983), pp. 41–9.

18 Jason Walford Davies (trans.), R. S. *Thomas: Autobiographies* (London: Dent, 1997), p. 41.

19 *The Guardian*, 13 April 2013.

20 See Dafydd Johnston, *Llên yr Uchelwyr: Hanes Beirniadol Llenyddiaeth Gymraeg 1300–1525* (Cardiff: University of Wales Press, 2005), pp. 190–4. For translations of some of Llwyd's poetry, see Joseph P. Clancy (trans.), *Medieval Welsh Poems* (Dublin: Four Courts Press, 2003), pp. 261–6.

21 Johnston, *Llên yr Uchelwyr*, pp. 222–9; Gilbert Ruddock, 'Siôn Cent', in A. O. H. Jarman and Gwilym Rees Hughes (eds), revised by Dafydd Johnston, *A Guide to Welsh Literature, 1282–c1550* (Cardiff: University of Wales Press,1997), pp. 150–69; Saunders Lewis, 'Siôn Cent', in Gwynn ap Gwilym (ed.), *Meistri a'u Crefft* (Cardiff: University of Wales Press, 1981), pp. 148–60. For translations of some of his poems, see Clancy, *Medieval Welsh Poems*, pp. 284–93. For Thomas's interest in Siôn Cent, see *Gororau'r Iaith*, 293–6.

22 Doubt has been thrown recently on this association between Siôn Cent and the Oxford School. See 'Siôn Cent, Saunders Lewis and the Oxford Philosophers: A Reassessment', *Cambrian Medieval Studies*, 80 (Winter 2020), 45–75.

23 Saunders Lewis had first discussed Siôn Cent in his *Braslun o Hanes Llenyddiaeth Cymru* (Cardiff: University of Wales Press, 1932), a volume that in all probability R. S. Thomas had read.

10

EPILOGUE:
THE CASE OF ROWAN WILLIAMS

> I read somewhere of a shepherd who, when asked why he made, from
> within fairy rings, ritual observances of the moon to protect his flocks,
> replied: 'I'd be a damn' fool if I didn't.' These poems, with all their crudi-
> ties, doubts, and confusion are written for the love of Man and in praise
> of God, and I'd be a damn' fool if they weren't.[1]

That, of course, is the concluding, typically jaunty and tricksy, pas-
sage from the Prefatory Note Dylan Thomas attached to his *Collected
Poems*. The flippancy of tone, and the provocative hint that religion
may be no more than superstition, will no doubt persuade some to
doubt the sincerity of this dedication. Revealing, though, is the careful
balancing of the 'praise of God' with the 'love of Man' – a parallel-
ing that his unorthodox Unitarian uncle, Gwilym Marles (hence the
Dylan Marlais), would surely have approved of. And we find the same
coupling of the human and the divine in a letter Thomas wrote, late
in life, about his motivating convictions as a poet, when answering the
question of an obscure Texas graduate student. 'The joy and function
of poetry', he there asserted, 'is the celebration of man, which is also
the celebration of God.'[2]

On this evidence, then, it would seem not unreasonable to conclude
that, occasionally at the very least, Dylan Thomas thought of himself
as a religious poet, however unorthodox a one, and however strong
his well-documented and thoroughly examined antipathy to the Welsh
chapel religion of his time. The earliest of his friends was certain of
it: 'Dylan believed', Trick roundly asserted, 'that every man has the
stamp of divinity in him, and anything that prevented that divinity

having full play was an evil thing'.[3] Nor was such a view that of Trick alone. One of the earliest important studies of Thomas was written by Aneirin Talfan Davies, himself an interesting religious poet, who was an Anglican and son of a Welsh Congregationalist minister. He had first introduced Thomas to the microphone in Swansea and had remained very good friends with him thereafter, as Davies began his own steady climb to a distinguished, and culturally very influential, position as Head of Broadcasting in Wales. Entitled *Dylan: Druid of the Broken Body*, his study argued that not only was Thomas's poetry steeped in the Bible but that it was profoundly sacramental in character – an approach that reflected Davies's own spiritual inclinations as a prominent member of the Church in Wales.[4] It was a reading of Thomas that particularly struck the teenage Rowan Williams in the Swansea of the sixties.

Given all this, why not include a chapter on Thomas in this study? His exclusion is partly because I am inclined to account him a religiose poet rather than a religious one – to view him, that is, as one who drew heavily on the religious culture of his early background only because it afforded him such a wealth of resources – from images to lexicons, from rhythms to tones and inflections – for fashioning his distinctive poetic rhetoric and even for setting the pitch of his memorable public readings. A more decisive factor, however, is my conviction that I have already addressed, to the best of my ability, the issue of Thomas's relationship to religion in several printed discussions, and have nothing new or useful to add on the subject.[5]

I have briefly turned my attention to it here, however, because Thomas's case affords a compelling example of the class of modern Welsh writing usefully identified by Rowan Williams when, writing of his own case, he made it clear that 'I dislike the idea of being a religious poet. I would prefer to be a poet for whom religious things mattered intensely.'[6] Another such case is that of Dannie Abse, whose valuable body of poetry was clearly informed by his respect and affection, as an avowedly secular Jew, for the long, varied, and immensely distinguished tradition of Jewish spirituality. 'I am a sucker for aphoristic sayings', he wrote. 'I love wisdom stories, parables, proverbs.' Throughout his life he drew on Talmudic, Midrashic and Chassidic jokes and stories as much in his poetry as in his prose, relishing their sly power to unsettle the mind from its comfortable axis, their ability to confuse, confound and perplex the tyranny of reason. He also loved their wry unillusioned irreverence, recalling for instance the

Jewish observation that 'If the rich could hire other people to die for them the poor would make a wonderful living'.[7] While he was a confirmed non-believer, he was chronically teased, tantalised (and even occasionally tormented) by the sadly illusory satisfactions of belief. He resolutely refused to abandon the physical in favour of the metaphysical although he was permanently fascinated by the mysterious aura of the inexplicable that experience, not least as a doctor, repeatedly taught him haunted the fringes of existence – the persistent presence of what in a very early poem he termed 'the uninvited' (*NSP*, 1). But in his poetry he deliberately confined himself to the evidence of his senses, believing that it allowed him margin more than enough for registering irreducible mysteries. 'I do not complain', he wrote: 'I start with the visible/ and am startled by the visible'.[8]

Despite this, there is considerable justice in Tony Curtis's claim that one 'could argue a case for Dannie Abse's place alongside R. S. Thomas, not only as a poet in the first rank of Anglo-Welsh writers, but also in the first rank of our religious poets' (*S*, 199). He was, Curtis added, 'drawn again and again to the possibility of God and to account for the power of the *idea* if not the *fact* of God in both his Jewish and his Welsh heritage'. One might describe him as a God-haunted agnostic. From the time he was a young poet he had a deep interest in the poetry of Rilke, recognising that its power lay in the German's attempt to use poetry to mediate the invisible to the visible, as Abse put it (*S*, 143). He pertinently quoted Rilke's comment that '"The Angel of the Duino Elegies … is the being who vouches for the recognition of a higher degree of reality in the invisible, terrible to us because we … still cling to the visible"' (*S*, 143).

One of Abse's finest poems arose from his attempt to recall and reproduce in English a poem about a Merry-Go-Round at night, the roundabout being 'a metaphor for Rilke: fairground spectators have the optical illusion of night's invisible creatures becoming tangible, as the roundabout turns them from darkness into light' (*S*, 143–4). However, in working from memory, Abse inadvertently combined his memories of the poem with his recent experience of seeing Mark Gertler's disturbing painting 'Merry-go-Round' at the Tate. The result is a poem rich in implication, suggestive not least of a meditation on the ephemerality and strange insubstantiality of human life:

> The roof turns, the brassy merry-go-round crashes
> out music. Gaudy horses gallop tail to snout,

> inhabit the phantasmagoria of light
> substantial as smoke. Then each one vanishes. (*S*,144)

It is a stanza worth placing alongside Abse's epigraph for his late volume *Ask the Bloody Horse*:

> While Freud was tracing the river to its source
> he met Itzig unsteadily riding.
> 'Where are you going?' he asks that wild-eyed rider.
> 'Don't ask me,' said Itzig, 'ask the bloody horse'. (*S*, 142)

And Abse added that he had also considered using a quotation from Martin Buber as epigraph: 'All journeys have secret destinations of which the traveller is unaware.' It is no coincidence, moreover, that having started as it does, his Merry-go-round poem ends by valorising the imagination of the children who ride the magic roundabout – and in the process it associates them implicitly with the imagination of a poet, who possesses the ability to dwell on occasion in that uncanny no man's land where alone fantasy can thrive:

> Faster! The children spellbound, the animals prance,
> and this is happiness, this no-man's land
> where nothing's forbidden. And hardly a glance
> at parents who smile, who *think* they understand
>
> as the scarlet lion leaps into the night
> and here comes the unicorn painted white.

It is worth recalling that Abse repeatedly emphasised that for a poet potent images seemed to emerge unpredictably out of the dark of the preconscious, glittering with mystery, just like the scarlet lion and white unicorn.

Dannie Abse's masterpiece on the subject of religion – and in that respect one of the major Welsh religious poems of recent decades – is 'The Abandoned', a poem whose importance for him is indicated by the fact that, whereas he began it in 1957, he did not complete it until 2008, a mere six years before his passing. From beginning to end it is infused with the humour that leavened much of his poetry, causing incautious readers to overlook and thus undervalue its seriousness. In this subtle, complex poem humour is freighted with a wide range of emotions, and is thus expressive of the spectrum of Abse's own feelings about any belief in God. And it is prefaced with two epigraphs, Rilke's 'Du Nachbar Gott' (You, Neighbour God) and George Herbert's lines 'thy absence doth excel/ All distance known'. The opening section turns on a suggestive inversion of normal human ways of characterising any relationship to the Almighty. In Abse's telling, that relationship becomes one of God's complete dependence on human succour and sanctuary. 'God, when you came to our house/ we let you in' (*ANSP*, 177). Concluding by describing God's progressive self-protective shrinking from human contact, the first stanza prepares the way for the second phase of the poem which is about God's absence, concluding with Abse scolding the Almighty: 'No need to be so self-effacing,/ quiet as language of the roses/ or moss upon a wall.// We have to hold our breath to hear you breathe.' The third stanza then begins on an exasperated note with 'Dear God, in the end you had to go./ Dismissing you, your absence made us sane./ We keep the bread and wine for show.' It develops into a villanelle in which the theme of God's dismissal and the residual retention of the elements of Holy Communion, now deconsecrated, recur, conveying a blended sense of guilt and relief, of release and of bewilderment. These feelings are openly acknowledged in the fourth stanza where mention is made of how former believers have been left 'bereaved, feel empty and alone' now that they have stopped yielding up 'fawning words' of praise. It also notes how thoughts of God still recur as humans search futilely for a scapegoat on which to blame disease, famine and war. Then the final stanza, in the form of an irregular sonnet, registers the kinds of feelings that are attendant on non-belief, even as Abse recognises that there can be no turning back:

> Last night, awakened, did we hear you call?
> Memory, father of tears, who was that knocking?
> That incautious noise. Was there someone knocking?
> Someone we knew when we were small?

The whole poem is a consummate inventory of the cost of what Abse the reluctant agnostic considered to be the maturity of unbelief. And it could also be read as his entering into conversation with his great Welsh contemporary (and in some ways rival), R. S. Thomas.

Then there is the intriguing, complex case of Tony Conran, another major figure on the post-war poetry scene in Wales. Although he himself recorded that he had been received into the Catholic

Church in the 1950s, the exact character of his faith remained uncertain. It was never directly expressed in a remarkable body of poetry that was nevertheless infused, as Jeremy Hooker has demonstrated in a masterly essay, with a profound acknowledgement of some kind of underlying universal order, indeterminate in origin. Conran proceeded to translate that vision – which he acknowledged he had derived partly from the example of David Jones – into a distinctive, signature poetic in which the validation of personal experience, which he believed to be the staple mode of all English post-Romantic poetry, was replaced by a recognition of social and cultural embeddedness and a primary valuation of the human web of interrelatedness.

As Jeremy Hooker has pointed out, these formative foundational beliefs made Conran into a performative poet, participatory and interactive, who particularly valued ritual and recognised its primal origin in the sacred, and who clearly perceived the relationship of ritual to communal cultural forms such as poetry and dance – Conran himself emphasised that he could best relate to the world through the heightened sensitivity to physical movement that had been occasioned by his cerebral palsy. 'We are', Hooker concludes, 'in danger of failing to recognise [Conran's] achievement as a religious poet. His deployment of impersonal modes, for example, serves a vision of religious wholeness.'[9] And he compares Conran in this regard with Jacques Maritain, the relevance of whose religious philosophy to the poetry of Saunders Lewis has already been demonstrated earlier in this volume.

Hooker's deep affinity, as a distinguished poet himself, with Conran's view of the world is very evident in the subtlety and perceptiveness of his analysis. While always remaining firmly attached to his native Hampshire, Hooker has chosen to spend most of his life in Wales, largely because of his appreciation of precisely those features of the culture that he identifies in Conran's work. One of those features is that ingrained spirituality of so much of Welsh writing which has been the subject of this present study. It has nurtured Hooker's own work, both as poet and as critic, since he finds in major Welsh poets such as Waldo Williams and R. S. Thomas precisely those qualities he admires hugely in the poetry of Mary Casey, also a native of Hampshire. 'Casey', he has written, 'shows an intimacy between the natural and the religious – in fact, an immanence of the religious in the organic world which only poetry is capable of registering'. Prose, he adds, can only be 'at best a partially sighted guide to what incarnational imagination shows'. And he concludes by remarking that

'Mary Casey's power as a poet derives not from a versification of doctrine or a general symbolism of the absolute or even an assured faith, but from the concentration in her poems of an intensely feeling and acutely seeing life'.[10] That is not only an accurate statement of Hooker's own practice and considerable achievement as a poet, it can also be applied to several of the poets whose work has been considered in preceding chapters.

In more recent times, several prominent Welsh women writers have produced poetry whose outlook on life is clearly marked by the religious backgrounds from which they come, even though those are never directly addressed in their poems. Ruth Bidgood is the daughter of an Anglican priest, Menna Elfyn of a Nonconformist minister, and Gwyneth Lewis is a committed member of the Church in Wales, and a poet with an impressive spiritual pedigree, since she is one of the very few Welsh poets whose gifts R. S. Thomas deigned to acknowledge, and she has also collaborated closely with Rowan Williams on several creative ventures.

Her moving volume in memory of her father is prefaced with a quotation from Psalm 46: 1–2.[11] While it is of course quoted in Welsh, in the King James version it reads as follows: 'God is our refuge and strength, a very present help in trouble. Therefore will not we fear, though the earth be removed, and the mountains be carried into the midst of the sea.' The volume is entitled *Treigladau*. The Welsh word for linguistic mutations, an essential component of Welsh grammar, to the preservation of which her late father was particularly devoted, the noun 'treigladau' also broadly signifies 'changes' of every kind. It is therefore appropriate for a collection in which Lewis traces her father's progress through life, from the family background in the Ogwr Valley to his post in Cardiff and onwards through his declining years to the last 'mutation' of all, the irreversible change from life to death. And for much of the volume, the physical equivalents for mutation are the travels (yet another meaning of 'treigladau') of her father on his motorbike 'Bess' of which he was so proud.

Written in the homely colloquial Welsh of her background, the poems are immensely effective in capturing some aspects, at least, of the intense and complicated relationships within Lewis's close nuclear family while at the same time they are typically sophisticated and complex explorations – by turns direct and oblique; sometimes delightfully light, playful and witty, at other times intensely serious and profound – of the nuances of the life they lived in common. Lewis has a Catherine-wheel of an imagination, that throws out profuse sparks of light in a great variety of unexpected directions. Her poems reach their inevitable sad climax in sensitively and unflinchingly charting her father's slow decline as he dies of cancer of the mouth. And it is in the poem uncompromisingly entitled 'Wedyn' (After) that Lewis comes clean about the role of religious faith in helping her maintain her emotional and mental balance. (She attributes her recovery from a lengthy period of alcoholism to her rediscovery of faith.) It is in the form of a prayer that opens with an unembarrassed direct request, forthright and simple as a child's, and all the more affecting because Lewis has such a highly subtle and sophisticated mind:

> Dduw Dad, edrych ar ôl Dad,
> Nid fel yr oedd, ar y diwedd, yn boddi,
> Ond fel mae e nawr, gyda Thi. (58)

[God our Father look after Dad, not as he was, at the end, drowning, but as he is now, with You.]

The poem suggestively notes that while his two daughters had always followed Welsh custom when addressing their father of using the plural form 'Chi' for 'you' rather than the intimate form 'Ti', the latter, following the example set by Christ himself in the Welsh Bible, was the mode of address they were accustomed to using when speaking to God. And the poem ends by beseeching the Almighty to ensure

> Nad yw'n tad, heb gorff, yn profi arswyd,
> Nac yn llosgi dan bwysau'r sêr,
> Nac yn rhynnu tu fas i amser.
>
> Nac yn galw arnat mewn fflachiadau:
> Dit dit dir da da da, rwy'n erfyn
>
> · · · _ _ _ · · ·

[That our father, fleshless, doesn't experience terror,/ nor burn under the weight of the stars/ nor freeze outside of time,/ nor call on You in flashes . . . _ _ _ . . . , I beg.]

That last, of course, is the morse code for SOS, universally recognised and respected by all sailors, and the reference is very appropriate in the light of the wartime years that Lewis's father had spent in the navy, while it also recalls the lighthouse lights flashing the far side of the Bristol Channel that used to be visible from the family's home in Cardiff.

One of Lewis's poems reflecting on life after her father's death is entitled 'Treftadaeth' (Inheritance) and central to it is the account in St Luke's gospel of the disciples meeting Christ on their way to Emmaus and failing to recognise him until the evening meal, when He blessed the bread. At that point, Lewis brings Caravaggio's great painting of the event to mind, 'Pan fo Crist, wrth y ford, yn lledu ei freichiau,/ Gan agor dimensiwn yn rhith y darlun i gyfeiriad newydd – i mewn i'r dyfnder' (T, 68). 'When Christ, at the table, opens wide his arms/ Opening a dimension that breaks the illusion of the painting out into a different dimension – into the depth'. It is a self-reflexive observation, as Lewis has herself quietly attempted exactly such a 'treiglad' (mutation) at some points in her remarkable collection.

Her singular talent makes Lewis a kind of exotic in the context of contemporary poetry from Wales. Admired by the likes of Seamus Heaney and Joseph Brodsky, she writes poetry astutely described by Gillian Clarke as 'Outrageously imaginative'. 'Witty and musical', Clarke goes on, '[her] poems are funny and bold, surreal and beautiful'. As an Anglophone poet of contemporary Wales, Lewis belongs to a class apart, and that a class of one. She considers herself to have been a religious poet from the beginning,[12] and her remarkable debut collection in English, *Parables and Faxes*, includes an arresting sequence that multiplies ways of obliquely exploring the absent presence of God in today's world as her virtuosic imagination pivots acrobatically around a core concern with silence, absence and self-forgetfulness.[13]

Her sequence opens with a poem that could be read as a riff on Wallace Stevens's great 'Snow Man', a hymn of praise to 'blankness' and vacuity', a theme to which she returns in the third poem which begins with her celebrating her marriage to nothing and proceeds to a confession of what she has gained since becoming a 'connoisseur[...]/ of blankness': it has hugely augmented her appreciation of such commonplace sights as 'scruffy ponies in a scrubland field/ like bits of jigsaw you can't complete' (*PF*, 31). The fourth poem begins by speaking of the transformation in humankind's understanding of its relationship to God during the later twentieth century in terms of a workman disappearing off the factory floor, and it ends with an appreciation of how his self-abnegation has made 'colours shades deeper than ever before/ and detail: the ratchets on a snail's sharp tongue' (*PF*, 33). Then in the sixth and final poem Lewis begins with an image of a monk saying nothing, 'finger to his lips/ and day begins within his silences' and it ends by acknowledging that 'our lives depend on his emptiness' (*PF*, 35).

When her husband was diagnosed with cancer and needed extensive treatment, Lewis digested the experience by eventually producing a remarkable poem, over 150 pages in length.[14] Entitled *Hospital Odyssey*, it is an epic created out of sheer desperate necessity, in which Lewis saves her own sanity by sharpening her intelligence into a counter-aggressive weapon. It tells the story of a psychosomatic quest undertaken by a character called Maris in a heroic struggle to save the life of her husband Hardy. In this crazy universe of hill health, which takes us beyond the looking glass that comfortingly mirrors normality, she encounters a matronly Greater Spotted Woodpecker, a Knight Templar of a consultant – keeper of the sacred sites of the human body – and comes across companionable allies like Wilson the lupine greyhound and Ichabod, the image of glowing good health. She also undergoes numerous hair-raising adventures, and narrowly avoids entanglement in the web of an insinuatingly predatory spider. The final section of the poem takes us on a journey in which Hardy's nearness to death leads to Maris embarking on a journey imaged in terms of what Lewis has termed a 'religious cosmology'. Like R. S. Thomas, and many other contemporary poets given to spiritual vision, Lewis is fascinated by the discoveries of quantum physics and of contemporary astronomy, and by the insights offered by both into a primary level of existence in which difference between body and world becomes dissolved as both are understood in terms of string theory and similar models of reality.[15] So, as Hardy comes perilously close to death:

> He was overcome
>
> By the knowledge that everything 'out there'
> Was in truth, his own body. We're filaments
> Of light, we're talking with everywhere
> At once, and we were never meant
> To be thought of as single, lines to be bent
>
> In the space-time continuum. (145)

A recurrent theme in Lewis's poetry is that spiritual belief alone can offer us a view of the world in its mysterious plenitude; its full, exhilarating, perplexing and troubling beauty. So, in 'The No Madonnas' she ponders the fate of the many ordinary women who, she imagines, must have refused God's approaches:

> But those who said no
> For ever knew
> They were damned
> To the daily
> As they'd disallowed
> Reality's madness,
> Its astonishment. (*PF*, 68)

'Reality's madness' is a perfect description of the world that Lewis attempts to capture in her incomparable spiritual poetry.

Nowhere in her poetry does Ruth Bidgood suggest that she has a faith as firmly grounded as, presumably, was that of her father. But her work does nevertheless carry important hints that her sensibility retains the imprint of religious conviction. Bidgood did not start to write poetry until she had reached her seventies and had moved to live alone in the isolated region of the Abergwesyn pass in mid-Wales, an upland area where homesteads are widely scattered and the whole land is swallowed up at night by a deep dark. It is hardly surprising therefore that her poetry places such a very high value on commemoration, or that it should so often record her awareness of the encroaching darkness of impending death. Her poems are as understated as they are undervalued, movingly unpretentious and unfailingly empathetic as they quietly capture 'the mystery/ that complements precision'.[16]

A key word in her vocabulary is 'haunted' – 'to accept as mine this given time,/ to live in the haunted present', as she puts it (*SP*, 125).[17] The adjective frequently relates to her interest in past lives, in speakers of a dead language (Abergwesyn had remained a thoroughly Welsh-speaking area well into the twentieth century) and adherents to a departed Nonconformist faith – in this respect she resembles Roland Mathias, sharing with him a sense of responsibility to honour those lives, that ultimately derives from a Christian awareness of dwelling in 'a cloud of witnesses'. Indeed, several of her poems are dramatic monologues, or imaginary letters of the long ago: 'I am a latecomer, but offer/ speech to the nameless, those/ who are hardly a memory, those/ whose words were always faint/ against the deafening darkness/ of remotest hills' (*NSP*, 81). In 'Church in the Rain' she repeatedly hears voices crying in the surrounding trees, as if seeking sanctuary: 'Hide me, they say, comfort me/ I want that which is no dream/ That which I want is no dream/ I want I want' (*NSP*, 115). Those voices clearly also bespeak unassuageable needs that she feels within herself, while that extended blank textual space left between the two 'I wants' is the visual signification of the sad futility of all such yearning for consoling spiritual presence.

The term 'haunted' further registers her sensitivity to those echoes of a past age still to be heard in old buildings, particularly churches: 'stone proclaims life', she writes, 'affirms a future/ by virtue of so many pasts,/ yet baffles questioning' (*NSP*, 30). Accordingly, 'haunted' signifies an awareness of a dimension of life that, while omnipresent, remains tantalisingly evasive, unreachable and unknowable. This sometimes moves her to recall legends of the past such as that recorded in Kilvert's diary claiming that anyone who came to Wild Duck Pool on Easter morning would 'see the sun dance and play in the water and the angels who were at the Resurrection playing backwards and forwards before the sun' (*NSP*, 144). Visiting the churchyard at Nevern that contains a legendary ancient yew tree, she thinks of 'Carn Ingli above' where Brynach walked with angels. She has also repeatedly been drawn to religious ceremonies, particularly those relating to the passage from life to death. 'A mindless ritual is not empty', she writes in 'Standing Stone': 'when the dark mind fails, faith lives/ in the supplication of hands/ on prayer-wheel, rosary, stone' (*NSP*, 78). In 'All Souls', one of her best poems, she resurrects the old custom of paying homage to the dead by ensuring that her own house 'sing[s] with light' (*NSP*, 71). Memory of Indian women launching candles on leaf-boats to carry prayers into the dark prompts her to emulate them so that her house is sent sailing into the dark, 'launched, with a freight of light' (*SP*, 101). She is attracted by the practice of the Maya, who 'broke bowls,/smashed weapons, shredded clothes,/ killed them, to let their souls go free/ into the owner's eternity' (*NSP*, 131). When she visits the ruins of the medieval Cistercian monastery at 'Ystrad Fflur', she senses a connection that is more than cultural, and, feeling its shadows 'fall benevolently still on your ancient lands', is moved to touch the stones 'not without homage'; and to end the poem with a kind of prayer:

'Take our laughter/ on your consenting altars,/ and to the centuries borne up/ by your broken pillars, add/ the light weight of an hour/ at the end of summer' (*NSP*, 41).

Bidgood's most explicit admission of what might be termed a troubled and problematic 'spiritual affiliation' comes, however, in the elegy she wrote for R. S. Thomas. The tone is set by its disarmingly simple and frank title 'Bereft', and it is hard not to hear in its child-like admission of helpless spiritual loss echoes of her relationship to her own vicar father. For her, Thomas's death has removed an invaluable intermediary and interpreter 'who had words to catch/ a wordless resonance'. It has forced her to recognise that now 'the argument is between us, unaided,/ and the great Absence' (*NSP*, 230). And the poem ends with a confession typical of those many in the twenty-first century who can find no firm footing in inherited faith:

> Bereft, we cling
> to his image of mercy
> in crevices of rock,
> to the hope of finding,
> as he did one day, the meaning
> of a sombre landscape
> in a single sunlit field.

The case of Menna Elfyn is not dissimilar. Although her poetry is clearly imbued with the values she absorbed as a child growing up in a manse, nowhere does she directly address her own religious faith. But a lifelong commitment to speak for the downtrodden and for oppressed individuals and persecuted, or unfairly marginalised, minorities has led to her travelling the world to read her poetry in solidarity with them and to form valuable links with peoples some of whose cultural circumstances remind her of that of her own Welsh-language community at home. Partly to that end, she has for years published her poetry in bilingual form, the Welsh text facing the English and interacting with it in ways that are often very fruitful. Her father had been a well-loved and highly respected minister with the Annibynwyr (Welsh Independents) and his life embodied those admirable qualities of gentle tolerance, ecumenism and social concern typical of that largely liberal denomination during the second half of the twentieth century. His daughter, whose feminism was early manifest in the powerful and daring poems she wrote about suffering a miscarriage, is a founding member of Welsh PEN, an avowed pacifist and notable activist who served several brief terms of imprisonment as a young woman for her peaceful law-breaking activities on behalf of Cymdeithas yr Iaith Gymraeg, the society of young people campaigning for legal parity of Welsh with English. Within Wales, she has for decades worked to broker more constructive relationships through her work between the majority communities of the country and marginal communities, including those of refugees and immigrants.

Menna Elfyn's excursions into the realm of the spiritual have been limited to occasional productions, such as the play she wrote to explore the remarkable life of Simone Weil, who remains one of her heroines. But as she moves through her late middle age, she is beginning to show signs as a poet of gravitating towards matters of the spirit – she is completing an English-language play provisionally entitled 'Gethsemane' for production by the National Theatre of Wales. Her latest volume is entitled *Tosturi*, a noun-verb meaning both compassion and to pity. She had toyed, she explains, with the plural form 'Tosturiaethau' (many acts of compassion) but had come to feel that it sounded altogether too grandiose, and even somewhat presumptuous, given that in the Welsh-language context the word inescapably brings to mind a famous line from a great Welsh hymn about God's loving compassion for mankind which is boundless as the vast ocean itself ('tosturiaethau fel y lli'). She has, she adds, long been fascinated by the way the simple word 'Amen' keeps recurring in so many different languages and resounds through so many faiths, and so has taken to collecting as many examples as she can. She speaks appreciatively of how one of her Arabic translators – Menna Elfyn's work has been translated into innumerable languages – had admitted to her that her father, trapped in Lebanon with his wife, had been musing on the word's meaning for most of his life. Similarly, she goes on to say, 'tosturi' is a seminal concept connecting all the great faiths. It confronts one as a constant challenge in this grimmest of ages, and is a reminder of the centrality of the question that Simone Weil so famously posed during the Second World War: of how to give meaningful expression through our lives to the pity we should feel for the plight of so many.[18]

Her poem 'Tosturi' begins by recalling that her father's favourite exasperated response whenever she misbehaved as a young girl was 'Trugaredd sy'n gwybod' ('Mercy alone knows') and that brings to mind the famous line from the hymn that has already been mentioned above. Faced by the monstrousness of the contemporary world, she confesses that once more she finds herself urgently inclined to aim for 'tir y tirion' (the land of the gentle and mild) while mumbling the same exclamation as her father, except 'heb yr ebwch hollalluog' – without the exclamation of spiritual authority of one who had been unshakeably secure in his belief in a compassionate Almighty.

The most arresting of the poets of Wales to explore the spiritual dimensions of reality is, however, Aled Jones Williams, a daring, restlessly original writer, who was R. S. Thomas's parish priest during the final years of his life, and who officiated at the memorial service held at the church in Porthmadog when his ashes were laid to rest there. No more appropriate priest for the occasion could have been imagined, since Jones Williams's experience of god (he prefers to eschew the capitalised version of the noun) uncannily resembles that of Thomas, a poet whom he immensely admires. Over a period of some thirty years, Jones Williams descended precipitately into several prolonged periods of severe alcoholism, requiring treatment in various rehab centres, and for a number of years he acted as manager of the L'Arche centre in Liverpool for individuals with intellectual disabilities. In 2002, he left the Church in Wales, opting to plough his own alternative lonely furrow as an agnostic who nevertheless remains a chronic spiritual seeker. He has admitted that in his time he has been attracted to Quakerism, Catholicism and Buddhism, as well as 'serving his time' in the Church in Wales – an institution with which he has become thoroughly disillusioned. One of his favourite writers is the great seventeenth-century seeker and mystic, Morgan Llwyd, and it is from Llwyd that he took the title for his remarkable confessional autobiography, *Tuchan o Flaen Duw* (Grumbling before God). In context the passage reads (in English translation): 'and if you are unable to pray, try to grumble before God, but set aside your Book of Common Prayer'.[19]

Jones Williams first established a reputation as a highly unconventional and controversial Welsh-language dramatist. But in 2010 he published *Y Cylchoedd Perffaith* (*The Perfect Circles*), a collection of poetry – his first love.[20] And there he begins to probe in earnest his acute awareness of the simultaneous power and insufficiency of words when brought face to face with spiritual matters. In 'Ti', for instance, he begins by emphasising that it is not so much the case that the absence of God means that He is not there but that He is the whiteness between printed words that allows their special scent to surface (*CP*, 68). In *Tuchan o Flaen Duw* he likewise insists that to accept the insufficiency of language is not to deny that nevertheless it can perform an invaluable service in bringing us into the presence of spiritual depths.

Jones Williams has understandably been shy of sharing his poetry with the public at large, preferring to circulate it privately among like-minded souls. And indeed 'poems' is a rather misleading term for what are, in truth, fragments, tentative meditative reflections on the mingled potency and impotence of words to articulate experience of the divine. It is revealing that one of his favourite painters should be Kurt Schwitters, that maestro of collages composed out of the detritus of living. And that he is interested in the Concrete poetry of the Vienna Group (1954–64) – he is particularly struck by their radical methods of engaging with language in the wake of the Shoah.

At one point in the privately printed little volume *Cerddaf o'r Hen Fapiau* (*I walk away from the Old Maps*), a collection of xeroxed hand-written scraps of poetry attractively enclosed within a striking abstract cover design, Jones Williams speaks of how, through the thrash of words, he reaches the hovel of language and there shelters 'thou' in the crib of stammering.[21] The layout of the poem, that sees words stagger across the page, textually enacts the meaning. Elsewhere, he talks of being gored by words and, wittily noting that 'brawddeg', the Welsh word for 'sentence', includes the word 'braw' (fear or terror), accuses himself of having walked away from that chilling truth, preferring to take refuge in the warm comfort of ordinary 'civilised' expression. Jones Williams is, like R. S. Thomas, an inveterate punster – a facility of which he is also very wary, recognising in it a dangerous capacity for dexterously avoiding confronting realities by cleverly deconstructing them. In fact, the collection as a whole is a brilliantly various exploration of the universe of language as experienced by one who knows himself to be an inveterate and everlasting spiritual 'seeker'. It is by means of such seeking that he stakes out the frontiers of human utterance and thus sensitively outlines by negation the image-less 'otherness' and 'beyond-ness' of 'god'.

To call such examples to mind is to begin to sketch a tentatively positive answer to the question, 'is the Welsh religious tradition examined in this study likely to survive into the twenty-first century?' The odds would seem to be very heavily against it – the country is now far more secular in character than ever it was in the last century, and most particularly so when compared to the period in which the writers

that have been examined here were maturing. But, as the foregoing
has shown, there are nevertheless interesting counter-indications, one
of the most fascinating of which is the poetry of Rowan Williams,
which is steadily growing in consequence with the appearance of every
new volume.

*　*　*

Rowan Williams has valuably clarified his own understanding of his
relationship to the tradition outlined in this volume in a private e-mail
exchange with me.

> I'd certainly say that the names you mention [of the poets considered in
> this volume] were all part of my own hinterland as a poet from early on;
> and I guess that, in relation to the Welsh tradition in general, it's always
> been important to me to try and write for the ear as well as for the eye/
> brain, and that an ear for assonance has always been there. But also I was
> appreciative of a properly contemporary and rigorous poetic tradition in
> which Christian topics were unselfconsciously there to be addressed – as
> they are, say in Polish poetry and a lot in Russian.[22]

At the time of writing, he explained, he was in process of translating
some of Euros Bowen's poems for inclusion in his next collection of
poems, to be published by Carcanet; and he added that 'I met him a
couple of times in the 70's (Donald Allchin), and he was encourag-
ing about my own very early and incompetent poems, so there is a
debt to pay!'

Williams has been a very skilful and productive 'free' translator of
the Welsh-language poetry of several of the poets mentioned in this
volume – most particularly Waldo Williams and Gwenallt – as well as
of the hymns of Ann Griffiths. He has also written illuminating essays
(some brief notes, others lengthy discussions) about Vernon Watkins,
Gwenallt and Euros Bowen, while identifying most closely with the
religious poetry of Waldo Williams and R. S. Thomas. Moreover,
the title – *The Wound of Knowledge* – of his important early study of
Christian spirituality from the New Testament to St John of the Cross
is taken from Thomas's poem 'Roger Bacon', a fact that he acknow-
ledges in the Preface, adding that Thomas 'has long since said most
of what I want to say'.[23]

As a Swansea boy, Williams naturally warmed to 'Swansea's
Other Poet', Vernon Watkins. On 11 March 2012 he presented an

outstanding hour-long feature on his poetry on Radio 3, during the course of which he described it as 'immensely sophisticated, metaphorically rich and technically brilliant', while conceding it was also 'demanding'. The work, he added, was some of the most distinctive produced in the twentieth century, and the voice speaking through it was 'compelling'. His affinity for another Swansea poet – this time a product of the heavily industrialised lower Swansea Valley rather than of the coastal and rural Gower peninsula – is apparent in the incisive introduction he furnished to a selection of Gwenallt's poems translated into English. He instinctively recognises him to be a poet who encapsulated 'the struggles of a whole era, a whole class of people' and who created 'a distinct imaginative world'. And he sympathetically outlines the background to the writing:

> His personal voice is matured in the context of an industrialism careless of life and welfare, first finding itself in the language of a Marxist critique and then falling into the rhythm and cadence of a bleak but honest and impassioned Christianity, with its vision of humanity reduced almost to animality (echoes of *King Lear*)[.][24]

Williams is perceptive and generous enough to offer his own cautious account of Gwenallt's defection from Anglicanism in later life:

> His growth towards a sacramental and Catholic perspective and his membership of the Anglican Church did not soften [his] vision, though it gave it far wider dimensions and a depth of underlying warmth and hope. When he abandoned Anglicanism, it could be seen in part as a protest in the name of the very catholicity he had learned in the Anglican Church, a protest against churchy intolerance and a bland indifference to the ways in which the gospel had woven itself into the culture and speech of *this* people and *this* place. For him ... 'Catholicity' was the freedom of Christ and the gospel to translate themselves into the familiar landscape of everyday Welshness (or any other local identity) – the landscape inhabited by saints doing ordinary things in the light and grace of God.

Into Gwenallt's poetry, he concludes, 'tragedy and generosity are woven ... in a way that gives it a rare spiritual authority.'

Williams's particularly close affinity with Waldo Williams is evident from the comments he has made on his own attempts to translate some of his work into English:

Waldo Williams's world is one that both invites and tests the translator. Because he can create an imaginative world so charged with light and with what I can only call a sense, an unmistakably Christian sense, of 'wisdom' embodied – a world charged with moral as well as visual vigour and radiance, charged with expectation of a personal but also a cosmic epiphany – the impulse to recreate is strong. The test comes in the economy of what he writes, an economy that is characteristic of the language itself, with its strong nouns, its ability to deploy various techniques to raise the affective temperature (apostrophe, intensified alliterative patterns) and its essentially concrete register ... Waldo's combination of density and luminosity makes him a specially significant partner in the complex engagement of translating, and a specially fruitful presence in the process of composition.[25]

Williams made these remarks in a lecture to the Waldo Williams Society on 'Poetry and Peacemaking', in which he homed in on Waldo's use of the seminal term 'awen' as he spoke of Waldo as 'a poet-pacifist on a par with Thomas Merton and the English poet Geoffrey Hill'. 'Awen' he understood to mean 'the primitive primordial energy coupled with the imaginative spirit', adding that '"awen" owns the world while "elw" (profit) is nothing but fantasy'. Awen connects and completes all things under the surface, working by means of recognition (hence Waldo's key phrase 'Awen adnabod') and when this recognition is embodied in poetry the words possess the force of peacemaking. This (see below) is very much in line with the kind of thinking advanced by John Milbank, his former student and distinguished Anglo-Catholic theologian of 'radical orthodoxy' – a contemporary variant of Episcopalian theology of which Williams is often described as a founder – who sees the 'Christian mythos' as uniquely offering a precious view of the world that saves it from operating as an arena of ceaseless violent social and ideological conflicts.[26]

It is natural for Williams to set Euros Bowen alongside R. S. Thomas, as both were priests in the Church in Wales. While recognising 'convergences' in their thinking and writing, he nevertheless points out the obvious divergences. 'Euros', he explains, 'is much more explicit in seeing the poet's work as a "setting in order," interpreting and harmonising the flow of the world's life in such a way that the shifts and changes of the world we perceive can be unveiled as transfigurations, epiphanies of God's life'.[27] As a consequence, he points out, the poetry is not dramatic in character, and is not 'sustained by powerful verbal and metrical tensions'. Instead 'many of the poems are slowpaced, a succession of images allowed to drift and circle before being settled into a final "frame" with some culminating, unifying turn. Short lines help to slow the pace, as do parallelisms, carefully placed repetitions, and, sometimes, the use of a loose poetic prose form'.

And then there is R. S. Thomas, the poet with whom Rowan Williams has for decades had a very special relationship, and with whom he has been conducting his own intense personal conversation. So subtle, nuanced, wide-ranging and distinctive has that conversation been that it is impossible to do justice to it here and so a few examples must suffice. Even then the sheer density of the discussions defies any attempt at adequate summary. Take, for example, the brilliant essay 'Dangerous Thoughts in R. S. Thomas' that appeared in *The Page's Drift.* A collection of essays to mark Thomas's eightieth birthday, it was published in 1993, but Williams's contribution is interestingly centred on that concept of 'The Wound of Knowledge' that had provided him with the title of the theological study he had published some twenty years earlier. By 1993, however, Williams had come to absorb, and to synthesise, aspects of the post-structuralist thinking of Jacques Derrida, the phenomenological existentialism of Heidegger, the new theology of figures like John Milbank, Vincent Gillespie and Maggie Ross,[28] and the remarkable poetry of Geoffrey Hill. He is fascinated by the phrase 'the adult geometry of the mind' that Thomas had coined in *The Laboratories of the Spirit,* and the essay is concerned with teasing out the complex, elusive meanings of the phrase for a priest who, as poet, understood he was under no obligation to evolve a systematic theology or metaphysics. Nevertheless, 'beyond the vigilant self-suspicion and self-subversion of the poetry', as Williams puts it,

> is something very like a theological option, an acceptance of the "foundational violence" identified in much modern and postmodern thought by John Milbank in his recent *Theology and Social Theory* – the assumption that conflict and rivalry (and thus: *ressentiment*) are somehow native to our being, because, explicitly or implicitly, the relation of beings to their final origin is itself a kind of flaw, "wound," violence. The particularity of the world of the multiple and contingent is at odds with the peace or self-coherence of "Being". Between origin and actuality, then, must be some kind of tragic fissuring, capable of being healed only in the fissures, the gaps, of language. Silence negates the negativity of a contingent world.[29]

And it is the acceptance of this by Thomas the poet, Williams concludes by suggesting, that makes his poems such compelling examples of 'exemplary failure', a phrase he takes from Geoffrey Hill.

Williams's doctoral study of the writings of the Eastern Orthodox theologian Vladimir Lossky (1903–58) may have inclined him to take a particular interest in such features of Thomas's religious writings as the above. Drawn, like Rowan Williams, to the mystical strain in the Christian tradition, a strain particularly evident in mystics, contemplatives and saints as opposed to the rationality of scholastic practice and of established ecclesiology, Lossky, like R. S. Thomas, favoured the apophatic approach to the mysteries of a radically unknowable divinity. Central to his theology was the recognition of the uncreated hyper-being, the Primordial One, or *Ousia*. A corollary to this would seem to be Williams's sensitivity to the traces in Thomas's poetry of a 'post-ethical' view of God. In the late poetry this often takes the form of speaking of God as a 'raptor', as Williams has pointed out in a second important essay which is significantly entitled 'Suspending the Ethical: R. S. Thomas and Kierkegaard'.[30] There he likens Thomas's concept of faith to that of Kierkegaard when exploring the strange, and on the surface sinister and repugnant, story of Abraham and Isaac. Abraham's faith is paradoxically expressed in the silence of his acquiescence to God's 'barbaric' command to kill his son. It is a silence that locates faith in a context where words fail. 'Faith', Williams concludes, 'is the unspeakable reality of affirming [the] relation ... between the individual and the absolute' (208). Williams adds:

> This is where Thomas's reading of Kierkegaard seems central to the business of his religious poetics: God can never be 'there' for examination, nor is God to be uncovered in analysis of religious emotion, religious experience, in anything like the usual understanding of such words. God can be established only in the depiction of a faith turned towards faith in Kierkegaard's sense. (209)

Also, for Williams as for Thomas, an important expression of faith is prayer, 'which is not a drama for the subject, but a suspension of the subject, the thinking ego immersing itself in the sheer process of the structured world as a means to identification with God' (*PD*, 82). Because 'we are "thought" before we think, "spoken" before we speak; our subjective lives are not privileged' (*PD*, 82). That is why

Thomas shares Heidegger's deep dislike for the 'subjectivism' of modern existence.

It seems, too, that Lossky's writings on the triune God of the Holy Trinity may also have a bearing on aspects of Rowan Williams's interest in Thomas, and central to this area of the Russian's theology is the concept of the uncreated hyper-being, the Primordial One, the *Ouisa*. As Father He is the uncreated essence and origin, as Son He is that uncreated essence become (begotten not created) flesh or existence and as Spirit He is the uncreated existence become the animator of all life.[31] The Holy Spirit and Christ are the hands of God the Father, reaching in from the infinite into the finite – a comparison apparently used by Rowan Williams, too, in an address he delivered in Cairo as Archbishop of Canterbury.

Williams's interest in Thomas's treatment of the Trinity surfaces in 'Suspending the Ethical' as a meditation on a poem from *Counterpoint* (12) where 'the selfhood of God' is imaged as 'two mirrors echoing/ one another', with the Holy Spirit as 'the breath clouding them'.[32] Thomas comes to accept, or so Williams proceeds to suggest, that any authentic relationship to God – one that does not involve grasping, or explaining, or strenuous search, or any other form of mastery by self of its 'object' – must involve acceptance of the inevitable 'clouding of the mirror'. It must accept it exists in and as that clouding – as a creation of the Holy Ghost. And it must accordingly accept the impossibility of proceeding beyond the conditioned nature of its very creation; therein lies its acceptance of the absoluteness of God in His otherness:

> When a person is engaged in desire without determined object, in the absence of an audience or an argument that justifies the decision to stay *still* with the desire, we see what it means to say "God," and what it means to deny that prayer is talking to oneself. (*EA*, 210–11)

> [But this] does not imply that absence itself is something we can settle down with. It must still be experienced as absence, because the mirror is there for the face to appear in. But what the appearance involves is frightening ... because it is something that both affirms our absolute singleness and uniqueness as created persons and yet has nothing at all to do with any of the available ways of reinforcing our sense of value or security. (*EA*, 212)

*   *   *

The conclusion of the essay on R. S. Thomas and Kierkegaard sees
Rowan Williams return to the role of poetry in Thomas's life of faith.
For him, 'Poetry is the construction of a more deeply and resource-
fully intelligible self which is achieved by pushing the inner tensions
of language to the point of new discoveries in form and metaphor'
(*EA*, 217). Williams sees Thomas's poetic enterprise as shot through
with paradox:

> Holding with Kierkegaard that the self is unintelligible and un-speakable
> without the absolute other, yet underlining relentlessly the radical nature
> of that otherness, Thomas cannot understand his poetic enterprise except
> as the pursuit of a presence – but a presence that can only obscure when
> it is actually present. Poetic "achievement", then, becomes a paradoxical
> act of consciousness seeking unselfconsciousness: speaking in such a way
> as to open up what is not said. And the unsaid is reality as the manifesta-
> tion of God, God as the ground of what is perceived (including the poet's
> own self and sensibility). (*EA*, 218)

It is an affirmation that needs to be set in the wider context of
Williams's apprehension of the Almighty, as explained in an inter-
view with Melvyn Bragg:

> God is first and foremost that depth around all things and beyond all
> things into which, when I pray, I try to sink. But God is also the activity
> that comes to me out of that depth, tells me that I'm loved, that opens
> up a future for me, that offers transformation I can't imagine. Very much
> a mystery but also very much a presence. Very much a person.[33]

And elsewhere Williams makes it clear his belief that the creative
impulse, which finds expression in his poetry, arises and is an articu-
lation from the same 'depth' that he mentions in the Bragg interview.
Hence, he perceives that poetry for Thomas is not a 'reproduction of
what is given' but 'the given in a new way'; 'it posits a new world which
is the depth of the old, not by denying the particular and immediate
but by seeking words for its unspoken setting, its setting within the
presence of God' (*EA*, 218).

Such an account of, and an accounting for, poetry, involving as
it does the recognition that in the case of the believer poetry is inti-
mately related to theology but is in no way ancillary to it, being its
own distinctive, precious, mode of apprehension, takes on new signifi-
cance once one remembers that Rowan Williams the theologian has

latterly developed into Rowan Williams the poet. His penchant for
the contemplative mode, so evident in his treatment of both Waldo
Williams and R. S. Thomas, is signalled by the cover image of his
poetry collection. It is Gwen John's beautiful painting of 'A Corner
of the Artist's Room in Paris, 1907–1909', so mysterious in its cap-
ture of what seems to be a gable room, empty save for a simple table,
book open on top, a wicker chair alongside, with a blue garment
carelessly draped over one arm. An open window on the far wall
allows a glimpse of a nondescript scene, where a rough masonry wall
largely blocks the distant view of a vague, anonymous woodland.
Nothing then here worth dwelling on, apparently, yet such is the quiet,
intimate, unselfconscious art of this shy composition that the whole
strangely luminous image is magnetic in its stillness, like a Vermeer
painting.

The first poem in the collection is a succinct portrait, in four short
sections, of Gwen John in Paris, and is also a kind of summation of
the life of an artist who, despite having been muse and mistress of
Rodin for a stormy period before finally retiring to Meudon and mute
communion with the nuns there, could, like her favourite St Thérèse
of Lisieux, be said to have largely lived her life 'not being seen' (*PRW*,
10). During her last years, John produced over seven hundred tiny
ink drawings responding to a photograph of St Thérèse and her elder
sister. In the first section of the poem the imagined presence of Gwen
John moves Rowan Williams to an intensely sensuous awareness of
the way the imagined blossoms in her jug 'throw their dense pollen
round the stormy room like a foam', a fine displacement of John's
early erotic infatuation with Rodin into the frank fertilities of nature.
In the third section of the poem, Gwen John recalls St Thérèse's
association of a photographer hiding his head under a black cloth
with her father likewise 'not seeing her' and the saint's reflection that
'Only when you can't see him do you/ know you're there'. It is, of
course, a paradox very much in line with Williams's understanding
of R. S. Thomas's relationship to God.

Williams's strong preference for flexible and contingent construc-
tions of faith, as distinct from the prescriptive rigidities of ideology,
doctrines and dogmas, is strikingly imaged in a poem on 'Drystone',
which opens by noting that these walls, typical of the uplands, are
totally devoid of mortar and wholly the product of the rural mason's
astute and sensitive eye for the consonance of 'unsocial' shapes that
enables the rough stones to be fitted securely together. Williams

notices how faithfully they follow the lie of the land, tracing a line that is 'rough, bumpy, contoured in jagging falls and twists' (*PRW*, 12). It is clearly for him an image suggestive both of a robust theology born of an appropriately flexible human response to the sacred unpredictabilities of God and His world, and of the poetics (such as that of R. S. Thomas) that corresponds to such a theology. So the craftsman is spoken of, at the poem's end, as one who 'conjured the dry aliens/ to run, one sentence crawled across the sheet,/ subtle against the wind, a silent spell, a plot'.

Williams is fascinated by the darkness of unknowing from which all existence proceeds and which still inheres deep within every being. This is captured in a beautiful stanza of the poem entitled 'Six O'Clock':

> When the sun
> levels its sights across the grass,
> it packs the blades and little animals
> so tight, so heavy that you wonder
> why they don't tumble over
> into their new, uncompromising shadow,
> into their inner dark. (*PRW*, 13)

It is a stanza that brings to my mind Edward Thomas's hauntingly strange poem 'Out in the Dark', a marvellous capturing of the uncanny and unnerving strangeness of all existence. Little wonder, then, that the word 'dark' recurs so often in Rowan Williams's poems. It is a word he repeatedly finds he needs the more his writing attempts to take on the mystery of things.

Rich as it is with the compaction of images, Williams's poetry is most often reminiscent of that of yet another Thomas – Dylan Thomas. It is a marked feature, for example, of his bafflingly dense poems of relationship, but also ubiquitous elsewhere, as in the grand declamatory rhetoric of 'Not till the gusty day/ when a last angel tramples down/ into the mud his dry foot hissing,/ down to the clogged forgotten shingle,/ till the bay boils and shakes' (*PRW*, 29) (lines appropriately enough about Oystermouth Cemetery); or when he produces hermetic lines such as 'Wind tight the press/ and mill our parching salt, our black and needful flour' (*PRW*, 30). Such writing is too rich for my palate. I prefer it when the writing is pitched in a lower key that allows Rowan Williams to display his real unshowy gift for a self-effacing sensuous precision: 'The wind is sharp as gulls/ past David's Pembroke window,/ lettering the stars across / a winter wall' (*PWR*, 37), lines that as a footnote explains relate to 'the unique "domestic" gallery established by David Jones's friend Jim Hide'. Such a style enables an empathic gentleness to surface, as in the opening to 'September Birds':

> Down in the small hollow where the currents shift
> slowly, and drop with the thinning sun, the crows
> float, crowding the shallow slopes of air,
> and vague as specks of stubble fire[.] (*PRW*, 38)

'That they are there', the important American poet George Oppen wrote in his wonderful little poem 'Psalm':

> In the small beauty of the forest
> The wild deer bedding down –
> That they are there!

And in the last stanza, Oppen makes it clear that his astonished humbled awakening to the sufficiency of the 'mere', mysterious, independent existence (of animals, of nature – yes, and of human beings) also involves an awakening to the proper use of words, a discovery of a style of writing that involves respecting even the most common and despised particles of language:

> The small nouns
> Crying faith
> In this in which the wild deer
> Startle and stare out.[34]

Rowan Williams's poetry is to me at its most attractive when it succeeds in sounding that note of quiet acceptance and affirmation.

That note is, for example, struck in a poem to his mother, Delphine Williams, which immediately precedes one to his father. It is a 'borderlands' poem in many respects. The setting is the Marches, and most specifically the area around Housman's beloved Bredin Hill, in Shropshire. That commanding height allows Williams to take his bearings, not just geographically but culturally. With the visionary eye of imagination, he sees 'Dead souls walk straight as Roman legions/

from fort to fort' along roads that run 'through the solid tribal world'
(*PRW*, 70). Thus prompted, he becomes what Hazlitt paradoxically
called 'a prophet of the past', as he intuits the implication of what
he is envisaging:

> The Roman road ignores the aboriginals, their maps
> and calendars. But we shuffling primitives can't fail to see
> this is the occupying power. Sooner or later, we shall have to learn
> to shape our mouths, measure our stride to theirs,
> and look nowhere but to the next grazed, wind-scrubbed summit.

It is a rare moment when Williams circumspectly hints at his own
situation as a Welshman, recognising that he belongs to a people with
long experience of 'occupation' of a complex kind. But, of course, it
is more than that, and it helps explain his particular attraction to the
'universalist' aspects of Waldo Williams's spiritual vision and poetry.
This becomes clear if one places the above passage from 'Flight Path'
(a title in which many meanings are compacted together) next to the
following lines from his translation of Waldo Williams's 'In the Days
of Caesar':

> Well, little people, and my little nation, can you see
> The secret buried in you, that no Caesar ever captures in his lists?
> Will not the shepherd come to fetch us in our desert,
> Gathering us in to give birth again, weaving us into one
> In a song heard in the sky over Bethlehem? (*PRW*, 86)

The conflation here of 'my little nation' with the 'little people' – that
is the vast multitude of the powerless, the subordinated, the margin-
alised and the oppressed throughout the world – is exactly the same
rhetorical move that one finds in Rowan Williams's poetry. In both
cases, it is their Welshness that allows them access to a wide, world-
embracing vision of the community of all humanity, a vision that is
underpinned and underwritten by their shared spiritual belief.

Rowan Williams follows his poem to his mother with one to his
father, Aneurin Williams, which opens thus:

> The quilt of willowherb muffles
> The stream before it drops
> Invisible to the beach;
> the moist whisper thinned

> to its straight seaward fall,
> the shore sound coming back up, dry
> as two palms rubbing steadily
> close to your ear[.] (*PRW*, 71)

That dialectic of take and give, of impulse and counter-impulse, is deeply typical of Rowan Williams's mind and writing, and at this point there seems the merest hint at the experience of ageing, understood as the psychological and spiritual experience of entering a hinterland between life and death, an uncanny borderland, a liminal region where in energy's decay one hears echoes, or intimations, of what is to come. It is at such moments as this that Rowan Williams's writing moves 'beyond the vigilant self-suspicion and self-subversion' evident in some of his other poems.

The poem for his father is located in Bae Creibwr in Pembrokeshire, but Rowan Williams is in general sparing in his references to Wales in his poetry. One exception, however, is his translation from the Welsh of T. Gwynn Jones's popular 'Ystrad Fflur', a simple lyric, romantic in tone, where the ruins of the Cistercian monastery are identified with the ruin of faith. Strata Florida, once a sacred place, a site of intersection of past and present, time and the timeless, is viewed by Jones with the sadly disenchanted and disenchanting eyes of the twentieth century. But, at the conclusion of Williams's very free translation, T. Gwynn Jones the confirmed agnostic seems to be unexpectedly unnerved by his failure to find either the language of elegy that alone can conclusively put the 'superstitions' of the past to rest or an alternative, secular, language adequate to assuage his own pain.

> Defeat, oblivion, rotting monuments
> of dead belief.
> Why is it then I find no words, here quietly,
> For private grief? (*PWR*, 85)

What is interesting, however, is that this version is a radical departure from the original Welsh, as is clear if one compares it with the fidelity of Joseph Clancy's rather pedestrian ending:

> But though I see upon faith's ruins
>   Sad death's oblivion,
> When I walk the earth of Ystrad Fflur
>   It eases me of pain.[35]

This ending suggests satisfactory emotional resolution, whereas that of Williams does not. And Clancy's more accurate version makes it clear that T. Gwynn Jones, still very much in thrall as he was to Victorian Medievalism, was writing in the popular eighteenth-century tradition of graveyard poetry and its sentimental melancholising. So why the alteration made by Rowan Williams? It could possibly be that he is prompted to hint at a nostalgia for belief, believing such must linger at the heart even of the most adamant of non-believers.

Another of his poems of Welsh place is a response to a very different location. Penrhys, the mountain separating the two Rhondda Valleys, has for decades been the site of a very large council house estate. It has come to have an unenviable reputation as a somewhat unruly place, which is hardly surprising considering its bleak, exposed site and the extraordinary lack of basic amenities such as shops there. But it is also an ancient pilgrimage site, the location of Ffynnon Fair, St Mary's Well, that in the later Middle Ages attracted pilgrims in large numbers from every corner of Wales. The Cistercians established a small chapel there that included a famous Screen, as well as a statue of the Virgin, and in the later fifteenth century a body of poetry was written in praise of the sacred location. The well, now carefully protected, is still there, and nearby is the statue of the Virgin. Unveiled in 1953, it soon attracted more than 20,000 visitors.[36]

In the poem, Williams is fascinated by this dramatic conjunction of the modern secular world, at its most sordid, and a site that has been regarded as sacred for the greater part of a thousand years at least. Rejecting the easy, obvious course of condemning the present and reverently celebrating the past, he opts instead in the end for a sensitive recognition of moving points of connection. At first, though, it looks as if he will go the easy route, as he registers the litter and debris being collected by a 'a dour council cleaner'; 'cartons and condoms and a few stray sheets/ of newspaper that the wind sticks across his face'. At this point, it even seems to him that the Christ child in His Mother's arms is urging repudiation of everything in the dispiriting and dispirited scene. Viewed in this light, the statue reminds him of Walter Benjamin's famous 'Angelus Novus', 'backing into the granite future, wings spread,/ head shaking at the recorded day,/ no, he says, refuse' – that last word seeming to gesture, via pun, to the refuse so liberally scattered around (*PRW*, 51).

It is at this point, however, that the poem sharply alters its perceived course, as advantage is taken of a subtle textual ambivalence.

The next phrase, 'Not here', is the grammatical completion of the Angel's injunction to 'refuse'; but it is split by a textual gap that isolates it from the sentence to which it grammatically belongs. Consequently, instead of reinforcing refusal, 'not here' seems to signal a new start, encouraging the reader to refuse to accept the Angel's refusal. This is a rhetorical trick straight out of the R. S. Thomas playbook – in his essays on Thomas, Williams has repeatedly shown himself to be a consummate student of Thomas's artful use of the textual breaks signalled by line-endings.

After that pivotal moment in the text, Williams concentrates on reconciling the secular present, in all its unredeemed character, with the sacred past, beginning with a sympathetic portrait of two young local council house girls, 'thin teenage mothers at the bus stop'. That adjective 'thin' immediately links them suggestively to the baby Jesus in the statue's arms who has already been described as 'thin'. And primed by that connection, we are ready to appreciate the spiritual double entendre in their chat: 'One day my bus will come, says one;/ they laugh. More use'n a bloody prince,/ says someone else'. Deeply informed by this sympathetic understanding of the young mother's plights, Williams can then move on to a conclusion that delicately implies, without grossly stating, the resemblance between their own condition and plight and that of the Virgin herself. So the poem leaves the girls 'Comparing notes, silently, on shared/ Unwritten stories of the bloody stubbornness/ of getting someone born'.

Given Rowan Williams's special relationship to R. S. Thomas, and the remarkable inwardness of his responses to Thomas's poetry, it is not surprising that one of the very best – and most ineffably moving – of his own poems should be written in Thomas's memory. The title 'Deathship' both brings to mind D. H. Lawrence's famous 'The Ship of Death' (with a nod too perhaps at Tennyson's 'Crossing the Bar') and also acknowledges the ultimate regal authority of death and the finality of its judgement, an absolute judgement allowing of no appeal other, for a Christian believer, than to the superior authority of Christ the Redeemer. In parts, the text deliberately raises echoes of the remarkable late poetry Thomas wrote in the little Jacobean stone cottage of Sarn y Plas, within earshot of the waves at Porth Neigwl, the little stormy bay whose restless, treacherous waters so fascinated him. In a beautiful image, Williams depicts him as aspiring, Christ-like, to calm the waters, by issuing 'words from a window,/ smoothing the sea, the iron back and forth/ to probe the fugitive wrinkles' (*PRW*,

73). Having begun low key with that intimate domestic image, sug-
gestive of the aged Thomas's voluntary confinement, the poem moves
outwards by cautious degrees, becoming increasingly charged in the
process with a static electricity that is discharged only at the last in
the wonderful visionary expansiveness of the conclusion. Thomas is
there imagined as setting a black boat

> to balance
> on the slow sea at dark, ready to sail.
>
> The smoke will rise, the cloudy pillar
> wavering across the sky's long page.
> At dawn, somewhere westward,
> the boat flares in a blaze of crying birds.

The Biblical allusions are as well chosen as they are effectively
deployed, just hinting at the Moses-like role R. S. Thomas played for
the likes of Rowan Williams, in helping to bring a benighted modern
people out of their spiritual captivity and into a more promising land.

* * *

The grouping of the Welsh translations at the very end of Rowan
Williams's collection of poems gives the impression of their being a
kind of sheet-anchor of the whole. Or perhaps, to change metaphor
abruptly, that they are an umbilical cord connecting him to a trad-
ition that continues to nurture his spiritual life. One of the poems by
Waldo Williams that Rowan Williams chose to translate was 'Wedi'r
canrifoedd mudan', 'After Silent Centuries', a poem in memory of the
Catholic martyrs of Wales by a Welsh Quaker who had no time for
sectarian divisions of any kind. And it is interesting to recall that in
his study of *The Wound of Knowledge*, Rowan Williams made appre-
ciative mention of Augustine Baker, the seventeenth-century Catholic
convert and Benedictine monk, who was a native of Abergavenny and
is best known for his contemplative work on Holy Wisdom, *Sancta
Sophia*.

 In the opening chapter of that work, Baker makes it clear that
the aim of a human being is 'eternal beatitude both in soul and body
in heaven, the which consists in a returning to the divine principle
from whom he flowed, and inconceivable happy union with Him,
both in mind, contemplating eternally His infinite perfections, and

in will and affections eternally loving, admiring, and enjoying the said perfections'. And to assist the human soul, Baker continues, God 'was [originally] pleased to the natural vast capacity of man's understanding and will to add a supernatural light, illustrating His mind to believe and know Him'. But in their Fall, Adam and Eve had forfeited this divine gift, restoration of it which only became possible in and through Christ's intervention in the world. Therefore, for human beings now to rekindle that original inner light they had to yield themselves entirely to Christ, most particularly through contemplation and prayer.[37] Williams's interest in Baker both indicates the Anglo-Catholic temper of his own theology and is an example of the inclusive, ecumenical approach to the Welsh spiritual tradition that he shares with Waldo Williams. It is an approach that owes something to his own experience of switching at a young age from the Welsh Presbyterian Church in which he was brought up during his early years in Cardiff to the distinctive brand of Anglicanism that he espoused in his spiritual maturity. And in the interview with Bragg, Williams drew attention himself to the line of continuity connecting the two phases of his religious life. 'The Presbyterian Church of Wales' (otherwise known as the Welsh Calvinistic Methodist Church), he went out of his way to explain,

> Was a very great institution in its heyday and more like the established Church than the Church of England sometimes ... we had a minister who preached with enormous fervour and intelligence, and even as a boy I liked listening. I thought, 'This is exciting.' A big world [was opened by] the hymns we sang, the lessons we learnt in Sunday School ... all of which combined to make me feel, Yes, there's reality here. And I think a lot of my mental world still is deeply shaped by not only Welsh Presbyterianism, but aspects of Welsh revivalism too. (*RW*, 31–2)

Given his distinction as a world-leading theologian and Christian leader of similar world significance, and bearing further in mind the extraordinary breadth and depth of his multilingual learning, it would be absurd, as well as demeaning, to treat Rowan Williams as a figure of significance primarily in the context of the modern Welsh tradition of spiritual poetry which has been examined in this volume. It would, however, also be diminishing of him not to recognise the significance of both of his connection with, and his distinguished contribution to, that tradition, a tradition of which he has repeatedly demonstrated a

keen awareness and appreciation. And his achievements in that con-
nection continue to be such as to offer some grounds for hoping that
there may be life to come yet in a tradition that, as this study has tried
to show, so memorably demonstrated its potential during the second
half of the twentieth century; it is, as Rowan Williams himself has
perceptively remarked, a tradition that bears witness to 'the richness
of the modern Welsh religious imagination' (*EB*, 9).

Notes

1 'Preface,' Dylan Thomas, *Collected Poems, 1934–1952* (London: Dent, 1964 reprint).
2 Walford Davies (ed.), *Dylan Thomas: Early Prose Writings* (London: Dent, 1971), p. 160.
3 David N. Thomas (ed.), *Dylan Remembered*, vol. 1 (1914–34) (Bridgend: Seren, 2003), p. 164.
4 Aneirin Talfan Davies, *Dylan: Druid of the Broken Body* (London: Dent, 1964).
5 M. Wynn Thomas, '"Marlais": Dylan Thomas and the "Tin Bethels"', *In the Shadow of the Pulpit: Literature and Nonconformist Wales* (Cardiff: University of Wales Press, 2010), pp. 226–55. M. Wynn Thomas, 'Marlais', in Hannah Ellis (ed.), *Dylan Thomas: Centenary Essays* (London: Bloomsbury, 2014), pp. 30–41.
6 Back cover, *The Poems of Rowan Williams* (Manchester: Carcanet, 2002). Hereafter *PRW*.
7 Cary Archard (ed.), *Dannie Abse: A Sourcebook* (Brigend: Seren, 2009), p. 140. Hereafter *S*.
8 Dannie Abse, *New Selected Poems, Anniversary Collection: 1949–2009* (London: Hutchinson, 2009), p. 37. Hereafter *ANSP*.
9 Jeremy Hooker, '"The Roles are Greater than we Know": Tony Conran's Religious Sceptism', *Imagining Wales: A view of modern Welsh writing in English* (Cardiff: University of Wales Press, 2001), p. 185.
10 Jeremy Hooker, 'Mary Casey: The Poetry of Aloneness', *The Presence of the Past: Essays on Modern British and American Poetry* (Bridgend: Poetry Wales Press, 1987), p. 44.
11 Gwyneth Lewis, *Treiglo* (Tal y bont: Cynhoeddiadau Barddas, 2017). Hereafter *T*.
12 I am very grateful indeed to Gwyneth Lewis for correspondence and discussion about this.
13 Gwyneth Lewis, *Parables and Faxes* (Newcastle: Bloodaxe, 1995). Hereafter *PF*.
14 Gwyneth Lewis, *Hospital Odyssey* (Newcastle: Bloodaxe, 2010). Hereafter *HO*.
15 Debates about the validity of supposing this date back to the dawn of the 'new physics' and to the intense inter-war debates between all its leading theorists.

Of them, the one most convinced of the need for a spiritual philosophy corresponding to the new philosophy of Einsteinian science was Wolfgang Pauli, who came to believe that the revolutionary discoveries made by him and his colleagues in the realm of physical reality needed to be complemented by the kind of understanding of non-physical reality that was manifest in some of the great mystical teachings of Eastern religions. He dreamt of a unified theory that would involve a synthesis of them both. See Juan Miguel Marin, '"Mysticism" in quantum mechanics: the forgotten controversy', *European Journal of Physics*, 30 (2009), 807–22.

16 'Little of Distinction', in Ruth Bidgood, *New and Selected Poems* (Bridgend: Seren, 2004), p. 16. Hereafter *NSP*.

17 Ruth Bidgood, *Selected Poems* (Bridgend: Seren Books, 1992), p. 125.

18 All the information in this paragraph is taken, with the author's kind permission, from an e-mail dated 29 September 2021.

19 Aled Jones Williams, *Tuchan o Flaen Duw* (Llanrwst: Gwasg Carreg Gwalch, 2012).

20 Aled Jones Williams, *Y Cylchoedd Perffaith* (Caernarfon: Gwasg y Bwthyn, 2010).

21 I am exceedingly grateful to Aled Jones Williams for kindly sending me a copy of this important self-publication.

22 E-mail, 29 March 2021. The content is reproduced with the sender's permission.

23 Rowan Williams, *The Wound of Knowledge* (London: Darton, Longman and Todd), p. x. Hereafter *WK*.

24 'Foreword', in Donald Allchin, D. Densil Morgan and Patrick Thomas (eds), *Sensuous Glory: The Poetic Vision of D. Gwenallt Jones* (Norwich: Canterbury Press, 2000).

25 *waldowilliams.com/?page_id=256&lang=en*

26 Williams summarises his relationship to this theology with typical graceful lucidity, in his seminal interview with Rupert Shortt, entitled 'Rowan Williams on Belief and Theology – Some Basic Questions', to be found online at the Fulcrum website. Hereafter referred to as *F*.

27 'Foreword', Cynthia and Saunders Davies (eds), *Euros Bowen: priest-poet/ bardd-offeiriad* (Penarth: Church in Wales Publications, 1993), p. 9. Hereafter *EB*.

28 Ross, an American theologically trained at Stanford and Oxford, has become an anchorite. In an interesting interview in *The Church Times* (16 January 2015) she observes that 'The churches are full of noise. There is an idolatry of spiritual experience. The situation is dire. They find support wherever they can, in silence and solitude if they can find it, or with like-minded people, if they can find them. In a sense they're fortunate – though it may not feel that way – because they learn quickly that the task is essentially solitary ... that communities are only as healthy as the solitudes that make them up; and that a life that is a prayer is about being, not doing.' Such remarks would obviously have resonated with Thomas. So, no doubt, would her further observations: 'It can't be said enough that kataphatic and apophatic approaches are two sides of the same coin. You can't have the one without the other. The most kataphatic praxis is set in an apophatic context. The two reflect the way the

mind works, as well as theological realities. For example, the mind identifies things by apophasis, telling itself what they are not rather than what they are. Crudely put, kataphatic relates to self-consciousness, and apophatic to deep mind. Ideally, there is a seamless flow between the story-making of self-consciousness, which is virtual, and the direct perception of deep mind, which reflects reality. In the end, we must all learn apophasis for the simple reason that we will die.' Available at *https:www.churchtimes.co.uk/articles/2015/16-january/features/interviews/* (accessed 7 April 2021). See also Vincent Gillespie and Maggie Ross, 'The Apophatic Image: the Poetics of Effacement in Julian of Norwich', in Marion Glasscoe (ed.), *The Medieval Mystical Tradition in England V* (Cambridge; D.S. Brewer, 1992), pp. 53–77.

29 Rowan Williams, 'Dangerous Thoughts in R. S. Thomas', in M. Wynn Thomas (ed.), *The Page's Drift: R. S. Thomas at Eighty* (Bridgend: Seren, 1993), p. 96. As he acknowledges, in his thinking here he is indebted to the phenomenology of Heidegger and his concept of the *Riss*, the fundamental and irreversible severance of the temporal order, the realm of existence, from that of Primordial Being. It is this rift that is the unbridgeable gulf between the One and the Many. And it is this rift, which dooms humans to live in the realm of multiplicities (which is also the realm of plenitude) that dooms language to be forever double-tongued or forked, every utterance being inescapably shadowed, and its integrity undermined, by the possibility of different utterance, without which it would not be possible at all. This, in turn, is what Derrida had in mind when speaking of the endless 'deferral of meaning' which rendered the finality of closure impossible. (See *Page's Drift*, p. 88.)

30 Rowan Williams, 'Suspending the Ethical: R. S. Thomas and Kierkegaard', in Damian Walford Davies (ed.), *Echoes to the Amen: Essays after R. S. Thomas* (Cardiff: University of Wales Press, 2003), pp. 207–19.

31 Here I shamelessly quote or paraphrase from an informative Wikipedia entry on Lossky: *https://en.wikipedia.org/wiki/Vladimir_Lossky* (accessed 23 June 2022).

32 R. S. Thomas, *Counterpoint* (Newcastle: Bloodaxe, 1990), p. 12.

33 Quoted in Rupert Shortt, *Rowan's Rule: The Biography of the Archbishop* (London: Hodder and Stoughton, 2009), p. 14. Hereafter *RW*.

34 *Poems of George Oppen (1908–1984), selected and introduced by Charles Tomlinson* (Newcastle: Cloudforms 4, 1990), p. 32.

35 Joseph P. Clancy (trans.), 'Ystrad Fflur', *Twentieth-Century Welsh Poems* (Llandysul: Gomer, 1982), p. 32.

36 Christine James, 'Pen-rhys: Mecca'r genedl', in Hywel Teifi Edwards (ed.), *Cwm Rhondda* (Cardiff: University of Wales Press, 1995), pp. 27–71.

37 The text of *Sancta Sophia* is available at: *https://.org/ccel/baker/holy_wisdom/holy_wisdom.iii.i.i.html* (accessed 23 June 2022).

INDEX